# Communal Organizations
*A Study of Local Societies*

*George A. Hillery, Jr.*

# Communal Organizations
## *A Study of Local Societies*

The University of Chicago Press. *Chicago and London*

International Standard Book Number: 0–226–33965–3
Library of Congress Catalog Card Number: 68–16696
The University of Chicago Press, *Chicago 60637*
The University of Chicago Press, Ltd., *London*
© 1968 by The University of Chicago. *All rights reserved*
Published 1968. Second Impression 1972
*Printed in the United States of America*

*This book is dedicated to*
*Vernon Joseph Parenton*

# Preface

Theoretical development in the field of community has been so encumbered by problems that it has reached an impasse. Several problems in particular are of strategic significance. First, and most disturbing, the range of things that are called "community" is so broad that "community" can mean practically anything. Perhaps in consequence, no satisfactory method for deciding what is *not* community has been developed. Finally (and the interconnections between these problems are extensive), there are no criteria for choosing among the bewildering variety of available theories. Even attempting to resolve the problem by fiat leaves one with the disquieting fact that for whatever theory is chosen there is an opposing one.

This book is an effort to solve these problems. The first approach began in a simple question: What is community? Attempts to answer this question resulted in an extensive survey of definitions. The concepts were in such a state of confusion, however, that no satisfactory order could be discovered. After seven years of trying to make theoretical sense of the field, I decided to begin at the other end: to study community by investigating the things that had been called community. This approach (which took another seven years) led me to look at case studies, first of folk villages, then of cities, and finally of prisons and mental institutions. These groups were selected because they represented a range of extremes of what had been called community. The method in using these studies was simply one of returning to the data and letting these determine the direction and choice of theory.

It is difficult for anyone to evaluate his own attainments, but as a minimum, I feel that three things have been accomplished. First, the theory developed here enables one to show where community theories are inadequate and where they are more useful. One is able to do this, moreover, on the basis of empirical rather than on *a priori* criteria. The basic criteria for such evaluations are the data: all theories must come to terms with certain carefully selected case studies of communal organizations, and particularly with models developed from them. Second, and because of this emphasis, one is able to trace the connection between some of the most abstract community theories and the most specific villages and cities. Third, and again because of the insistence that theories must come to terms with data, one is able to show what is and what is not a communal organization. And communal organizations are still the kinds of groups in which almost all people live.

There are several things that are not attempted. Social change, for example, receives little emphasis. Nor is there much consideration of the place of community within the larger social structure. There is no treatment of community planning or development. These are important topics, but, as a beginning, I have chosen to discuss only a cross-section of communal and non-communal types that have existed in recent times.

In presenting the findings, I have written for several audiences. Because of the importance of communal organizations for understanding human social behavior, the book has relevance for anyone interested in social science. There is most to say to specialists in community, of course, including those in urban and rural sociology. But there is also something to be said to those interested in formal organizations, to the criminologist, and to the student of mental health. A major finding is that communal organizations must be contrasted with formal organizations (after recognition, of course, of their common underpinnings), and that we learn much of both types through this contrast. Further, although certain deviates (such as criminals and the mentally disorganized) are products of communities, they are treated in formal organizations. The difference is not to be dismissed lightly.

# Acknowledgments

A year on a postdoctoral fellowship, granted by the University of Florida, made possible the work which carried the research for this study past the idea stage. During this period T. Lynn Smith acted in the capacity of a seasoned elder statesman. His counsel as well as his patience are gratefully acknowledged. I also want to acknowledge the assistance of Professor L. E. Grinter, through whose office the fellowship was administered.

Gideon Sjoberg and Thomas R. Ford read the first drafts of the manuscript. Their enthusiasm in no way diminished their criticism and I am grateful for both. Robin M. Williams, Jr., also read an earlier draft, and his encouragement has been deeply valued. Frank A. Santopolo read and gave suggestions on most of the manuscript. Willis A. Sutton, Jr., has offered comments on my work probably over the longest span of time of anyone. These and all of my colleagues at the University of Kentucky are given special thanks for suffering with me as well as suffering me during the years in which this book was being written. Specifically, I wish to mention Howard W. Beers, Robert Straus, James S. Brown, C. Milton Coughenour, Jiri T. Kolaja, Ralph J. Ramsey, John H. Mabry, J. J. and Sylvia Mangalam, Harry K. Schwarzweller, Joseph C. Mouledous, Eugene Gallagher, Basil Sherlock, John A. O'Donnell, Marion Pearsall, and Thomas P. Field. A. Lee Coleman, as departmental chairman, gave encouragement and understanding when I had little to show except zeal.

My debts, however, go beyond my colleagues at Kentucky. Numerous scholars have been kind enough to react to my ideas and questions, both in conversation and in correspondence. Some have contributed more than others, and I find it impossible to do more than list them: Nels Anderson, Wendell Bell, Earl Brewer, William Caudill, Irwin Deutsher, Allen D. Edwards, Ray H. Elling, Alex Frazer, Joseph H. Fichter, Charles Fritz, Erving Goffman, Ward H. Goodenough, Whitney H. Gordon, William Gum, Rudolf Heberle, George C. Homans, Robert W. Janes, Christen T. Jonassen, J. H. Kolb,

Robert K. Merton, Horace M. Miner, Charles H. Page, Donald S. Pitkin, William Query, Irwin T. Sanders, Frank R. Scarpitti, S. Frederick Seymour, William H. Sewell, Eshref Shevky, Eldridge Sibley, Gresham M. Sykes, Harley M. Upchurch, Sloan Wayland, and W. M. Williams.

To my students—my captive audience—goes appreciation for reaction beyond and above requirements. They have shared with me the exciting discovery of knowledge gained through scientific inquiry. I recall with particular fondness (and I trust they do, too) their taking me at my word and "really" criticizing me. Blake Hill, Bruce Mayhew, Dennis Poplin, Robert Roberts, and April Lillard must be particularly singled out in this regard.

Of course, I specifically want to assume full responsibility for the way in which these innumerable suggestions have been used.

It is impossible to say where my debt to my wife begins. Perhaps her contribution is not truly a debt, but it is more important for that.

Finally, several secretaries have typed several drafts of the manuscript: Linda Holt, Jean Thomas, Ruth Zimmerman, Margi McCroskery, Mary Oordt, Betty Sue Clarkson, Rosa Lena Brumfield, Nancy Charitana, and Madeline Hillery.

GEORGE A. HILLERY, JR.

# Contents

xi

# Figures

# Tables

# Introduction: The Study of Community

"... we shall discover the laws of social forms only by collecting such societary phenomena of the most diverse contents, and by ascertaining what is common to them in spite of their diversity."—GEORG SIMMEL

Few social entities are more basic in the study of sociology than the community. The community is obviously a social fact, one with which almost everyone is acquainted, and yet it is one that few understand. This lack of understanding is probably most in evidence among sociologists, if for no other reason than that they have examined what others have taken for granted.

This book attempts to provide the reader with certain fundamental community concepts, fundamentals pertaining both to the nature of community and to its taxonomic relationship with other social systems. In other words, although most of the discussion in this book concerns community, an important part concerns that which community is *not*—a frame of reference which it is hoped will serve the reader as a means of evaluating other theories.

## THE PROBLEM

When students of human society speak of community, they most often disagree. The unknown researcher contradicts the recognized authority, both may sound equally convincing, and the impasse obscures a simple but fundamental point: As far as science is concerned, the important objective is not what someone says the community is or is not; the scientific goal involves an understanding of the phenomenon which the word is describing. There is no way to reconcile the numerous contradictions unless a careful examination is made of the object being discussed.

The question before this book, then, is: What do communities look like?

The strategy that has been used in making this investigation is based upon a three-fold approach. First, one particular kind of social system or human grouping is assumed to be a community, primarily because virtually no researcher has denied that it contains at least *some* aspects of community. This particular kind of system is called here a "folk village." Second, the folk village is then compared to the city, a social system which has both been given and been denied the designation of community. Finally, both of these systems are then compared with a third class of objects, represented by prisons and mental hospitals, which are called "total institutions" (Goffman, 1957) or "custodial systems." Although this third kind of system has also been called community, it is one hypothesis of this study that it differs sharply and qualitatively from the other two social systems—especially from the folk village.

This study therefore begins in the area of community and extends into other areas of the sociological landscape. In essence, it is a collection of living groups and attempts to classify them. With such a classification, we can describe other variations, such as approximations to folk villages and cities. In any case, throughout this study, "real" social systems are used as the basis for the argument.

One implicit goal of such an investigation, then, is of course a taxonomy of social groups. An interest in discovering the nature of something, demands a concern with that which the "something" is not. And such distinctions amount essentially to a taxonomy. This taxonomy will be presented later, after some of the variations of community have been described and discussed. The concern of the book is only partially with taxonomy, however, just as it is only partially with definitions. Other theoretical concerns are equally and even at times more important.

Some of the findings are new. Some are merely old findings that have been reorganized. And some will probably be considered "obvious." But the method of science requires that all available material be utilized—the obvious with the not-so-obvious. (And who is to make the distinction?) It is the attempt to answer the question of the nature of community that is important.

DEFINITIONS

One of the simplest ways in which to document a need for clarification in the field of community research is to examine the definitions. Murray's ("Oxford") *English Dictionary* furnishes an appropriate beginning. According to it, the original Latin word, *communitatem,*

> was merely a noun of quality from *communis,* meaning "fellowship, community of relations or feelings"; but in [medieval Latin] it was, like *universitas,* used concretely in the sense of "a body of fellows or fellow-townsmen," . . . and this was its earlier use in English. . . .

Additional meanings have become obsolete; for example, community could mean "vulgar," or "common" (it could even refer to a prostitute). However, as the word has come down to us, it has three interpretations. First, community is used as a quality, generally referring to people having something in common, whether goods, rights, or character. The second meaning concerns a body of people, or, in modern sociological parlance, a social system. Third, sometimes but not always associated with either of the first two meanings, community pertains to people with a common land or territory.

The sociologist has added to the plethora of meanings, perhaps because he sees so many complexities in the object itself. Sociologists have employed no less than sixteen concepts in formulating ninety-four different definitions (Hillery, 1955). And no two authors use all sixteen concepts. For example, some writers say that community is a social group inhabiting some territory; others say that community is not social. Some say that communities are self-sufficient; others deny it. At least four concepts emphasize having things in common, but at least two concepts stress interdependence. (See also Gould and Kolb, 1964, pp. 114–15.)

What does *community* mean then? Having something in common, a group of people, a piece of land? A group of people having land in common? A group of people having something else in common? or perhaps something else. The term as it exists in the general as well as in the technical sense, has too many meanings to be understood. One may *believe* that his audience understands him when he says "community," but in fact his audience will supply its own interpretation, and chances are that the interpretations will differ. Consequently, even if a precise meaning were arbitrarily assigned, it would be misunderstood because others would still be using their own definitions.

The moral to be drawn is a scientific one: Our definitions must be wedded to facts—those things which we perceive through the senses. The error which is so often encountered in definitions and concepts of community is what may be referred to as the "sin of pronouncement." Students have "pronounced" the traits they felt "should" be contained in community, and *then* they have proceeded to look at the facts (if, indeed, they have looked). Since anyone is free to "pronounce," if he does not tie his "pronouncement" to some data, many different things have been "pronounced" under the heading *community*.

Our concern is to examine some of the objects that have been "pronounced" upon—those objects that can be found in the real world. If the reader can accept the assumption that the folk village is a type of community, then he possesses a useful tool for distinguishing communal from non-communal forms. The significant question concerns the nature of social groups, not whether a ninety-fifth definition of community is possible.

PREVIOUS STUDIES

The general orientation of this study is closest to the work of Robert Redfield, especially Redfield's concern with community as a holistic phenomenon. The most pertinent study is his *The Folk Culture of Yucatán* (1941). There are two major aspects of this investigation which are similar to the present one. First, Redfield examined the continua or spectrums between the rural and urban aspects of society. Second, these continua were studied by means of case studies of ongoing social systems. The differences, however, though not as important as the similarities, are at least more numerous. First, Redfield confined his analysis to the societies within a single culture—that of Yucatan. In contrast, the present study includes a variety of cultures in order to obtain as wide a variety of observations as possible. Second, many more social systems are used, and third; the works of many more investigators are employed than were used by Redfield. Fourth, the author has continually endeavored to test alternative hypotheses. Redfield never really questioned the assumption of the rural-urban continuum. In this book, the continuum is reexamined. The possibility is entertained that the rural-urban continuum may not in fact exist. On the other hand, there is also the possibility that other continua may extend from the rural or urban extremes to the total institution.

The case study approach has also been used extensively by Maurice Stein in *The Eclipse of Community* (1960), although primarily as a means of illustrating a theory rather than developing one (see Stein, 1960, p. 9). Stein undertook this study with the observation that:

Social theories about the forces transforming Western society during the past four centuries converge on three kinds of processes—urbanization, industrialization, and bureaucratization, as the central sources of change. . . . On the basis of this agreement, and the conviction that all three could be observed at work in American communities, the decision was made to search for their effects as these are reported in the various community studies examined [p. 5].

Thus, Stein developed a theory and set out to find supporting evidence. This book takes the opposite approach: from a collection of data pertaining to certain entities, what kind of a theory can be developed? Further, how does this theory compare with others?

The use of case studies in an attempt to ferret out information concerning community is by no means new. Even before Redfield's publication, Zimmerman (1938) employed the technique extensively in his analyses of community change. Other researchers have studied the same social system in different points of time: Mead (1956), Redfield (1950), and even the Lynds (1929, 1937) in their studies of city life (to mention only studies used in this report). There have also been restudies of the same social system by different investigators, of which Lewis' study (1951) of "Redfield's" Tepoztlán is probably the best known, especially for the criticisms it raised (in this connection, see Miner, 1952). Hatch's restudy (1948) of Zimmerman's earlier description is used in this work.

Similarly, the cross-cultural approach to the understanding of communities is also an old one. The earlier works, such as those of Gomme (1912) and Maine (1871), lacked the focus on specific social systems which characterize later works, including the present. (But for an important recent study in this tradition, see Sjoberg, 1960a.) Other studies that have analyzed specific communities and have chosen these communities from different cultures, have not focused on community structure and function, per se.[1]

The Human Relations Area Files (HRAF: Murdock *et al.*, 1950, and Murdock, 1958) is actually a research tool rather than a completed study. It is useful because it cross-indexes a variety of studies with the aim of facilitating cross-cultural comparisons. But whereas the HRAF describes similar ways of life (that is, cultures), the present study is concerned with concrete and identifiable social systems. For example, the HRAF may describe a given trait as occurring among the Maya Indians. For the HRAF, the location of such a culture within a broad area, such as the Yucatán Peninsula, is sufficiently precise. This book, however, asks the further question, which village (or town or city) is being described? We must know the social system that is involved in the analysis and we must know what it contains and what it does not contain. Merely specifying the culture is not enough. Both specifications, of course, are equally useful, but for different reasons: one focuses on culture, the other on society.

[1] Reference is made particularly to the Comparative Study of Values in Five Cultures Project of the Laboratory of Social Relations at Harvard University. Although specific communities were studied, the research resulted either in the study of a given community (as with Vogt, 1955) or in a comparison between communities from the same culture (Vogt and O'Dea, 1953).

One of the chief differences of this study from others lies in the use of whole social systems. Students of community have been negligent in the systematic use of their data. To what extent, for example, is the work of Hiller (1941) or MacIver (1917) founded on relatively complete descriptions of existing societies? We can do no more than suppose. Is a village more like a city than it is like a prison? How does one know? Specifically which villages and which cities and which prisons is one talking about? When a theory is constructed without linking it directly and systematically to concrete evidence, misunderstanding is invited.

The cause of such misunderstanding—perhaps confusion is not too strong a word—can be seen to rise from many sources. But the cause is not the major point of interest. We are concerned with establishing some basis by means of which to order the excellent work done in the field of community. If this work is to be useful, it must be firmly oriented with respect to its data. Our task is to provide this orientation.

THEMES

The major themes developed in this book fall into two broad classes: methodological and substantive. The methodological themes were intentional. They may, then, be properly labeled "purposes." In this sense, the method of this study is at least as important as any other feature.

The methodology is treated in detail in Chapter 1. Here, we will only call attention to the major reasons why the research took the direction it did. There are four methodological themes: (1) conceptual clarification, (2) emphasis on objects, (3) emphasis on induction, and (4) developing a taxonomy.

1. It seems evident that we must have clarity of terms if we are to communicate. When concepts are sharpened and are linked more firmly with their data, then a theory of community is forthcoming.

2. Throughout the discussion, communal organizations are treated as objects. Regardless of whether community is regarded as a process, a state of mind, or what-have-you, it is accompanied by traits that can be seen, heard, felt, and smelled. At the same time, I now believe that one of the most important

things about community is that it is an organization based on symbolic behavior, and certainly this is not an object. Nevertheless the manifestations of the organization—buildings, streets, people—are very much objects, and it is from these that the research started.

3. There is a decided emphasis on induction. In oversimplified terms, rather than testing hypotheses derived from theory, theory is instead built from data.

4. Finally, much of the effort in these pages is devoted to a classification of human groups. In the social sciences, we are trying to understand why people behave as they do. A taxonomy appropriate to this end, therefore, should help to predict or identify the types of behavior found in various systems.

These four purposes were clearly evident from the start of the investigation. The substantive findings, on the other hand, arose inductively; they were products of the investigation. Again, four chief themes may be identified: (1) rural-urban variation, (2) the fact that communities cannot be defined by specific goals, (3) structural freewheeling, and (4) levels of communal organization.

1. One of the most significant variations between certain types of communal organizations is also one that has been recognized the longest: the variation between folk (or rural) and urban ways of life. This variation pervades most of the components of villages and cities—and, at the same time, it unites them. Villages and cities are different, but only in degree.

2. Communal organizations lack any single unifying goal. Unlike business organizations, labor unions, and (as we shall see) prisons and mental hospitals, communal organizations do not exist for one purpose. This is a difficult concept to demonstrate, since it is a negative one. But in spite of the difficulty, this concept is an extremely valuable tool for separating communal organizations from other forms of social systems; it has a high taxonomic value. It also stands as a warning to those who believe that the community can be understood in terms of its temporary goals.

3. "Structural freewheeling" means simply that a change in one part of a communal organization does not mean that a mathematically predictable change must occur in another part of the system. There is, in other words, a relative lack of organi-

zation in communities (and probably in all human social systems) which means that some parts will "spin their wheels" (that is, "free-wheel") before they mesh with the other parts. But such a mechanistic analogy is useful only to a point, no matter how often it may have been used by others. The simple fact is that human groups are linked by means of symbolic ties, and since symbols by nature have different meanings for different people (no matter how slight these differences), we can expect that changes will take place differently than in systems where the links are those of metal or flesh.

4. Communal organizations exist on levels. Families are regarded as the basic building blocks (that is, families in households). These coalesce to form neighborhoods which coalesce to form villages or cities which coalesce to form regions, culture areas, or nations. This finding means that communities quite often are contained within communities. But it also means that one must be careful to distinguish the level of inclusiveness. Since communal organizations exist on levels, some types of communal organizations—such as families—are apt to contain components of other types of systems—such as cities—both because they are taxonomically related and because they are actually contained in the other object. Nevertheless, the objects can be distinguished conceptually, which means essentially that we are able to predict that different types of behavior will be found among them, in spite of a substratum of behavior common to all.

The methodological themes, directly or indirectly, underlie the entire book and provide its basic direction. To give but one example, in order to clarify the concept of community, a description must be given of non-community. This is accomplished in Appendix C, where the total institution is considered as an object. On this basis, inductively, a taxonomy is developed. The point is not whether we feel the total institution is or is not a community. To be consistent with the methodological themes, the evidence for our conclusion must be presented, regardless of whether it is positive or negative.

The substantive themes, on the other hand, receive different degrees of emphasis in various chapters. The first parts of this book are organized around folk-urban variation. For the remainder, the lack of goals in communal organizations, their

structural freewheeling, and their organization into levels comprise the basic taxonomic principles by means of which communal organizations are classified and are distinguished from
other systems.

PLAN OF THE BOOK

Since the goal of this book is to develop a theory of community,
emphasis is placed on models and on higher levels of more
generalizing explanation. To facilitate the development of this
theory, the treatment of the data—the analyses of the folk villages, cities, and total institutions—is presented in the Appendixes. Though it was from these analyses that the theory was
developed, presenting them with the theory would impede the
presentation. The reader thus may proceed in three ways: (1)
The book may be read in the order in which the study progressed, that is, the Appendixes would be read after Chapter 1,
then the remainder of the book. (2) The analysis may be read in
conjunction with the development of each of the models. Thus,
Appendix A would be read with Chapter 2, Appendix B with
Chapter 3, Appendix C with Chapter 7. Or (3), the reader may
choose to read all of the theoretical part and then check the
closeness of the integration by turning to the Appendixes. (This
latter course has been chosen in the ordering of the material for
book presentation.)

After Chapter 1, the book proceeds inductively for the most
part. In Chapters 2 and 3, models of folk villages and cities are
established. These models are then combined into a more
general one, the model of the vill (Chapter 4). This model, as a
model of one type of community, is used to evaluate various
community theories that have been developed by others (Chapters 5, 6, and 7). After this evaluation, a model of the total institution is developed that stands in contrast to the model of the
vill and thus delineates a conceptual boundary around the vill
(Chapter 8). On the basis of this boundary and one other, various other types of communal organizations are briefly surveyed
(Chapter 9). The concluding chapter offers generalizations from
the findings of this book toward establishing a basis for a theory
of communal organization.

# I

# Approaching the Problem

In sciences with a relatively long history, the researcher's exposition of his method can be confined rather narrowly to the problem at hand. For example, the use of statistics in population analysis is obvious, given the nature of the field as it developed over the centuries. In areas of study with more recent foundations, however, such as community, the reasons for choosing alternatives of investigation are less obvious. To provide a relatively complete picture, therefore, the presentation of the methodology of this study will briefly trace the major idea from its first broad and vague stages to the relatively specific concerns which emerged.

The inquiry began in an attempt to discover the degree of consensus which had been reached by students concerning the meaning of community (Hillery, 1955). Most students would agree that the human community is a social group inhabiting a common territory and having one or more additional common ties. But such "consensus" is disturbing. First, there is no agreement on the nature of the common ties, and thus the degree of consensus is relatively superficial. Second, many who would agree to the formulation would also argue that common territory is not the really important feature. And third (without attempting to be exhaustive), what of those who disagree?

It is important at this point to comment on the relative lack of theoretical precommitment at this stage of the present research. This study began from an investigation of theory. But the contradictions were too numerous to resolve and the solution seemed to be to return to the data. In at least one case, evidence was sought to support a theory before the evidence was examined—that prisons and mental hospitals did not contain the family—but, for the most part, theories and concepts were introduced because the data suggested them, not because a conscious search was made for supporting evidence.

It was in this way that I came to the conclusion reached by Hanson (if in a different sense): "The issue is not theory-using, but theory-finding; my concern is not with the testing of hypotheses, but with their discovery" (Hanson, 1958, p. 3). I proposed to discover theory, which included setting our concepts in order. This meant discovering which of our theories are most useful. Knowing this, we should be able to generate (discover) even more useful hypotheses.

The major stumbling block seemed to lie in the fact that no one had developed a taxonomy of community. Many suggestions existed, but none were based on a relatively complete or even broad sample of existing communities. The problem became, then, one of obtaining complete information on which to base types. More specifically, it was felt that inventories should be compiled of traits found in various communities, and these inventories should be organized so that they would resemble as completely as possible the objects from which they were constructed. If feasible, the study should begin with that system which offered the most significant consensus regarding its community status. Whatever the disagreement concerning the "essence" of community *within* this object, the problem therefore became one of finding some object which would be the locus of the phenomenon.

The small agricultural village seemed to fit the research needs quite well. In fact, no definition could be found which clearly stated that the phenomenon of community was *not* to be found in such a social system. The "village" was then assumed to be a community (the adjective "folk" was added after the research on the village had been completed). It was further assumed that other types of social systems could also be community.

A thorough study of a community, one which would permit an inventory of its traits, is a laborious process. As much use as possible therefore had to be made of the existing "case studies." Several criteria were used to select these: (1) they had to agree with the minimum formulation of community as set forth above ("a social group inhabiting a common territory and having one or more additional common ties"); (2) at least initially, they had to be small enough to permit a relatively complete inventory of their traits; and (3) preference would be given to villages from different cultures in order to maximize the extent of coverage. (Other criteria arose as the study progressed. They are discussed later in this chapter.)

The next step consisted of exploring the taxonomic limits of community. For this purpose, groups whose status as communities was controversial were of particular interest, for such groups should have the highest chance of being the kinds of social systems that would be on the borderline of the phenomenon called community. The basic assumptions were two: (1) Groups of controversial status are likely to be controversial because they are in fact in a no-man's-land with respect to classification— that is, they are neither completely one thing nor the other. Examining such groups would be observing social systems which were probably lacking some of the features of the subject of more central interest—the community. (2) A comparative analysis is more fruitful for describing an object than an analysis which concentrates only on the object itself.

Cities appeared to represent one of these borderline cases. The village is assumed by many to be on a continuum with other locality groups, such as hamlets, towns, and cities. Cities would thus represent the opposite extreme from the village on this continuum. However, cities are controversial according to several prominent rural sociologists. Sorokin, Zimmerman, and Galpin (1930, p. 329) would have their "cumulative community," by definition, limited to rural areas. Sanderson (1919, p. 85) is even more explicit in excluding cities from the province of community. (See also Hillery, 1955, p. 119.) Further, although cities do fit the minimum definition of community given above, it will be recalled that the definition was considered superficial, and in fact it is possible that community may cease to exist somewhere on the continuum between the village and the city. Accordingly, Louis Wirth's definition was used as a supplementary one: "For sociological purposes a city may be defined as a relatively large, dense, and permanent settlement of socially heterogeneous individuals" (Wirth, 1938). The study therefore assumed that the city *may* be a community, not that it was one.

The other borderline system was originally called a "quasi-community," after the suggestion of Reiss (1954). A search was made for a type of social system which approached the community in certain significant respects and yet which was not community. Prisons and mental hospitals seemed a priori to represent such systems, particularly in that they lacked the inclusion of the family in their social structure. But as research proceeded, it became apparent that the term "quasi-community" was likely to prove troublesome, especially in its assumption of a theoretical relationship to community. Thus it was with particular welcome that the concept of "total institution" (Goffman, 1957) was encountered, a total institution being a social system that not only tended to regulate the total lives of its inmates but which also set barriers to social interaction with the outside. Included in the list of total institutions are orphan asylums, mental hospitals, prisons, army barracks, monasteries. Even more to the point:

Whether a particular total institution acts as a good or bad force in civil society, force it may well have, and this will depend on the suppression of a whole circle of actual or potential households. Conversely, the formation of households provides a structural guarantee that total institutions will not arise. The incompatibility between these two forms of social organization should tell us, then, something about the wider social functions of them both [Goffman, 1957, p. 48].

By focusing attention particularly on total institutions, the research would test Goffman's concept as well as achieving a test of its own. The test is especially significant since at least two types of total institution—prisons and mental hospitals—have been called communities by their investigators (see Hillery, 1963, p. 779, n. 1).

Therefore, in discovering the possible meanings of community, it seemed that a profitable line of attack would be to proceed toward gaining an understanding of three types of social systems: villages, cities, and total institutions. The same source would be used for each type: case studies from different cultures gathered by other investigators. In addition, a case study of a city (compiled by the writer) was included.

In considering the possible relations between these three things, one may simply assume that each system could vary from the others in either degree or in kind. Variation in degree would mean that the objects could not be clearly differentiated from each other, that is, they would represent related phenomena. Variation in kind—discrete or qualitative variation— would show the reverse: the various objects would represent different kinds of things and should not be included together. Combination of the objects and the type of variation furnishes eight possible sets of relationship, each of which may be graphed as in the accompanying chart (Fig. 1).

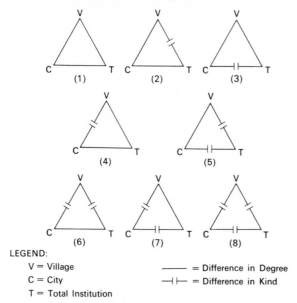

LEGEND:
V = Village
C = City
T = Total Institution

——— = Difference in Degree
—⊢⊢— = Difference in Kind

*Fig. 1*—Schematic of the Eight Possible Sets of Relationships

These possibilities give the following hypotheses (corresponding to the order presented in Fig. 1). Apparently, only one of the hypotheses can be verified. The problem thus involved discovering the appropriate hypothesis.

1. There is no clear distinction between folk villages, cities, and total institutions. If the folk village is considered a community, then these other social forms must also be so considered. Differences are in degree and distinctions can only be arbitrary (though possibly useful).

2. There is a continuum between communities and total institutions, proceeding from a condition of community to conditions where community is represented in ever-diminishing degree; villages representing the essence of community, total institutions representing its absence, cities in the middle.

3. There is a continuum between cities and total institutions, but villages occupy the middle of the continuum. If folk villages are the essence of community, then there are qualitatively different dimensions along which the quality of community changes. Cities and total institutions are not related.

4. Villages and cities, though different in kind, do not differ significantly from total institutions. This hypothesis implies that the phenomenon of community is not a useful conceptual tool.

5. Villages and cities are both communities, varying from each other in degree, and both are distinct from total institutions.

6. Villages are distinct from cities and total institutions. The latter two exist on a continuum and are not significantly different from each other. Neither cities nor total institutions should be considered communities.

7. Cities are distinct from villages and total institutions. The latter two exist on a continuum and are not significantly different (or distinctions are arbitrary). Total institutions and folk villages are communities, cities are not.

8. Villages and cities are conceptually distinct entities, and both are distinct from total institutions. The word "community" would be used to represent qualitatively distinct and separate things if it were to be applied to all. The term would more profitably have its narrowest rather than its broadest meaning—that is, community as a folk village rather than community as any set of social relationships.

A consideration of these hypotheses underscores the frame of reference employed in this study. The starting assumption was that the folk village was a community. What else was to be called community remained to be seen. The task required examining the objects first and *then* deciding on the nature of their relationships.

The research was designed to establish variety—either within the field of community or between the community and other types of social systems. Types which were closely related to the folk village—or to the city, or to the total institution—were purposely avoided. Thus, the research design makes no claim that its typology exhausts possibilities.

CONSTRUCTING MODELS

In keeping with the initial research decision to return to the data, information was collected which pertained to identifiable social systems. The intention was to develop a model of each type of system that would approximate as closely as possible the empirical reality—even though, of necessity, it would abstract from this reality only the common features. The model would thus be an *empirical abstraction.*

There was no intention to develop ideal types (see McKinney, 1954, for a detailed discussion of this method), since emphasis was to be placed on accuracy of description rather than on logical closure. As McKinney has noted (1954, p. 144), though ideal types are objectively probable, they are "a little more out of touch with perceptual reality than other constructs are." The emphasis on empirical abstractions sacrifices some generality, but the data are kept more clearly in view.

The nature of empirical abstractions can be more readily perceived in terms of a simplified classification of types of models. (1) *Replica-working* models are completely scaled and operating reproductions of the objects they represent—for example, a model home or a model airplane. (2) An *empirical abstraction* shows only part of the object it represents. There are several reasons for this incompleteness: only uniformities are used, an otherwise simplified picture is involved (for example, in this study, we are interested in community, and thus we say little about racial composition), or the empirical abstraction may not be complete in its content (for example, if an item is missing from the data, regardless of its importance, it will be absent from the empirical abstraction). (3) *Cybernetic* models do the same kind of job or function as the object they represent, but they do so only partially and by means of different processes. Thus, electronic computers simulate one function of the human brain, but this function is performed by different methods and by means of different materials than those used by the brain. (4) Finally, *ideal types* are purely conceptual models of some aspect of reality as it conceivably would work if unaffected by extraneous influences. Frictionless surfaces and the perfect vacuum are examples. A major difference between ideal types and cybernetic models is, whereas both models rule out extraneous influences, cybernetic models are able to do this in practice and ideal types do so only conceptually. Thus, the model is called an ideal or pure type, since (as in reality), the ideal or pure state cannot be attained except on a conceptual level.

No invidious comparison is intended between ideal types and empirical abstractions. Rather, the problem at hand simply did not call for ideal types—for a number of reasons. One of the most perplexing questions was, *which* ideal type to use? The literature abounds with ideal types, not only of communities but of varying kinds of communities. Furthermore, it would not be feasible to develop original ideal types, since such development would presume some knowledge of the system to be studied and its relation to other systems. This knowledge could come only *after* the particular systems had been examined and combined into models.

Although the decision had been made to avoid a priori reasoning, there were nevertheless certain technical objectives. First, the models would be qualitative rather than quantitative. The available data (largely, studies made by other persons) were not sufficiently coordinated to make possible a statistical treatment. Second, some sort of trait list of the contents of the various systems would be needed. The traits, however, could not be integrated until the data had been gathered. Conceivably, the "model" might turn out not to be integrated at all.

No formal method was used to isolate the traits, although as the research proceeded it came to be guided to some extent by the universal culture pattern of Wissler (1923) and particularly by the elements of the human group as formulated by Homans (1950). Later, the concept of components (Sanders, 1958) was adopted for subelements. Essentially, the approach was an approximation of the "point to point" method employed by W. I. Thomas.[1]

The investigation began with a comparison of two villages (Hilltown and New Peri). A model was built from their common elements. Another village was compared and the model was modified. This procedure continued until an inventory of three consecutive villages yielded no further changes in the model. The inventory procedure consisted of reading the case study and marking those passages which confirmed or denied the presence of a given component. Then, each marked passage was copied on a sheet which pertained only to the given component. In this manner, all villages could be systematically compared, component by component. (Or, the passage sheets could be arranged to summarize all components for any village.)

The process of analysis accordingly advanced in stages:

1. Two initial village case studies were selected.
2. A survey was made of their common components.
3. A tentative trait list was compiled.
4. Relevant passages were copied from these studies corresponding to the components in the trait list.
5. Another village case study was analyzed.
6. A survey was made of the components common to the three villages.
7. The trait list was modified.
8. Relevant passages were copied from this third study corresponding to the components in the trait list.
9. The original studies were compared with the modified traits.
10. Relevant passages were copied from the original studies corresponding to the components in the modified trait list.

Then, beginning with step 5 and continuing through step 10, seven more village case studies were examined. In all, ten villages were eventually surveyed.

This procedure yielded a trait list for the system being studied. The trait list is not the model; the model is integrated. The folk village model used in this study is, therefore, a model constructed

---

[1] In Blumer, 1939, pp. 166–67, 172, 190–91. Though Thomas was not speaking so much of an individual research effort as of the efforts of "science" in general, the writer believes that the conceptual transfer is valid (Thomas hints as much: see p. 172 in Blumer).

from an integrated trait list compiled from case studies of ten specific folk villages. The models for the city and the total institution were constructed in the same manner.

## PROBLEMS OF VALIDITY AND RELIABILITY

An observation is valid when its description corresponds with that which it is supposed to describe; it is reliable when repeated observations yield similar reports. Validity and reliability are regarded as two aspects of a larger problem of truth, which is here given the name of *fidelity*, or faithfulness. In attempting to be valid and reliable in our observations, we attempt to be as faithful as possible to the data at hand.

In the following discussion the folk village is used in illustration, but the remarks apply equally to all the systems.

The sources used in this study were mainly accounts of other investigators, and the analysis which evolves from such sources is properly termed secondary analysis. However, the usual meaning of secondary analysis is that the user of the data has used them for ends other than those for which the data were first gathered (see Goode and Hatt, 1952). But most of the accounts used in this study were done with the purpose of describing the village, and only with that purpose. In other words, most of the studies used were done for precisely the task at hand, and the analysis is to that extent less secondary than it might at first seem.

The attempt was made to compare each of the villages as thoroughly as possible in order to allow the villages themselves (through their investigators) to provide their own descriptions. It would appear probable that the greater the number of villages examined, the greater the number of different frames of reference. Therefore, the problem of constructing a frame of reference common to all the sources became paramount. It was reasoned that if each of the investigators had described the same kind of thing, and if their reports were sufficiently extensive, then purposely or inadvertently most or all of the things important to the object under investigation would be mentioned. In other words, if some same things could be communicated from separate investigators to the present writer, the observations were reliable.

This criterion of reliability is accordingly described as "inter-individual verification." What one investigator sees may be his own biases. But, if investigators A, B, C, . . . O are all able to communicate a given item of information to an additional researcher—who is, further, at one remove from the scene—then that researcher has an assurance that he too would perceive the same thing and that the reporting is probably reliable.

If the observations are reliable because they are consistent, then they are valid for probably the same reason, for they were all made independently. In other words, we know that the description of each researcher was apparently faithful to his data because it agrees with the descriptions of other researchers who were not in contact with each other or with him. The description, then, very likely corresponds with that which it was supposed to describe, and it is a valid (as well as a reliable) observation.

The data extracted from the sources were essentially qualitative. The main questions were: Which traits do all villages have, and (the more difficult question) which do they lack? Six problems were encountered in establishing the presence of these qualities.

1. Cross-cultural comparisons were used in lieu of a representative sample. A representative sample would, of course, have been preferable. However, there is no assurance that villages in the literature are in any way representative of villages in general. The task then becomes one of maximizing whatever the village studies do in fact represent. By limiting the analysis to only one village from any given culture, the researcher is at least assured that if his villages are peculiar, the peculiarity is not confined to one culture. In more positive terms, with a cross-cultural approach a picture is obtained which is more likely to be reliable for folk villages in general.

The concern regarding the importance of a cross-cultural approach arose also from the feeling that students of human behavior tend to speak too often of American communities. Such an approach fails to consider that the American scene is of extremely brief duration, historically, and that the American population is but a small fraction of that of the world. America is in both these senses atypical.

2. No two villages were examined by the same investigator. This approach was prompted directly by the criterion of inter-individual verifiability. The reliability of observations can be increased by using a multiplicity of researchers.

3. In a qualitative study of a few cases, the problem of missing information of course becomes quite important. If a phenomenon is reported for all villages, then it is probable that this phenomenon is indeed found in the system generally. But should a component be missing from any one village, three interpretations are possible: (1) The item was overlooked in the study of that village. Where the description is extensive, however, such an oversight is improbable. (2) The component was really missing and the villages which included it are atypical. (3) The village which lacks the component is atypical. The correct interpretation, however, is often found in the sources.

Should data for a component be missing from all studies, the item must be excluded from the model. This necessitates certain interpretations of the model, to be mentioned presently, but it is important to note that not always is a component clearly lacking. For example, sometimes when a component is not mentioned its existence can be inferred from knowledge of the culture generally. The case of the New England village, Hilltown, is such an instance. None of its studies give any mention of magical beliefs, beliefs which were present in all of the other villages. However, anyone familiar with even contemporary American customs of "bad luck" and "good luck" would find it hard to doubt such belief in Hilltown, also. In addition, Hilltowners were Congregationalists (Puritans) initially and for a large part of their history. This denomination waged an active war against witches, thereby acknowledging the existence of magic. In this instance, one is probably justified in inferring that all of Hilltown's investigators simply ignored this component, but that it was present.

Even where evidence is totally absent, one should be careful not to assume that avenues of future research with respect to that trait are closed. A trait may receive what can be termed "minimal validation." For example, it was demonstrated that all persons in each of the ten case-study villages are ethnocentric about some subgroup in the village and about the village itself. It was further demonstrated that all except the Chinese village showed ethnocentrism for some larger social system, usually a nation. In this instance, one may conclude that a hierarchy of ethnocentrism has been minimally validated, but that the validation extends only to the village and its subgroups. The hierarchy *may* extend beyond the village, but, at least for one village, evidence is lacking.

The methodological concept of minimal validation, then, establishes the existence of a given trait and, in addition, leaves open the possibility—even raises the possibility—that further elaboration of the trait may be possible. The concept also guards against temptations to overgeneralize. If one trait is unmentioned, though it is a trait mentioned in nine other villages, it may actually not be generic to the phenomenon under consideration. The concept of minimal validation points up the fact that some traits may in fact be only minimally validated—as in the case of ethnocentrism. It distinguishes between minimal and maximal validation. (Applying this concept to this study as a whole affords an interesting perspective.)

4. The use of contradictory evidence plays a central role in the process of validation, the rule being that contradictory evidence is sufficient to discard any component from the model. Numerous examples could be cited of hypotheses which were sacrificed on this principle. To name only one, the hypothesis that the nucleus of all villages was in or near its center was destroyed by two instances in which the residences and service buildings were clearly and entirely to one side of the fields.

5. The sources were limited to case studies. One characteristic of case studies is extensiveness. Because there is no agreed-upon frame of reference for community analysis, short (journal-length) reports of villages are likely to overlook important or necessary components. On the other hand, extensive (book-length) accounts increase the probability of mentioning a greater variety of objects. Even if an investigator has an inadequate framework, a detailed examination of a given object means that he will necessarily mention more things, items that in a briefer account would have been omitted as of lesser importance.

Those who employ secondary analyses must accordingly develop sensitivity to the inadvertent remark. Quite often components which were in fact common to the villages were treated lightly or incidentally by the various reporters: ethnocentrism, spatial patterns, mobility, stratification, socialization—the list would include many of the components.

6. Case studies further imply the description of entities. But

since emphasis is on induction, it is important that the entity be sui generis—self-made, so to speak, rather than a construct imposed on the data by the researcher. The distinction is not always easy to make, but a useful rule of thumb in the present case consisted of relying on the people themselves: a given system was designated an entity if it was so considered by the people being studied.

The problem of the meaning of entities requires an extended comment. An entity stands relatively alone or is relatively complete in and of itself. It is a unit, that is, something which cannot be subdivided without losing its identity. Sorokin has distinguished six kinds of entities or unities (1947, pp. 145–46), but only the kind he terms *meaningful-causal* pertains directly to the kinds of entities used in this study. A *meaningful* unity, according to Sorokin, is one related by some logical ($1 + 1 = 2$) or aesthetic (a Beethoven sonata, a painting by Raphael) connection; but a *meaningful-causal* unity has in addition the quality of necessarily possessing activity. Whereas a meaningful unity is a *product* of human activity, a meaningful-causal unity is a *characteristic* of human social activity. And only human societies have this characteristic. Thus, two or more persons in social interaction (a useful definition of the human group) not only have some sort of meaningful relation between themselves, by definition, but they also cause each other to behave differently than would be true if each were alone.

An examination of any of the concrete objects that we will call community will reveal that they contain all of Sorokin's unities. Cities, for example, can contain piles of sand and boxes of bricks (Sorokin's two kinds of *spatial* unities) as well as houses with furniture. They also, of course, contain human beings (Sorokin's *direct-causal* unities). In addition, cities have laws and customs (*meaningful* unities). Yet, none of these unities give us the city, even when added together. The city, in other words, is a *meaningful-causal* unity in the sense that it is an interrelated set of human groups.

Sometimes the other types of unities will be important for explaining things about social behavior. The most obvious examples are the spatial unities. These will be seen to influence human interaction in communities, and thus they must be considered as important to the particular kind of meaningful-causal unit that we call the city. However, no entity is relevant if it fails to tell us something about the way in which the people themselves get along.

One final question needs to be answered: What assurance is there that a sufficient number of common components have been uncovered?

In the absolute sense, there is no such assurance. But this lack of certainty is part of the experience of any science. No scientist ever knows that he has covered a sufficient, let alone a significant, part of his subjects. Even the pragmatic test (that is, it is sufficient because it works) provides no certainty. A model may be right for the wrong reasons.

But on a more positive side, there are two relevant considerations. The first is the method itself. To the extent that the sources used are broad in nature, the number of components extracted from the sources will also be broad in coverage. Further, choosing case studies from several cultures increases the chances that the components will be sufficient for cultures generally. The method, then, is designed to strive *toward* the goal of sufficiency. But there is also another test of sufficiency. Do the models that are developed help to correct or substantiate other theories? That is, does the information advance knowledge in the field? This is a question that is the concern of several chapters (see especially Chaps. 5, 6, and 7). Sufficiency, then, is relative as well as absolute. The method is relatively sufficient if it can improve our understanding of community.

# 2

# A Model of the
# Folk Villages

The basic theme of this chapter concerns the features common
to ten folk villages from as many cultures.[1] These villages are
identified in Table 1; their common features are summarized in
Table 2. (The villages are discussed more fully in Appendix A.)
In the tables the parts have been gathered so that they may be
worked on. The remaining task is the construction from this
information of a working model of the folk village.

The term "model" as here used means a general picture
which describes an entire class of social objects. The model of
the folk village has two major parts: a list of components, and
the concepts that integrate the components. These concepts will
be organized, later in this chapter, into a unified concept—an
"integrating construct." Neither part of the model, alone, can
provide an adequate picture. The integrating construct
organizes the list of parts and gives them a focus—or, more precisely, a series of foci. The list of components, on the other hand,
provides a more complete picture of the things which the foci
emphasize.

Thus, in the formal sense, no definition is given for the folk

[1] Much of the material for this chapter is taken from Hillery, 1961.

Table 1. Selected identifying characteristics of the ten villages in the comparative analysis

| Village | Culture | Population | Major economic activity | Time of study | Investigators |
|---|---|---|---|---|---|
| San Ildefonso | Pueblo Indian | 128 | Corn, pottery | 1936–39 | Whitman, 1947 |
| Suye Mura* | Southern Japan | 58–194 | Rice, silk | 1935–36 | Embree, 1939 |
| New Peri | Melanesian | 200–300 | Fish | 1953 | Mead, 1956 |
| Romonom | Micronesian | 230–240 | Fish, horticulture | 1947–48 | Gladwin and Sarason, 1953; Goodenough, 1951 |
| Chan Kom | Maya Indian | 251 | Corn | 1930–31 | Redfield and Villa Rojas, 1934 |
| Hilltown† | New England, American† | 1,000–1,825 | Diversified agriculture, lumbering | 1938, 1945 | Zimmerman, 1938; Hatch, 1948; Homans, 1950 |
| Kaihsienkung | Lower Yangtze Valley, China | 1,458 | Rice, sheep, silk | 1935 | Fei, 1939 |
| Dragalevtsy | Bulgaria, Southeast Europe | 1,669 | Diversified agriculture | 1934–37 | Sanders, 1949 |
| Shamirpet | Central India | 2,494 | Diversified agriculture | 1951–52 | Dube, 1955 |
| Silwa | Upper Egypt | 3,500 | Wheat, millet, diversified agriculture | 1951 | Ammar, 1954 |

* Represented by Kawaze buraku.
† Only Hilltown in the nineteenth century is considered here.

*Table 2.* Summary description of the elements (traits) of a folk-village model

| Element | Description |
|---|---|
| **1.0** *Interaction* | |
| 1.1 Personal contact | Interaction is characteristically direct rather than indirect. Almost everyone is aware of all other village members. |
| 1.2 Social processes | Cooperation is most in evidence, though conflict and competition are also described. |
| **2.0** *Space* | |
| 2.1 Spatial integration | Space inhabited by each village is integrated into a whole, though noncontiguous parts may be included. |
| 2.2 Spatial patterning | Village has a nucleus formed of various services clustered in a given part of its space. |
| 2.3 Boundaries | Village boundaries are vague; that is, though present, they are either conflicting, partly lacking, or unstable, or the inhabitants are uncertain of them. |
| **3.0** *Activities* | |
| 3.1 Base of operations | Village space is the location for village activities and from it the villagers operate in journeying to the outside world. |
| 3.2 Mobility | Horizontal mobility is low. Most villagers are native-born to village or its immediate vicinity. |
| 3.3 Continuance | Villages are able to persist in time. |
| **4.0** *Sentiment* | |
| 4.1 Ethnocentrism | Villagers display a hierarchy of ethnocentrism involving at least the village and its subgroups. |
| 4.2 Awareness | Villagers are aware of the village in that they give it a name and invest a ruling body with central authority. |
| 4.3 Homogeneity (mechanical solidarity) | Villagers are homogeneous with respect to place of birth, in having family connections within the village, and in performing similar economic activities. Organic solidarity is also universal, though rudimentary. |
| **5.0** *Norms* (Institutions) | |
| 5.1 Family | Families are sexual, socializing, and economic units, having male rulers and spatially retentive qualities for their members. |
| 5.2 Economics | Primary production industries dominate (agriculture, fishing, or both). |

*Table 2 (cont.)*

| Element | Description |
|---|---|
| 5.3 Religion | Villagers profess both religious and magical beliefs. |
| 5.4 Government | There are both rulers and self-governing tendencies. |
| 5.5 Mutual aid | Mutual aid characterizes economic and other institutional behavior. |
| 5.6 Stratification | Statuses are grouped into strata. |
| 5.7 Socialization | Schools are developed to some degree through outside influences. Indigenous socialization is achieved primarily, though not exclusively, through the family. |
| 5.8 Recreation | Festivals, adult games, and music are practiced in traditional and in group forms. |

NOTE: For sources used in compiling elements of the model, see Table 1. Note that all of these elements are found in each of the ten villages described in Table 1.

village. The integrating construct can be used in the place of a definition only if it is used as an introduction to the trait list itself. Here, the reasoning of Arensberg is followed:

Nowadays it is clear that a model rather than a definition serves to represent the complex variables of a complex situation, thing, or process. . . . Definitions are too shallow and too full of verbal traps; summaries of propositions are too slow, piecemeal, and cumbersome [1955, p. 1145].

Although the purpose of the model is essentially descriptive, the description is on a theoretical level beyond that of the studies upon which it is based. The model, in other words, generalizes from the specific studies to a particular type of social system. The model is based on data from ten cultures and thus applies to folk villages in general. It applies to *all* of the villages in *each* of the model's details. There are no exceptions, unless these are specifically noted. Finally, important as the folk village is to this study, it should be repeated that the folk village is only one type of community. Until the analysis is extended to other systems, theoretical conclusions must be limited.

DEVELOPING THE SYNTHESIS

The synthesis is based on several considerations, the most basic of which is that the synthesis is built only from common components. (These are isolated in Appendix A.) The task of this chapter is that of searching for integrating components around which the other components group. Integrating components must possess two characteristics: they must be stable, and they must be distinctive.

Little effort is required to see that only stable components can act as integrating components. For example, the institution of stratification is relatively unimportant to the daily lives of the people of Chan Kom in Yucatán, and is therefore not an integrating force equal to the integrative power of stratification in the Indian village of Shamirpet, where the institution is very highly developed.

But stability alone is not sufficient. Hypothetically, we are dealing with a distinctive type of group, and thus the components that are used to build the synthesis should also be distinctive. Otherwise, the model will not distinguish the folk village from other social forms. Since the folk village is the one constant among all these data, it follows that what is more "of" the village will be more constant and distinctive.

*Stable and unstable traits.* The most apparent variation among the villages occurs in their institutions. As the different villages are compared with each other, the type of family is found to be either patrilineal or matrilineal (with or without the related forms), extended or nuclear, exogamous or endogamous with respect to the village, and monogamous or polygynous. Economic forms emphasize either fishing or agriculture. Property relations fluctuate markedly. No three villages share the same religious belief. Mutual aid extends beyond the economic sphere into quite different institutions. Governments differ in the manner of using formal councils, and chiefs are elected or hereditary. Stratification varies from mild to extreme. Schools are indigenous or imported, and socialization methods range from permissive to authoritarian patterns. In recreation, however, there is a stable core of festivals (including feasts), adult games, and music, though there is more diversity in dances, stories, and children's games. (This diversity may be due more to a lack of evidence than to real differences.)

The least degree of variation among the institutions is probably to be found in mutual aid, indigenous socialization, and recreation. On the other hand, important similarities are also present in familial and economic institutions (see Table 2). Stratification, government, and religion are the most variable.

Reasoning from the premise that whatever is distinctive of villages is not likely to be most variable *and* least constant, then stratification, government, and (particularly) religion become improbable as distinctive features. This is not to imply that these institutions are not essential to the village, but rather to state that variation in these forms is so rife that it is difficult to isolate anything about them that the villages have in common. The institutions, of course, can be identified in each village; but in respect to each institution, the villages show more differences than similarities. To phrase the matter more generally, the forms in which these institutions appear vary too widely upon too shallow a base to permit the identification of any consistent position they may occupy in the structure of the folk village.

The familial and economic institutions stand in contrast. Though there were marked variations within each of these institutions, there was also a hard core in each from which there was no deviance. The families in each village not only were economic units but were also found to have a nucleus of bio-social practices (child-rearing and sanctioned sexual relations) and the same basic membership structure of husband, wife, and children (polygyny was rare). The economic constant for all villages was that of primary production: more than half of the population in each village was engaged in either agriculture or fishing or both. Such constants were absent in the status structures, governments, and forms of worship. One may conclude, therefore, that if the family and economics show as much variation as the other three institutions, they are also different in showing important features which were qualitatively constant.

*Non-distinctive traits.* An additional criterion can bring the synthesis closer to the integrating construct. Since one of the major reasons for constructing the model is to show the distinctive features of the system in question, components which help distinguish the system from others should be used as focal points around which the model is developed. When taken together, the components used should be of such a nature that they are found in no other social system.

According to this criterion, several other components also become unlikely integrating concepts. Numerous different types of social systems continue for extensive periods of time, ethnocentrism is regarded as one of the universal traits of human groups, and awareness is one of the criteria usually attributed to social systems. But even if exceptional cases without these traits could be found, the main principle would still stand: their presence is not distinctive to the groups in question.

Economic activity provides a peculiar problem. In a specific sense, there is no common form: all ten villages are devoted primarily either to agriculture or fishing or both. On the other hand, in an abstract sense, these specific occupations can be combined into the more general one of primary production. There is, however, an even more general institution which includes economic behavior as well as other kinds—mutual aid. Thus, wherever economic activity could be suggested as an integrating concept, mutual aid is even more of one. Economic institutions are therefore eliminated in favor of the more general institution, mutual aid.

Satisfying the criterion of distinctiveness will not provide a complete model. Common to all the cases used in building the model is the trait list, and it should not be overlooked. The criterion of distinctiveness does help in separating the system in question from other systems, but it should not be forgotten that other elements may be equally important to the operation of the system. A case in point is the element of interaction. No social system can exist without it, but by the very token of such universal necessity, the element of interaction is not likely to be distinctive.

*Integrating traits.* Nine components have now been found to be unlikely integrating concepts. The ten remaining traits are the three components of space and the components of base of operations, mobility, homogeneity, and the institutions of family, mutual aid, socialization, and recreation. Which among these ten will be used? If the entire list of components is to remain as part of the model, then the components selected as integrating traits must be shown to be linked or associated with all of them. The question then becomes, what are the fewest traits that will link all of the others together?

At first glance, the components appear to be grouped into two classes: those associated with space and those which (in the folk village) operate generally through the family. According to this arrangement, folk villages could be described as a localized system of families. But the question immediately arises, what are these families doing? The most inclusive answer is that they are cooperating; that is, they are bound together through institutionalized practices of mutual aid.

The hypothesis is therefore advanced that the integrating construct for the folk village is composed of space, family, and mutual aid. Functionally, the construct may be expressed as follows: *The folk village is a localized system of families cooperating by means of mutual aid.* The construct is offered as a hypothesis, since an important task remains—the components must be shown to be associated with all other items in the trait list.

### INTEGRATION OF THE MODEL

*The system.* One of the most basic features of the folk village as a social system is found in the fact that interaction is primarily direct and face to face. Everyone may not know everyone else intimately, but such a condition is approached; at the least, all strangers to the village are recognized as such. According to the integrating construct, the form of interaction most basic to the model is cooperation. The families engage in other forms of interaction—they compete, conflict, and so on—but cooperation is a common thread. It also extends beyond kinship to the other institutions.

The discussion at this point, however, concerns cooperation as a process. As such, the element involved is that of interaction. (The institutionalized aspects of cooperation are discussed with mutual aid; see p. 36.) Villagers may not necessarily love one another, but they *do* cooperate.

*Localization.* The locality inhabited by village families is not always a single, contiguous area, but—even so—the area is integrated into a unit. Though political, economic, and other methods are used, this integration takes place also—and in each case—by common recognition that all territorial parts belong to the village. Further, there is but one location for the folk village, it is relatively permanent, and it displays certain spatial patterns (that is, various services are clustered or nucleated in a given part of the village area). The vagueness of the village boundaries, however, attests to the lack of rigid patterning or complete integration.

None of the villages is isolated or self-sufficient in anything approaching an absolute sense. Large numbers of people leave their village for brief and for extended periods. Each village is in significant contact with other villages and with the larger society, but villagers are slow to change their group membership. Their village is used as a base of operations rather than as a place from which one may permanently move (though permanent moves do occur). In addition, the village is able to continue—to persist in time.

That families are aware of their membership in the village is shown by their recognition of a village name and a ruling body. They are also ethnocentric, though this sentiment is not confined to their village. Mechanical solidarity is revealed in the high proportion of persons native to the area, the importance of the family, and the dominance of the same rural occupation.

*The family.* The construct specifically mentions familial rather than individual cooperation. Such an emphasis does not deny that individuals cooperate—of course they do. But by far the most important form of cooperation is not that between individuals but between individuals as family members. Such a statement can be made even on the basis of incomplete data. There are several points to note. First, the family, not the individual, is the procreative, socializing, economic, and even the stratification unit. Second, evidence indicates that most or all adults are married (or have been) and probably none is without some village kinship ties. Third, though it is difficult to say which institutions are in fact more important to the continued existence of the village, one can gain a rough quantitative measure of such importance by noting the amount of time spent in certain institutionalized activities. Village members spend more time with their families and at their job than they do in connection with any other institution, and when one also adds time spent in socialization and as a member of a stratified position—both of which are family-based—then the role of the family as a time-occupier becomes at least equal to that of economic pursuits, if not actually supreme. Fourth, the individual cannot escape his kinship status in a social system where everyone or almost everyone knows everyone else. And finally, though data on the importance of the family have been limited to four of the eight institutions, the remainder are omitted only because information is not complete—not because it is contradictory. Consequently, one may conclude that the basis of village cooperation is familial rather than individual.

*Mutual aid.* Cooperation is most conspicuous among the institutions. Its institutionalized form, mutual aid, exists in all the villages, particularly in connection with economic pursuits. However, for most of the villages, mutual aid extends beyond the economic sphere into other institutions (the data are not clear for the villages of Shamirpet and Silwa). The institution is thus more than an economic one.

Cooperation as a process appears also in the other institutions, although it is difficult to attach to it the specific designation of mutual aid. There is never a case of a ruler who is unresponsive to the people; some democratic processes are always at work. Differences are also turned to the end of cooperation. The upper strata have roles of leadership and prestige in the community, even where differences between strata are weak, and as strata become increasingly well defined, solidarity becomes increasingly organic. That is, to a greater and greater extent, differing strata have varying roles.

Thus, the student of the folk village is faced with a mixture of traits. All villages contain both organic and mechanical solidarity. In some, such as Chan Kom and San Ildefonso, organic solidarity in the form of a division of labor does not appear relatively very significant. But in others, such as Shamirpet, Dragalevtsy, and Hilltown, organic solidarity becomes important. In no instance is either trait absent, and this is particularly true of mutual aid. Since the villagers are homogeneous in having family connections within the village, in being born in the area, and in sharing the same type of occupation, mechanical solidarity (including mutual aid) is considered the basic binding power of folk villages, though it is never the sole source of cohesion.

Religion provides a negative test. What happens when cooperation is actively denied? The two most important examples here are Hilltown and San Ildefonso. In both there was a religious schism which severely threatened the integration of the village. In San Ildefonso, the schism spread to the governmental institution and to the location of family residences. The village was in the process (not completed) of splitting apart. The incompleteness of the split is to be noted. Much, even most, of the religious and political cooperation between the two emerging factions was destroyed and, indeed, the factions were defined by their lack of cooperation in these areas. But in spite of this separation there was occasional cooperation not only in religion and politics but in other institutional behavior as well. Thus, at the time it was studied (1936–39), San Ildefonso was in the process of becoming two villages because of a restructuring of the channels though which cooperation functioned.

In the folk village of nineteenth-century Hilltown, the religious schism between the Unitarians and the Congregationalists was prevented from severely affecting the political sphere through a tradition of majority rule. Although antagonism existed between the two sects, one gained control of the governmental machinery and the other recognized and acquiesced in that control. Nevertheless, antagonism not only developed but also survived among members of both groups, even to modern times. Although haste in making causal connections should be avoided, it is significant to note that rather early in the twentieth century Hilltown was in a discernible state of disorganization. In fact, a little more than two decades after the schism, the population of the village began declining. Today, Hilltown is no more than a suburb of nearby industrial cities. Although it once did fit the model, it now does not and thus at present cannot be given the designation of "folk village." But the time lag— if the suggested connection does in fact exist—should not be surprising. The evident rift in San Ildefonso had been in the making for twenty years.

The islanders of Romonom witnessed a similar schism (this time political), a schism which had largely but not completely healed by the time of their study, but which had occurred almost fifty years before. And the villagers of neither Romonom nor San Ildefonso had developed the elaborate mechanism for adjusting to and living with disagreement as had those of Hilltown. A folk village is a thing composed of many interlocking parts. To judge from the evidence, if one part is damaged, the whole can be seriously threatened; but the full repercussions are slow to take their effect.

The discussion so far does not refer simply to the development of heterogeneity in the folk village, but rather to the existence of *negative* sanctions to cooperation. The cases given are those in which cooperation between the parts is denied and prohibited. The village of Shamirpet, however, provides a different case: one without sanctions. The village, predominantly Hindu, includes a Muslim minority (comprising about one-tenth of the population). Cooperation is not enjoined, but neither is there antagonism. Shamirpet, then, furnishes a case in which there is no religious cooperation with one of its parts—but the part is a minor one and there is no antagonism. And the village shows no tendencies toward disintegration.

Of course, it is not religious cooperation which is so important. The thesis maintains that the folk village is a social system which is built on cooperation *in general*. Religion has been discussed because it provides an important instance of possible consequences of failure in cooperation. (Loss of cooperation is of course not the only cause of village disintegration—Kaihsienkung was destroyed by the Japanese—but even for Hilltown it is not certain that unhealed religious schism was the decisive factor; the schism began before, and continued through, the disintegration, but that is all that can be said.)

Recreation provides evidence of another kind. Far from affording instances of disruption, recreational behavior in its institutionalized aspects is one of the more consistently patterned and cohesive forms appearing in the villages. It is never absent, even where it is disfavored (as it is in Silwa), and several varieties are common to all ten of the villages studied. In San Ildefonso, recreation furnished one of the notable occasions (mutual aid was the other) when the villagers forgot the quarrels associated with their schism.

These data suggest a possible role which recreation may fill, though no definite conclusion can be reached on the basis of the present evidence. Perhaps the importance of recreation lies in its role as a stimulator of cooperation. Certainly one must cooperate to some extent in order to take part in group forms of recreation (the only forms discussed here), but the significance of recreation extends farther. Recreation makes cooperation a pleasant affair. Institutionalized play may be the stimulus, therefore, which the folk villagers use (or need) in order to keep cooperation at its peak efficiency.

The hypothesis has therefore been demonstrated: Though

each of the components is not integrated directly with all other components, the three foci, taken together, are.

One final point should now be clear: Folk villages vary in the degree as well as in the type of their integration. Variation in type has been treated in noting the different importance of organic and mechanical solidarity, and differences in degree are equally evident. Hilltown and San Ildefonso were both in some stage of disintegration at the time they were studied. Romonom was healing a rupture and thus would stand between Hilltown and San Ildefonso and those which possessed more stable solidarity. The ultimate in disintegration was achieved by Kaihsienkung; that is, it was finally destroyed. A picture of the folk village as an impregnable bastion of group strength, then, would be extremely erroneous. Folk villages die, as they are born, and to judge from these data, weakening of the forces which integrate their components is a chief symptom of such a death—if, indeed, it is not a cause.

Therefore, though all ten of the villages studied have the qualities contained in the model, and though they all have common focal points around which these qualities are integrated, the integration, itself, is variable. But such variation in no way detracts from the model's usefulness. It merely recognizes a prevalent condition in the objects which it describes, just as a model of man must take note of his age.

SIGNIFICANCE OF THE MODEL

From the apparently endless variety of things found in the folk villages, nineteen general types of phenomena have been found in every one. These nineteen classes of items focus on three aspects—space, cooperation, and the family—but these foci are by no means descriptive of the village in its entirety. Rather, they serve as central or key components to which all other parts may be related.

By describing the folk village as a localized system of cooperating families, and by integrating this construct with the inventory of the components of the folk village, a generalized picture of one type of community can be drawn. This model thus becomes a kind of theory of community.

A theory should explain. We have offered an explanation of

how a folk village works: through the cooperation of its localized families. This, at least, is the expectation that the theory produces (Meehan, 1968).

In spite of its descriptive emphasis, the *general* nature of the model should be stressed. By "general" is meant the quality of referring to more than one entity. The model of the folk village is general in at least three ways: (1) It refers to more than one village (2) in more than one part of the world (3) in more than one culture. ("More than one" in each case here means ten.) This general picture, furthermore, is both extensive and systematic. It is extensive in that it refers to many parts of the folk village and it is systematic in that it refers to all of these parts in all of the villages studied.

We have thus attained a theory which describes and explains the workings of a particular type of social system. To be of significance in spite of its limitations, this theory must now exert some influence on ensuing collections of data and on future theory formation. Specifically, all considerations raised in this book from this point on must either incorporate the theory or show it to be inaccurate or incomplete. The model then becomes a kind of bench mark from which observations can be made.

# 3

# A Model of the Cities

One of the central tasks of this book is to compare various types of social systems, in the form of models, to the folk village. The basic assumption, it will be recalled, is that the folk village is a type of community and that other types of social systems can be adjudged communities as comparison shows them to be similar to the folk village. The major hypothesis of this chapter, therefore, is that both the city and the folk village are conceptually similar. If this hypothesis is correct, then it follows that various conceptual deductions can be made concerning the city, based on the findings in the folk village.

An important difference between this chapter and Chapter 2 is in the possession now of empirically based theory for at least one type of community—the village. (Given the inductive approach, no theory was available in the previous chapter to guide the construction of the folk village.) The difference necessarily makes the integration of the city's model different from that of the folk village, since the model of the city will be constructed with reference to that of the folk village. Thus, though the model of the city to be developed is inductive in that it is built only from data gathered from the traits common to the five cities summarized in Table 3, the model is deductive in that it follows the same general outline of the model established for the folk village.

The attempt to synthesize the elements of the city's model, therefore, will generally follow the procedure outlined for the folk village. Deviations will be made only when the previous theory shows them to be expedient. Accordingly, the first step is a summary of the components common to all of the cities. This summary is provided in Table 4. It describes the elements of the model of the cities. (As with the folk village, in order to understand the nature of this table, it is important to recognize that the table itself is not the model. It contains only the elements of the model. The integrating construct—given below—is needed, *in addition to* the trait list provided by the table, before the model is complete.)

*Table 3.* Selected identifying characteristics of the five cities in the comparative analysis

| City | Major ethnic groups | Population (estimated) | Major economic activity | Time of study | Investigators |
|------|------|------|------|------|------|
| New Orleans | "White," Negro | 659,768* | Commerce, transportation, manufacturing | 1950 | Hillery, 1951, 1952, 1954, 1957; Gilmore, 1944 |
| Merida | European, Mayan, and mixed | 96,660 | Commerce | 1934 | Redfield, 1941; Hansen, 1934 |
| Middletown | "White" | 47,000 | Manufacturing | 1935 | Lynds, 1937, 1929 |
| Ch'u | Chinese | 31,000 | Market center, small and hand industries | 1947–48 | Fried, 1953 |
| Timbuctoo | Songhoi, Arab, Tuareq | 6,000† | Commerce, transportation | 1940 | Miner, 1953 |

* Urbanized area, U.S. Bureau of the Census.
† Minimum permanent population.

*Table 4.* Summary description of the elements (traits) of a city model

| *Element* | *Description* |
| --- | --- |
| **1.0** *Interaction* | |
| 1.1 Personal contact | Interaction is both direct and indirect, with emphasis on quantity of contacts rather than quality. The role of the stranger is integral. Some form of mass transportation is present. |
| 1.2 Social processes | Both cooperation and competition are frequently displayed, though cooperation (contractual) appears more basic. Conflict is also in evidence. |
| **2.0** *Space* | |
| 2.1 Spatial integration | Urban territory is integrated economically by a market or markets, partially integrated by political rule, and integrated organically to a degree by locating different status groups in different parts of the city. |
| 2.2 Spatial patterning | Processes of segregation, centralization, and decentralization are evident. Each city also displays an elaborate network of paths and streets. |
| 2.3 Boundaries | City boundaries are vague in that they are conflicting or otherwise unstable. |
| **3.0** *Activities* | |
| 3.1 Base of operations | Cities are bases of operation for both localistic and cosmopolitan activities of citizens and others. |
| 3.2 Mobility | Territorial mobility is extensive and horizontal mobility is considerable. City-dwellers do not as a rule remain in one place or retain contacts with only one group during their lifetimes. |
| 3.3 Continuance | Cities have been in existence between one and ten centuries, or an average (mean) of five centuries. |
| **4.0** *Sentiment* | |
| 4.1 Ethnocentrism | Although inhabitants of all cities display some form of ethnocentrism toward varying groups, only three cities display ethnocentrism toward the city as a whole. (No data are given for the two smallest cities.) |
| 4.2 Awareness | Citizens are aware of the city as manifested either in their ethnocentrism, in the name they give the city, or in their recognition of the city as an entity distinct from other social groupings. |
| 4.3 Heterogeneity (Organic solidarity) | Cities were not consistently homogeneous in respect to any trait. A division of labor was noted in all institutions described under Norms, below. Mechanical heterogeneity (as opposed to mechanical solidarity) was also found for several institutions in all cities. |

*Table 4 (cont.)*

| *Element* | *Description* |
|---|---|
| **5.0** *Norms* (Institutions) | |
| 5.1 Family | Families are sexual units, economic consumption units, and often socialization units. Most adults are married, but there are also significant segments of unmarried, divorced, or separated adults in all cities. |
| 5.2 Economics | Secondary production, distribution, and service industries dominate, characterized by specialization both between cities and among individuals. |
| 5.3 Religion | Religious bodies have sacred and/or secular hierarchies. Magical beliefs are also present. |
| 5.4 Government | A division of labor was observed between administrative, enforcement, and judicial components (though not necessarily legislative components). No city was governed totally by power (as contrasted with authority). |
| 5.5 Cooperation | Contractual behavior characterizes economic and other institutions. |
| 5.6 Stratification | Distances between strata are great in all cities and all strata have some degree of vertical social mobility. |
| 5.7 Socialization | All cities have established schools. Socialization also occurs in the family, though not exclusively. |
| 5.8 Recreation | Feasts and festivals, games, and music are practiced in traditional and in group forms. Recreation is also partly commercialized in all cities. |

*Stable and unstable traits.* The next steps consist of eliminating components of the model which are not likely to be integrating ones. Following the procedure for the folk village, the most basic consideration is that the synthesis is to be built only from common components. The first step is to isolate the more unstable components: Given this collection of similar things, which are the more variable? The assumption is that those things which are more central to the city will appear from city to city in relatively unchanging form. On the other hand, if one can make no more than a superficial prediction about a given component —such as, for example, that religion will be found in all cities— then that component must not be one which is intrinsic to cities. The component may be *in* cities and may be important to cities, but the probability is that it will neither be distinctive of cities nor will the city be integrated around it.

As in the folk village, the most noticeable variation among the cities is in the element of continuance and in the institutions. The cities—at least the five studied—seem to have existed longer than folk villages—the range for the cities being from one to ten centuries. Among the city's institutions, variations similar to those in the folk village were found and in some cases even additional variations. Tracing only the more important, families may or may not have economic production functions; some persons (though a minority) may not live in the married state; and those who are married may be childless and thus not act as a socialization unit. The type of economic activity varies not only in reference to the specialties but also in regard to the dominant economic activity, whether it is serving local or foreign markets or producing by means of hand or factory industries. Religions have little in common other than being religious (and magical) systems and in having an internal division of labor. The same remarks can be made for governments: they govern in part by means of a division of labor. Institutions of contract vary in the extent to which they occur with institutions of mutual aid (though mutual aid was never more than imperfectly developed). Stratification in the city shows somewhat more uniformity than it did in the folk village, but only in that the highest and lowest strata are vertically more distant from each other. Cities could operate under a caste, slave, or open class system and still be effective as cities. Socialization shows more uniformity than the folk village and more differences: all cities had schools that the cities themselves had established, but the role of socialization was not as often fulfilled within the city family as it was in the folk village's. Recreation, again, was consistent in displaying festivals and feasts, games, and music. It varied in other forms, and it varied also in the extent to which it had been influenced by commercialization.

One should probably note also that the *evidence* for the sentiment of ethnocentrism was not complete for all cities, but no conclusion can be made that ethnocentrism was lacking in any city (relative to the city as a whole).

The least degree of variation is probably found in the institutions of contract and in recreational forms. Important similarities, however, are also to be seen in the family, economic institutions, and socialization. The importance of the similarities in contract can be seen especially in comparison with the other components of the model, as given in Table 4. When linked with the component of heterogeneity, the institution of contract is associated with a well-developed division of labor in all of the city's institutions. Cooperation, therefore, in its institutionalized form of contracts, occurs more frequently than the institutionalized forms of the other social processes, competition and conflict.

The features of the family consistently found in all of the cities were its function as a unit for the performance of sanctioned heterosexual relations and as a unit of economic consumption. Socialization was present among families with children. Economic institutions were consistent in that they emphasized secondary rather than primary production industries and contained also distributive and service industries. Primary production industries (agriculture and fishing) were in the minority. Further, the city's economic institutions were universally characterized by an elaborate division of labor. A consistency in socialization is only to be found in the fact that all the cities had schools and that the family was most often so structured that socialization was one of its functions.

*Non-distinctive traits.* Four components, therefore, vary too widely to reveal a distinctive pattern in any of the cities: We may expect (1) the city to continue, (2) to have religion, (3) to have government, and (4) to have stratification, and we may also expect differentiation within each of the three institutions—but no more than that. There is no way of knowing, for example, what kind of religion will be found in the cities, what kind of government, or what kind of stratification. The fact that the institutions have internal specialization is not characteristic of these institutions, but it is characteristic of organic solidarity and the accompanying institution of contract. Therefore, we cannot expect to build a model of the city which would give a central place to these four components; they exist, but they do not display a common pattern.

Still following a negative approach, another component of the city model can be isolated which will *not* serve as an integrating factor—the institution of economics. It appears in all of the cities in a rather consistent form—non-primary production industries—and of course it is vitally important to the continuation of each city. But the economic institution per se is not an institution that integrates the others. The marked individuality and accompanying competitive and even conflicting sentiments and processes that accompany economic practices disqualify it as an integrative factor. Rather, it is the institution of the contract that integrates.

The fact that contracts probably find their highest development in the institution of economics is perhaps the reason it is often mistakenly assumed that the economic institution is the most important of the city's components. But the single institution that pervades all of the other institutions and each of the other elements of interaction, sentiment, activities, and space is not economic; it is, rather, the institution of contract.

*Integrating traits.* Following the concepts advanced in the description of the folk village, the elements of space, interaction, and activity, together with the component of awareness from the element of sentiment, can be summed up under the concept of a localized system. The sentiment of organic solidarity, as revealed in organic heterogeneity,[1] may be included as an aspect of contract (which is, in turn, a type of cooperation).

In light of the importance of the familial institutions in the folk village, these institutions deserve special treatment. The most obvious point to note is the increased importance of the individual in the city; nevertheless, the city family still occupies a major position. More systematically, this dual importance of the family and the individual can be stated as follows: (1) most citizens are married; (2) the family is a consistent component of cities; (3) similarly, the individual is consistently a significant minority; and (4) individuals make contracts *as individuals.* Thus, we cannot speak simply about cooperating families. The process of cooperation must be clearly separated, since it can and does occur on an individual basis. Accordingly, the individual is related to the city in at least two ways: individuals acting for themselves, and individuals acting for their families (most often for their wives and children).

Thus, the initial hypothesis has been followed: The city can be treated conceptually in the same manner as was the folk village. The foregoing analysis reveals that only quantitative modifications of certain qualities are necessary in order to

---

[1] For a discussion of organic heterogeneity, see Appendix A.

satisfy the hypothesis (as contrasted with abandonment of the qualities). The most important of these modifications is the decreased importance of the family. Accordingly, the following statement is offered as the integrating construct for the city: *The city is a localized system integrated by contracts and families.* This is not a complete description of the city, no more than the corresponding construct for the folk village completely described that type of social system. For a complete description (relatively speaking), the model of the city should be consulted. The integrating construct is intended to be distinctive and integral rather than exhaustive.

### INTEGRATION OF THE MODEL

*The city as an interactional system.* Whereas the folk village is bound together by a system of ties based on primary-group interaction, the type of interaction which renders the city a system is clearly a combination of both primary and secondary ties. Primary groups are found among various other kinds of groups, particularly in families. Primary ties, however, do not unite all families to each other. And in each city there is a significant minority of individuals with no family connections. The chief type of interaction binding families and individuals together is the contract, which is generally a secondary form of interaction. (The contract as an institution is discussed later in this chapter.)

The types of social interaction in the city may be viewed as operating on three levels. Most individuals have primary ties with some other individuals, especially via marriage and the family. Some individuals, however, are excluded from this level. On another level, other persons are in contact through secondary ties, especially by means of contracts. And, finally, there is a level of interaction which is characterized by anonymity. This last level may include those in contractual and other types of relations, and it does include the stranger to the city (or quarter) as well as the normal resident.

The same basic interactional processes that were found in the folk village were found in the city (though there were probably others as well): cooperation, competition, and conflict. Of these three, only one is consistently institutionalized and only one pervades the other elements of the city—cooperation in the form of contractual relations. It is for this reason that cooperation is judged most basic of the three processes in the cities.

To conceive of the city without competition and conflict, however, would be as erroneous as to ignore the people themselves. Competition is quite in evidence, especially in the market place. Conflict appears here, too, in the form of theft. How important these two processes are is difficult to say. The contention is advanced, however, that they do not permeate the city (or at least the five cities studied) to the same degree as does contractual cooperation. At the very least, there is no evidence showing the pervasiveness of the other processes and much to show the pervasiveness of cooperation.

Mass transportation is important to the city in several ways. First, it helps to keep the various parts integrated at a more efficient level than would otherwise be the case. Second, it keeps the city in contact with the outside world. And third, mass transportation represents an articulation of the interactional element with that of space.

*The city as a localized system.* Perhaps the most apparent feature of the system of the city is its localized aspect. The fact that space is not paramount, however, becomes clearly evident in that social factors invariably modify the spatial configuration. Space in the city is integrated economically by the market, to some extent by the government, and also to some extent by the organic interrelation of its strata—certain areas are allocated to given status groups, be these classes or castes. The city, in other words, is not integrated merely by the fact that people are near one another, though proximity undoubtedly is a significant part of the picture. The other part of the picture is the social one. (It should also be noted that the city is not necessarily integrated by geographical features, whatever importance geography may have in a specific case. For example, all these cities are located near large bodies of water, but they are not uniformly related to these bodies either economically or socially.)

Another indication of the secondary importance of space is found in the nature of the spatial patterning. Cities do not group their institutions in the same place. The more important fact associated with the spatial pattern is not the location of groups or institutions but the interaction of social forces under the limiting influence of space. Thus, there is not a common relation between ecological zones, but there are common ecological processes, particularly segregation, centralization, and decentralization. Similarly, there develops in all cities a communication network of paths and streets as a consequence of the interrelation of space, permanent buildings, and interactional processes. The same result is seen in the vagueness of boundaries. It is not space which determines man's interaction or his activities; if it were, one would expect to find discrete and distinct boundaries to the social system. Instead, the people recognize one set of boundaries politically, another set socially. Further, all of these boundaries, conflicting as they are, tend to change as the city changes.

The city, then, is first and foremost a social system. It is, further, a peculiar social system in that it is localized. But the spatial quality is more limiting than determining.

The localized aspect of the city's system extends, as might be expected, to the daily activities of the people. The city is a base of operations for the activities of the residents (and visitors) both in a cosmopolitan sense (in journeying to the outside world) and in a localistic sense. Locally, the individual repeatedly journeys from one part of the city to another. In a cosmopolitan sense, the city is a cluster of things—people, sentiments, norms, etc.—which the city-resident leaves when he journeys to the outside world, and to which he returns.

The implications of territorial mobility for the integrating construct have been noted in connection with mass communication (transportation) and in the discussion of the city as a base of operations. The city is obviously not a collection of static residents. It is a site of frequent moves which involve a large proportion of the city members. Indeed, natives to the city are at times in the minority, and non-natives involve a significant segment of all the cities. Permanent moves occur often, and evidence exists that horizontal mobility—that is, change in group membership—is even more frequent than territorial mobility. This fact is of importance in understanding such components of the city's model as secondary-group membership, contractual cooperation, and heterogeneity.

The fact that the city is a system is attested to in many ways, but the most elequent testimony is to be found in the ability of the city to continue. These fluid and dynamic complexes of forces have existed as clusters (or, more completely, as entities) among the five cities for no less than one century and in at least one case for more than ten centuries.

More data are needed on these cities in order to be certain of their ethnocentrism, but the analysis in Appendix B suggests quite strongly that ethnocentrism toward the city as a whole was not well developed. In fact, the lack of attention which the investigagors of Ch'u and Timbuctoo gave to ethnocentrism is evidence in itself, under the assumption that a virile ethnocentrism would have been asserted more strongly to the investigators.

In all probability, the significance of the contract can be invoked in explanation of this (possibly) weakened sentiment. If ethnocentrism is weak, it is probably a consequence of the specific nature of the ties which contract engenders. One's relation to the city is rarely to the city as such or even to a significant part of it. The relation is rather to selected segments of the city, and, because of the specific nature of the contract, a relation to one part of the city does not necessarily involve a relation to another part. In support of this claim, evidence is found in all of the cities that some types of ethnocentrism were felt by their inhabitants, even though information may not have been divulged concerning ethnocentrism toward the city per se. Further, one of the findings in Appendix B is that loyalty to these cities, even where it undoubtedly exists, is never complete; that is, other interests arise in successful competition, interests such as identification with one's ethnic group, identification with a given residential quarter of the city, etc.

The inhabitants are aware of their city, but the weakness of their ethnocentrism detracts from the unity of the city as a system. The presence of awareness acts in the opposite direction; that is, awareness is a necessary element in the existence of any meaningful-casual entity.

*Heterogeneity and contract.* At this point, an alteration is necessary in the order of treatment of the integration of the model's components, and the institution of contract will be discussed next in conjunction with the sentiment resulting from heterogeneity, that is, organic solidarity (as opposed to discussing contract with the other institutions).

A few definitions are necessary here (see Appendix B for fuller explanations). *Organic heterogeneity* is nearly synonymous with *division of labor*, except that no solidarity is implied. Organic heterogeneity thus differs from organic solidarity. *Mechanical heterogeneity* refers to differences that do not involve a division of labor.

The social facts most available are organic heterogeneity, its pervasiveness, and the presence of certain types of limited contracts in all of the cities. As shown in Appendix B, the city is characterized by an extensive division of labor, a division which is found in all of its institutions and which is elaborately developed in practically all of them as well. But the city is not composed solely of a division of labor. There is mutual aid and there is heterogeneity of a type which is not involved in a division of labor (mechanical heterogeneity). These aspects of city life, however, do not seem of importance in understanding what happens to most of the people most of the time. Further, organic heterogeneity is not limited to the social institutions. Its influence can be found in social interaction (particularly in secondary relationships and in the social processes) and in spatial relationships (especially in the territorial distribution of status groups). In addition, since activities are influenced by interaction, space, sentiment, and norms, activities are obviously conditioned by the city's organic heterogeneity. Finally, if the conceptual leap is made from organic heterogeneity to organic solidarity (see Appendix B), the social fact of a division of labor is seen to manifest itself in the element of sentiment as well.

Thus, the second social fact, after first noting the presence of organic heterogeneity, is its pervasiveness. No element of the city's model is without the significant influence of this type of specialization.

The third fact is the obvious importance of contracts to all of the cities, even when contracts are looked at in the narrow sense. There is, first, the contractual nature of the market place—and markets are central to the urban economy. Second, there is the presence of money in the five cities. Money may be looked upon as a contract in at least two ways: (1) between the society which sanctions and upholds its use and the individuals who use it; and (2) between the partners to the exchange who recognize the limitations placed upon themselves.

Contract is even more important than this, however, as can be shown by a careful examination of the concept. According to Parsons, contract is a form of cooperation in which the content, means, and risk of the interaction are limited; there is also some society-wide recognition of these limitations (1960, pp. 144–45). In other words, for a contractual system to be *fully developed* (there can be approximations), there are limitations placed on what is involved in the contractual operation, what methods can be used to carry out the agreement, and the extent to which the agreement involves the persons concerned. For example, when buying a theatre ticket in Euro-American cultures there is general social recognition that such tickets *can* be purchased (as contrasted with the purchase of children), that money is to be used in such a purchase (as opposed to the use, say, of human life), and that buying the ticket obligates the manager only to give the patron a seat and to permit him an unhindered view of the stage (the patron has no rights, say, in the manager's wife). Implicit in this example is the fact that these limits are recognized by others, that is, by a segment of a social system larger than the immediate parties to the transaction of ticket-purchase and sale.

Given the above definition, it follows that what was described as organic heterogeneity is really a system of contracts. The contracts may not always be written, nor may they always be consciously recognized as limited agreements, but they are there nonetheless. And, as important a consideration as any, the contractual system extends beyond the economic sphere. Parsons recognizes that the contract is "the more general and central institutional focus" of the economic complex (1960, p. 144), but contractual relationships are also quite in evidence in such specialized roles as judge, priest, teacher, and minstrel. In fact, the principle may be now advanced that all of the specializations that have been described as manifestations of organic heterogeneity represent varying approaches to contract—except those specializations which result from force. (An example of the latter would be robber and victim, and here the process involved is domination rather than cooperation.) Thus, one could define *contract* as a voluntary and mutual agreement to engage in a purposely limited cooperative endeavor.

Contractual cooperation, therefore, is the binding force that holds the city's heterogeneity (generated by the division of labor) in some kind of unity. Organic solidarity is thus actually a system of contracts. Durkheim claims that the division of labor and its resulting interdependence held certain types of society together. According to the findings here, however, it is not the interdependence or its recognition which is of such importance, though of course interdependence is involved. Rather, it is the agreement to limit cooperation which is the chief binding power. Interdependence enables the society to survive; contract permits the interdependence to function. Seen in this light, the remarks on contract become an elaboration on Durkheim's concept of organic solidarity.

What then of the presence of slaves in some cities, particularly in Timbuctoo and (earlier) New Orleans? A system of slavery is logically contradictory to a contractual system, as set forth above. How does slavery come to exist in an urban system, and what is the relation of slavery to the contract?

The existence of slavery in the city must be studied with the full facts in view that the contract—to which slavery is antithetical—is the more pervasive component in the model, and that slavery exists only in some cities, not in all. Apparently, therefore, slavery is not intrinsic to urban development per se. More logical is the contention that slavery exists in spite of urbanization. The genesis of slavery, of course, rests in the presence of a powerful politico-economic elite, and these (with slavery) have existed outside of urban configurations. The Kwakiutl Indians of the Northwestern American coast are one such conspicuous example, and even closer to this discussion are the nomadic Tuaregs of the Sahara, a non-urban people who owned slaves, the slaves in turn dwelling in Timbuctoo. What happens, then, is that the politico-economic elite can and do bring their slaves into urban settings. (This happened also among the planters who had residences in New Orleans.) Others in the city may obtain slaves as part of the process of cultural diffusion. In general, then, though slavery does occur at times in some cities, it is not to be regarded as something produced by the city.

Once slavery is a part of city life, what relation does the system develop to a contractual one? The evidence is clear for both Timbuctoo and New Orleans. The slave participates in the contractual system as does everyone else—with one exception: He has a non-contractual (that is, a subordinate and compulsory) relationship to his master. He may or may not contract on his own right. Often he does both; that is, he may contract for himself and for his master. In fact, he may even purchase his freedom or, in terms of the present discussion, he may dissolve or destroy his subordinate role through his participation in the contractual system.

*The family among other institutions.* The topic of slavery, a non-contractual institution in *some* cities, provides an interesting contrast with the family, a non-contractual institution in *all* the cities. Though contracts are typically made with individuals, most city members spend much of their lives in familial relationships, that is, non-contractual ones. Indeed, the family is so important that it exists in opposition to contractual relationships. Further, the family should be recognized as the most extensive component of non-contractual relationships in city life.

Unlike slavery, the family is not to be regarded as something which exists in spite of the city (though to look at the relative instability of families in some cities, such a conclusion may seem warranted). But the inescapable fact is that the family is well entrenched in all of the five cities, even Timbuctoo. Though that city had an astronomical divorce rate, there was not a corresponding number of unattached inhabitants. It is true that contracts and families produce opposing consequences: specific as contrasted with diffuse obligations and rights. But to attempt to label the family as thereby not essential to the city is to fail to explain the family's continued and vigorous presence. Relative to the folk village and to the contract (in the city), the family is weak, but it is nevertheless a significant urban component because it integrates the city in several ways.

Since the assumption is often made that the family is of no importance to the city, the nature of this integration should be given in some detail. Of five components in the model of the city that the family integrates, probably the most far-reaching consequences are found in the component of personal contact. The family integrates persons into the city who would not otherwise be integrated, specifically children and spouses (notably, wives). The point here, though simple, is crucial. Many if not most of the inhabitants of the city are in it *only* because they are members of a family. This is integration in its literal and most direct sense.

The family helps to integrate the city spatially through its households. (Note that this type of integration occurs in the folk village, also. It is more apparent in the city probably because of the paucity of other integrating functions.) In fact, the spatial pattern of the city is to a large extent a pattern of households. Moreover, the base from which most persons operate is the household, which is the seat of the family. The household is of further importance in that it also helps integrate non-kin inhabitants of the city.

The family is the first rung on the hierarchy of ethnocentrism. Whatever may be the data on ethnocentrism for the city as a whole (it will be recalled that such evidence was not given for two cities), there can be no doubt about the importance of the urbanite's ethnocentrism toward his family.

Probably the family is involved in all institutions, just as it is in the folk village, but the evidence from the five cities is not clear. Certainly, one can participate to a large extent as an individual in religious and governmental affairs, in recreation, and of course in the contract. In the remaining institutions, however, the role of the family is clear, even if limited. Economically, the family is a consumption unit; it is fully a unit of stratification; it always participates effectively in socialization. Even with respect to the contract, the individual is not so important as the fact that contracts are made with individuals and that through the individual the contract operates on the family.

In brief, therefore, families are both integrating units and units of integration. The existence in the city of the two opposing institutions of contract and family has not yet been satisfactorily explained (but see Sjoberg, 1960a, p. 330), and to look to opposing personality needs is only to shift the problem to another level, not to mention the fact that such needs have not yet been demonstrated. For the present, one can only note that the behavior of city residents cannot be fully explained without recourse to familial relationships, just as they cannot be explained without recourse to contractual relationships. (What will eventually happen to the family in the city is, of course, highly speculative. In this connection, see the discussion of the kibbutz in Chap. 9.)

The foregoing would be misleading, however, if one were to conclude that contractual relationships do not influence the family (and vice versa, though the latter is a more difficult question). The influence of contractual relationships can be seen as operating against the family in the greater degree of instability of the family in the cities relative to the stability of families in the folk village. Contracts are made for limited ends, whereas familial relations are generalized. With the contract so important to the city, it is small wonder that the urban family has felt its influence, that the general ties of the family are frequently broken as if they were limited ties of contract. But the fact remains that within the family the obligations and rights are still general and that they are not limited by specific rules as are contracts. In this sense, the so-called marriage contract is no contract at all (even admitting that historically and in special cases some contractual limitations have occurred in some marriages).

Probably the most striking fact about the city family is that it is so well preserved even when compared with its more fully developed counterpart in the folk village. Whereas mutual aid as an institution disintegrates virtually to the point of disappearance and is superseded by contract, the family remains quite conspicuous. There is, however, an important similarity: both mutual aid and contract are types of cooperation and, in this sense, only the form of the institutional process has changed. Cooperation is found both in the model of the folk village and in the model of the city. The same can be said of the family. In the folk village, the family is more stable and embraces more functions. In the city, it becomes a more fluid institution and there is a paring down of its functions. But the family, like cooperation, occurs in both models. The presence of greater individualism in the city relative to the folk village, represented by increasing contractualism, stresses the fact that a change has occurred. The change, however, is one involving basically the same components in both cases, as well as the same basic organizational principles.

The economic institution has been essentially accounted for. The contract reaches its fullest development here, probably because the economic institution is of such immediate importance to survival. The family, of course, also has this immediate importance, but contractual relationships simply do not meet the opposition in economic institutions that they do in the family. On the contrary, as is obvious, economic institutions probably flourish more luxuriantly under contract than under mutual aid.

The interrelation between economic, contractual, and familial institutions can be summarized quite simply by noting that a city resident can make a living in two ways—by engaging in contractual relations with others or by possessing familial relations with someone who has such contracts.

It might appear that the above discussion of economics is too brief a treatment of such an important institution, but the question should be put: Important for what? The economic institution is crucial for man's biological survival, and any importance it has for the rest of the social system hinges mainly on this importance. Thus, for treating what is *in* the community (as opposed to what is *of* or central to the community), economics deserves extended consideration. Other institutions, however, are important for other things—and socialization and the family are vastly more important than economics for the continued *social* existence of a community. The thesis here is that space, contract, and the family are much more important than economics in integrating the components of the city and in distinguishing the city from other social forms.

*Peripheral institutions.* The components of the city around which the others are ordered may be termed "of" the community. But not all things are as important to cities, and these others we can call "in" the community rather than "of" it. The remaining institutions to be discussed fall in this category, specifically, religion, government, stratification, socialization, and recreation. They may be treated on the order of dependent variables, that is, they may be explained by other factors. These factors may be grouped into two complexes: the components of the integrating construct (space, contract, and family), and the position which they have on the continua between the folk village and the city. The continua must now come in for greater emphasis, since they appear to be the only means of explaining the variation among these institutions and their position in the city. (The plural *continua* is used because there are several continua, each qualitatively distinct, joining the folk village and the city.)

The position of religion in the model is probably a consequence chiefly of the system of contract and the position which any given city occupies on the village-city continua. The structure of religion mirrors the division of labor appearing elsewhere in the city. The strength of religious beliefs and their importance to the people is probably inversely related to the degree to which the contractual institutions have been developed. Religion has probably more influence on the lives of the inhabitants of Ch'u and Timbuctoo than it has on the residents in the other cities, and the division of labor in the two smaller cities is more poorly developed.

The prevalence of mechanical heterogeneity in four of the cities (Timbuctoo excepted) attests to the peripheral nature of urban religion. It makes little difference to any city whether it possesses one religion or fifty; it can be just as much a going concern either way. In fact, a minority can be atheists, and the city goes on as ever. (The kibbutz is significant in this connection—see Chap. 9.) But if mechanical heterogeneity can be used as an index of the nearness which any of the cities are to the folk village (although all are indubitably cities rather than folk villages), then this index is seen to correspond to that given for the division of labor: Ch'u and Timbuctoo have the fewer religions (or sects). These two cities thus have less organic heterogeneity, as well as less mechanical heterogeneity, in their religions as well as their other institutions.

Government, like religion, reflects the division of labor characteristic of the city. That it should be influenced by the city's system of stratification is not surprising, especially since stratification is similarly influenced by the contractual institution. But the relation in this instance is by no means complete. New Orleans and Middletown are ruled by the business elite, but professional politicians are apparently not without influence in New Orleans. Ch'u is ruled by government officials who seem ipso facto to have high status. Timbuctoo was ruled by a combination of the conquering French, the religious cadis (judges), and political chiefs. The data are not sufficiently clear to permit comment on Merida. Apparently, then, government in these cities is in a position similar to religion: persons in various strata can rule and varying kinds of government can operate, and the city will function, no matter.

Stratification, as mentioned, is heavily influenced by the city's contractual system. Two important facts with which to begin are (1) that the vertical distance between strata is small in folk villages, whereas it is much greater in the city; and (2) that the political and/or economic elite are at or near the top of the urban strata. Add to these facts the additional one that each of the cities gives achievement a prominent place in the status hierarchy. Achievement is not of uniform importance—family and possessions can take precedence—but it is always of importance. The role of contractual relations thus becomes evident at several points. First, because the upper strata are increasingly isolated through the processes of specialization, a greater social distance appears among the classes. When the possibility of achievement and its consequent enhancement of wealth is added to this isolation, the potentiality of creating vast distances between strata are markedly increased.

Socialization is also influenced by the urban characteristic of specialization. But as mentioned earlier, the family is also quite important. True, all "families" do not have this function (for example, the childless married couples do not), and the method is often no method at all. Nevertheless, the children learn the language and elementary customs of their culture first in and near the home.

The closer position of Timbuctoo to the village end of the village-city continua must again be noted, this time in the poorer development of its schools. In the North American cities, on the other hand, the specialized educational system takes over rapidly from the family. Not to be ignored for any of the cities are the apprentice systems. The close relationship of these to the contractual institution needs no comment.

Recreation follows the other institutions in reflecting greater specialization than occurred in the folk village, especially in the universal and marked (though not complete) commercialization. Ch'u and Timbuctoo, again, are closer to the villages in that their recreation shows a lesser degree of specialization.

The sensitivity which recreation shows to contractualism indicates that its function as a medium for reinforcing cooperative norms is apparently as undiminished in the city as in the folk village. The consistency with which both specialization and commercialization appeared from city to city shows merely that the form of cooperation has changed from that of mutual aid to that of contract.

## CONCLUSIONS

Two major conclusions emerge. The first shows the value of treating the city as a variation of the same type of thing as the folk village. The two models are best to be viewed as varying from each other in degree, that is, as existing on continua.

The second conclusion concerns the error of attempting to view the folk village and the city as being connected with one, unidimensional spectrum. The three foci of the city are qualitatively distinct, and as such they represent no less than three dimensions. Probably more accurately, one should speak of three complexes of dimensions, each operating to a large degree independently of the others and yet each influencing the others.

If this interpretation is correct, we should expect any given number of cities to be placed at different points on any of the three continua, depending on which continuum is being considered. Thus, family structure would be expected to be capable of changing at a different rate than cooperation, and both could change at different rates than spatial influences. And yet, since the city is a system (or at least a system of systems), each of the foci will affect the others, and thus the *tendency* will be for the three foci to change together.

Because of this necessity for three continua, it should not now be surprising that a well-developed and stable family system can occur in one city along with a fairly well-developed system of contracts. Thus, Ch'u is not much different from the folk village on the familistic continuum (though it is different), and it is further along the cooperative continuum (more contractual) than on either the familistic or spatial continua. Similarly, Timbuctoo is not as different from folk villages along the spatial continuum as it is on the others (though, again, it is different). Merida is farthest along the spatial and cooperative continua and only somewhat farther than Ch'u along the familistic one. The two U.S. cities apparently have had more even development on all three continua.

# 4

# The Vill

The models developed in Chapters 2 and 3 may both be described as theories of a low level of abstraction. They remain close to their data and do not permit very many generalizations which would apply to other social phenomena. When folk villages were discussed, specific instances of folk villages could be cited. When cities were discussed, specific instances could again be cited. It is now profitable to move to another level of analysis, a more general theory that includes both folk villages and cities. We must now use theories to explain our more general theory, where before we used data drawn directly from the living social systems.

The more general theory is by no means the ultimate in abstraction, as will become apparent. And thus, since even more general theories are possible, the more general theory is a theory of the middle range (Merton, 1957). The problem arises, what shall this middle-range theory (or model) be called? The most obvious answer is that it should be called a model of community —but the meaning of "community," of course, presents troublesome problems. To apply such a term to the middle-range model means that other people will give this model more meanings than we will assign to it. A term is needed, therefore, which will refer *only* to folk villages and cities and which will refer to *nothing else*, unless other things can be shown to be related to folk villages and cities in the same manner that these things are related to each other.

The word to be used for this middle-range model is "vill." It has the virtue of already existing in the English language and its meaning can be extended to include both cities and villages. Literally, it refers to a township or a subdivision of a county; more important, the word is used so seldom as to be capable of severe restriction. Thus, in the most immediate sense, *the vill is a more general model which includes both the models of folk villages and cities.*

The evidence that such a model can be developed is found in the following manner. Inductively, one need only refer to Chapters 2 and 3: the same things (things capable of being described with the same concepts) were found in both folk villages and cities, the important distinction being that these same things were found in differing and varying degrees. Deductively, one may reason that should such a more general model be valid (that is, truly general), then additional evidence for such a model will be found. The more general model should also provide a reinterpretation of the models which it contains—otherwise, nothing new will have been added. The more general theory should also be able to predict the existence of other social systems. Finally, the more general theory should help to show the strengths and weaknesses of theories developed by others and it should show how it adds to these theories. All of these points will be considered (the last, in subsequent chapters).

### THE THEORY OF VILLS

*The foci on a general level.* In the synthesis of each of the models for folk villages and for cities, the components were seen to be integrated around three foci—space, cooperation, and family. It follows, therefore, that any common model should also be integrated in the same manner.

Although the model of the vill is composed of two other models, it differs from them in two ways: it is more general and it is composed of continua. The presence of continua may be viewed as the most important manifestation of the quality of generality. Continua were not as important for the folk village or the city; each of the models could be described according to its own qualities (the folk village is a relatively homogeneous grouping in space of families engaged in mutual aid, the city is a relatively heterogeneous grouping in space of individuals, with their families, engaged in contracts). The model of the vill, however, must include all of these variations. The localized groupings range from more to less homogeneous (or from less to more heterogeneous); the organization of the members ranges from virtual complete dominance of the family to the presence of the family among other institutions; and the mode of cooperation varies from mutual aid to contract. The description of these ranges is accomplished by continua. Instead of referring to any specific trait, we refer to a range of variation in traits.

As with the models of the folk village and city, the model of the vill is described by means of an integrating construct and a list of components. The trait list for the vill can be described at this point simply as a combination of the two trait lists developed for folk villages and cities. (The combined trait list is given in Chap. 8, Table 7). The integrating construct, which will receive most attention in this chapter, may be stated as follows: *The vill is a localized system integrated by means of families and cooperation.*

By *localization* is meant the quality of being located in only one place outside of which the system has no identity. Contrast, for example, factories, schools, and other social systems which may *in practice* operate in more than one place or whose members do so. The use of the term *system* is intended to emphasize that there is some integration in the vill. It is not just a collection of things. Uppermost is the *social* system in which members interact more with each other than they do with outsiders. Also important, however, is the *ecological* system which traces the relation of the members of the system to their environment, especially the spatial aspects of the environment. The concept of system thus refers both to the localization and to the social aspects of vills.

No vill is composed only of individuals. Most individuals are attached to the vill in part because they are *family* members. Folk villages rely almost exclusively on this type of social organization, whereas in cities the familial attachment is supplemented by relations with contractually oriented groups.

*Cooperation* takes place within the local system in two ways: in in terms of mutual aid (in folk villages) and contracts (in cities). Though both forms of cooperation are institutionalized, mutual aid emphasizes relationships that are more personal and, in the purest sense, the activities associated with mutual aid are never defined rigidly; they are instead diffuse. Contracts, on the other hand, are more impersonal and the activities related to them are more specific.

The variation in each of the traits occurs as noted in the contrast between folk villages and cities. The principal variation in localization is in spatial differentiation, which varies from relatively homogeneous to more heterogeneous. Cooperation varies from mutual aid to contract. Finally, the groups change from family-dominated to groups formed *more often* on the basis of contract.

As was true for the models of the folk village and the city, none of the three foci, alone, is sufficient to describe the vill. Like its subtypes, the vill is a complex of foci. No vill is without spatial, cooperative, *and* familial orientation. Further, each focus in the complex affects the others not only directly but through the other components in the model with which it is integrated. This statement must necessarily be as true of the vill as it is of its subtypes. Extended discussions of the integration in the models of these subtypes have been given in Chapters 2 and 3. For the present, we need only assume that the foci are similarly integrated with all of the other components in the more general model, just as they are in the models of the folk village and the city. This integration will be explored more fully in Chapter 8.

*Some theoretical implications.* It is not possible to give priority to any one focus at the present state of knowledge. We know only that families stay together and that they cooperate. Whether they cooperate in order to stay together, or vice versa, or whether they raise families in order to cooperate, no one can yet say. Certainly, each of these three things is functional for the others, but even then, dysfunctions are also apparent. For example, it is obvious that proximity may also breed strife, and thus proximity (localization) may become dysfunctional for cooperation.

Nor can one seek to argue the importance of any one focus by deemphasizing the other two. For example, it is true that cooperation is present in all vills, but so is conflict, and thus co-operation has a serious threat to its existence in vills generally. Similarly, one could almost view space as a means rather than a focus of community activity. And yet a close look at the fifteen vills shows clearly that spatial relationships play an important role in maintaining the organization of community. (This, of course, is part of the message of the human ecologists.)

Thus, no attempt will be made to argue the importance of any of the three foci. Instead, our concern is with the manner in which the foci relate themselves to each other. To understand this relationship, it is helpful to view the manner in which the picture of vills has emerged. First, from the total range of things that are relevant to such things as folk villages and cities, nineteen components common to them all were selected. Then, from these nineteen components, three were chosen which were integrated with all of the other sixteen. Thus, the vill is a selected picture of reality according to given criteria, particularly the criterion of common possession of a wide range of traits.

Because of their role in linking the other elements, the foci are understandably quite different from each other: space is a physical and essentially non-social phenomenon; the family is a biosocial unit (although more social than biological); and co-operation is more completely social. Since all of these things comprise the vill, it follows that the vill is not a purely social thing. Accordingly, it is most appropriate to characterize the vill as a social system in an ecological context.[1]

The relation between these two aspects of vills has probably been stated most clearly by Amos Hawley (1950, pp. 73-74). Human ecology, he claims, deals with the central problem of sociology, the development and organization of the community (that is, the vill). But human ecology does not exhaust that problem. Man's collective life includes psychological and moral as well as ecological integration. These other forms of integration, however, should be regarded as complementing rather than as separate aspects of the community. "Sustenance activities and relationships are inextricably interwoven with sentiments, value systems, and other ideational constructs" (Hawley, 1950, p. 73). From the point of view of this book, the spatial relationships would reflect the more purely ecological

[1] I am indebted to Robert E. Roberts for this phrase.

aspects and the other elements in the vill's model would be more social. The "sustenance activities and relationships" would reflect the integration of these components.

Accordingly, to know the vill as a whole, it must be considered from the point of view of all three foci. If one is interested in the more sociological aspects, he will consider vills as structured and functioning in reference to families and cooperative institutions. When that point is granted, then it must be recognized further that such a system also has a spatial basis, and a basis of such importance that familial and cooperative interactions, norms, activities, and sentiments are limited and at least to that extent determined by factors of distance and thus of space. To understand the patterns that develop within such limitations, space must enter into consideration, no matter how great is the interest in the social aspects of vills.

Some quite valuable research in sociology and anthropology might seem to argue against giving cooperation the degree of importance it is given in this book. In particular, the works of Lewis and (to a lesser extent) Coleman may appear to challenge such an emphasis. Oscar Lewis (1951, 1953) has become one of Robert Redfield's most severe critics, particularly in criticizing Redfield (1930) for ignoring the numerous elements of conflict in the village of Tepoztlán. Lewis is justified in this particular criticism (see Chap. 7), I think, but his criticism should not cause us to lose perspective. Of course there was conflict in Tepoztlán, but so was conflict noted in all fifteen vills (five cities, ten folk villages) studied in this book. No doubt some serious conflict has probably appeared in every vill which is more than a generation old. But what have we said when that has been stated?

An answer has been given by James Coleman (1957). He provides a detailed description of community conflict in American cities. But for all of Coleman's careful analysis, he does not argue that conflict within the community is essential in integrating the community. On the contrary, his argument is the obvious but very important point that conflict is a divisive force, and that only the presence of certain other forces keeps the community from annihilation.

Conflict is important to understanding the vill for the same reason that pathology is important to the study of physiology.

But we should not confuse the nature of the importance. Vills exist *in spite of* conflict. Occasionally, conflict can become too strong, as in Hilltown and Kaihsienkung—the first collapsed from internal conflict, the second from external conflict. Indeed, the argument can be advanced that the reason vills continue to exist in the face of conflict is found in their cooperative activities. In San Ildefonso, mutual aid was still practiced even when the village was splitting in two; it had to be practiced if the people were to survive. In New Orleans in the late 1950's and early 1960's, contractual relations continued side by side with racial strife; they had to continue if the people were to survive. Sometimes, of course, the cooperative organization is not strong enough to stem the tide of conflict and the vill literally dies. But the germ which kills this kind of social organism is proof enough of how the organism functions.

*A note on the integration among the foci.* One of the most important points to emerge from this study is the consistency with which certain patterns emerge. Nevertheless, there is also an important inconsistency: The exact position of a given vill on one continuum cannot be predicted from its position on other continua. There is, of course, a tendency for vills consistently to occupy the same relative position for each focus. For example, New Orleans and Middletown *tend* to appear as the most urbanized vills for trait after trait. But erratic shifts do occur. Thus, Kaihsienkung is least differentiated spatially but has the highest proportion of single males for any folk village. Dragalevtsy has the lowest proportion of divorces but the highest literacy and the most spatial differentiation of any folk village. Finally, Timbuctoo has the highest divorce rate of any vill but the least spatial differentiation of any city. These vills are in the minority, to be sure, but equally important is the fact that they *do* deviate, pointing to the conclusion that there is a relative independence among the foci of vills.

There is often an implicit assumption among social scientists that the parts of a social system are as closely linked as those of a biological or even a mechanical system. But a moment's reflection will show that in social systems there is a greater independence of parts. Families may leave a village, new positions can be filled by different people, slight population changes can occur, new roles can be created or old ones abandoned without a necessary immediate or even an ultimate noticeable influence on the system. Or a city may be virtually totally destroyed by war and it can rise again—often with the same persons at the same location (Iklé, 1951). Even more important, serious schisms can appear in a village and the village can continue to operate for many decades before dissolution occurs—as happened in Hilltown and as was happening in San Ildefonso.

All of these features point to a connection between the social parts which is quite different from connections between biological or mechanical parts. If we were to assume there was no difference, we would have to say such things as: an animal can swap feet or heads with another animal without serious effects, or a machine can be cut in half and continue to operate for several years. Animals and machines cannot, but social systems can act in these ways. Human groups are held together by symbolic connections, and the lack of mechanical or biological tissue joining individuals introduces a freedom in the structure of human social units which is unknown in mechanical or biological units. This relative autonomy of parts we can call "structural freewheeling."

All of which is not to deny that changes have impact on social systems. Reference is rather to the lack of immediate impact, to the quality that social systems have of continuing in old patterns even in the presence of drastic modifications, and of the slowness of the repercussions of such modifications. It is probably in the light of these qualities that variations in group integration should be viewed but, in any case, the relative autonomy of the parts of social systems must be recognized. It is this relative autonomy which the vills display concerning their foci. The foci are related, but it is possible for changes to occur in one focus without its full effects being noted in the others. To put the matter more directly, it is conceivable that a folk village could become relatively contractual and, as long as it maintained its familial structure and spatial homogeneity, that it could still exhibit most other aspects of a folk village—at least for some time.

Nor should it be forgotten that structural freewheeling is not often displayed. Most folk villages tend to show a high correlation among their parts, as do most of the cities. It is probable that any vill will usually have its familial, contractual, and spatial patterns generally in the same stage of development. But, equally important, changes can and do occur in one focus without corresponding changes in the other foci; this is the principle of structural freewheeling.

There have been at least two predecessors to this theory, and it is instructive to consider them. Ogburn's theory of cultural lag (1922) is the better known. Ogburn's theory, however, refers primarily to pathological conditions and to the lag of non-material culture behind material culture. The theory of structural freewheeling is not limited to either condition. For example, the failure of the family system to change with the growth of contractualism may or may not develop pathological manifestations. Nor can one properly speak of a lag. In either case, we are considering the relation between one part of "non-material" culture and another, instead of the lag of non-material behind material culture. Thus, Ogburn's theory can be considered a special case of the theory of structural freewheeling. In fact, structural freewheeling indicates why there is a lag: the parts are not mechanically or biologically integrated.

Much the same comment can be made of Sjoberg's contradictory functional requirements. The concept is admirably descriptive: it refers to "the operation of contradictory structures, each 'essential' to the system, yet at odds with one another" (1960b, p. 330). It thus refers to a different process than the theory of cultural lag, in that there is no possibility of the strain being permanently eased—the structures are at the same time essential and inconsistent. Again, because there is not the one-to-one cohesion posited by usual theories of integration, the theory of structural freewheeling gives a basis for the existence of contradictory functional requirements.

Structural freewheeling thus includes both lags and contradictions. The question then arises, what is the manner of integration in human societies which permits structural freewheeling? In all probability, the answer is to be found in the fact that human groups are integrated by human interaction, and that most if not all human interaction is ultimately symbolic. This means that human groups are integrated by means of agreements, whether by force, conditioning, or voluntarily. The agreements, in turn, are arbitrary; that is, the agreed-upon symbols *could* mean any of an infinite number of things; the meaning that they have is only arbitrarily assigned to them by implicit or explicit agreement. Because the cohesion of groups thus has an arbitrary basis, the group is capable of operating by means of other agreements at the same time. The agreements, in fact, are never solidified or irrevocable. They can shift, even change radically, and as long as some sort of agreement remains—regardless of how contradictory to other agreements— the group continues to cohere.

Whatever the ultimate reasons, we are nevertheless faced with the fact of structural freewheeling, whether it appears as cultural lag, contradictory functional requirements, or in some other form. We can only suggest that as long as human groups are integrated by symbolic agreements—rather than by mechanical or biological ties—such manifestations are to be expected.

# 5

# An Evaluation of Classical Theories

Since the vill as a phenomenon falls within the scope of community—as community is conceptualized by most sociologists—the theory of the vill can be used in evaluating various theories of community. Because the basic assumptions of community theories have seldom been explicitly questioned, such theories cannot be expected to correspond precisely with the theory of the vill. But because the vill is a *kind* of community, many existing theories can be expected to match the theory of vills, at least to a limited extent. (We are not yet ready to develop a theory of community on the basis of the preceding chapters.)

Precisely because the theory of the vill is an evaluative tool, it is able to discriminate between other theories according to their empirical usefulness. Thus we are able to rely on the accumulated experiences of others to elaborate the theory, to show where it may be expanded, and to show depths and facets that the theory itself does not explore. In this sense, the evaluation becomes a process of theory construction in its own right.

The nineteenth century saw no development of a theory of community which is pertinent specifically to vills. Scholars such as Gomme made precise and penetrating analyses of communities in specific cultures, but they made little attempt to generalize. Several theories in this period, however, sought to isolate the principle ingredients involved in social change, social differentiation, or both. Four of these theories have a particularly close relationship to vills. In order of their appearance, they include Maine, Toennies, Durkheim, and (much later) Becker. Max Weber's work pertains specifically to cities. Since these men were not always considering the vill, their theories can only be compared to that of the vill, not judged right or wrong. Also, these scholars were essentially trying to solve an evolutionary or historical problem. The theory of the vill, on the other hand, is developed essentially from conditions in the contemporary world and is thus, not by intention but due to the limitations of its data, ahistorical.

### HENRY SUMNER MAINE

Maine's essential argument is that society has evolved from a condition in which the family was dominant to one in which the individual is dominant. "The movement of the progressive societies has been uniform in one respect. Through all its course it has been distinguished by the gradual dissolution of family dependency and the growth of individual obligation in its place. The individual is steadily substituted for the Family, as the unit of which civil laws take account" (1861, p. 138). The resulting society, however, is not one of atomized individuals. ". . . The tie between man and man which replaces by degrees those forms of reciprocity in rights and duties which have their origin in the family. . . . is Contract." The laws governing family laws were designated by Maine as "Status laws," and thus the evolution of "the progressive societies has hitherto been a movement from *Status to Contract*" (1861, p. 139).

From this statement of Maine's thesis, it is apparent that he did not give any attention to the importance of space in communities (cf. 1861, pp. 123–24). His interest was not in communities (and thus not in vills) but in societies in general. Insofar as the discussion of society applies to the discussion of vills, however, the analysis in the preceding chapters is in essential agreement with Maine's.

Nevertheless, one is struck by the difference in emphasis that

Maine gives to certain features found in vills. For example, the model of cities shows families to be quite important, just as the discussion of the folk village shows contractual relationships to be present. Thus, the evolution has not been *simply* from status to contract. Rather, if the folk village is taken as the prototype of the city, the evolution has been from a system in which the family is dominant to that in which the family is one among other institutions; and the evolution has been from that in which status cooperation (that is, mutual aid) has been the dominant form to that in which contractual cooperation has been dominant. Thus, if we may infer from the theory of vills to the evolution of society, there has not been one continuum from status to contract but two (at the very least), the continua of an increasing multi-institutional orientation and an increasing cooperative specification.

Further, the evolution (again deducing from the theory of vills) has not been from families to individuals but from a system in which families are dominant to that in which the family loses some of its functions to other institutions. Although the general theory of vills permits one to agree with Maine that in "primitive societies . . . the individual creates for himself few or no rights, and few or no duties" (1861, p. 430), this is no less true of modern societies. In our terms, Maine's remarks apply equally to folk villages and cities. For the city dweller, too, creates but little. His chief difference from the villager is that he has more from which to choose. But, on the other hand, he also has more group influences and constrictions to which he is subject, if only because he is in contact with more groups. From this point of view, the growth of individualism is not as important as the relative decline of family power (though not its absolute decline), together with the relative increase in the power of other subsystems in the vill.

It is logical to suppose that the growth of other subsystems or institutions is a consequence of an increase in importance of contracts. The burgeoning of contractual relationships is also responsible in a sense for the growth of the importance of the individual. That is, if freedom be defined as the release of an individual from the power of others, and if power be defined as the ability to use force, and if force be defined as the reduction of alternatives (after Bierstedt, 1950), then any increase in alternatives will (1) decrease the use of force, (2) decrease the power which others have over the individual in question, and (3) increase individual freedom. The city dweller is thus free in that he has more choices. But to equate this freedom with a proportionate decline in group constraints is to ignore the increased number of groups in the city. In the extreme case, the villager is a member of two groups—his family and his village. The city dweller, on the other hand, is *at least* a member of his family, his city, and his job, and more often he is a member of his neighborhood, district, or quarter, his ethnic group, his church, his recreational associations, etc. Relative to the villager, the city dweller thus substitutes a contractual for a personal constraint. However, he is not an individual in the sense that he stands alone. On the contrary, in this sense he is even less an individual than the villager, for he has many more contacts. He is more of an individual only in that he has more choices. Furthermore, it should never be forgotten that these choices are entirely within a social context. He may be lonely, but he is not lonely as the farmer in his field is, or the fisher in his boat. He is, of course, lonely in the crowd.

In general, Maine offers confirmation for the theory of the vill which, in turn, offers support for his own theory. As noted, one cannot speak of evolution of the vill—the data are not of that kind. One can only speak of differentiation. But to the extent that the difference between folk villages and cities can be explained as a product of differential evolution, then Maine's thesis is justified—there has been an evolution from status to contract. But there have also been other evolutions. Maine's remarks do not deny these other evolutions, but because of the brevity of his statements, they are apt to be overlooked. The continuum between vills is not a single but a multiple one.

### FERDINAND TOENNIES

Although acknowledging the influence of Maine (among others), the theories of Toennies took a quite different direction. There is an overlapping, to be sure, but the facile identification which is so often made between Maine and Toennies (and others) warrants a careful comparison of the concepts these scholars were trying to develop. Essentially, Maine was attempting to trace the history of mankind, especially as it manifested itself in legal channels. His approach was at least as inductive as deductive. He relied on the evidence in law as much as he did on the guiding principle of social evolution. Toennies, in contrast, was essentially concerned with deducting from a general theory and with finding illustrations to support that deduction. The data and even their exposition are secondary to the task of developing the theory itself. As much evidence as is needed for this thesis can be gained from the fact that Toennies never explicitly defined his basic concepts. Indeed, he clearly stated that the conditions described by *Gesellschaft* can never be found in this world (1957, p. 91). Maine, on the other hand, was trying to describe existing and past data as accurately as possible.

The types which Toennies was using have come to be known in sociology by their German names: *Gemeinschaft* and *Gesellschaft*. Loosely, they may be translated as *community* and *society*, respectively. This choice of words is probably the best, and it has important implications for the theory of vills, but Toennies himself would probably abhor the limitations introduced by such precision. Essentially, he conceived of humans acting through their own volition in either of two ways—naturally or rationally. Complete action in terms of natural will (*Wesenwille*) gave rise to Gemeinschaft types of social relations, whereas complete action in terms of rational will (*Kürwille*) gave rise to Gesellschaft types of social relations. Gemeinschaft is relatively simply translated in terms of the theory of vills. The folk village is a Gemeinschaft-like type of society. But before the identification is made too simply, an extended quotation is needed:

The Gemeinschaft by blood, denoting unity of being, is developed and differentiated into Gemeinschaft of locality, which is based on a common habitat. A further differentiation leads to the Gemeinschaft of mind, which implies only co-operation and co-ordinated action for a common goal. Gemeinschaft of locality may be conceived as a community of physical life, just as Gemeinschaft of mind expresses the community of mental life. In conjunction with the others, this last type of Gemeinschaft represents the truly human and supreme form of community. Kinship Gemeinschaft signifies a common relation to, and share in, human beings themselves, while in Gemeinschaft of locality such a common relation is established through collective ownership of land; and, in Gemeinschaft of mind, the common bond is represented by sacred places and worshipped deities. All three types of

Gemeinschaft are closely interrelated in space as well as in time. They are, therefore, also related in all such single phenomena and in their development, as well as in general human culture and its history. Wherever human beings are related through their wills in an organic manner and affirm each other, we find one or another of the three types of Gemeinschaft. Either the earlier type involves the later one, or the later type has developed to relative independence from some earlier one. It is, therefore, possible to deal with (1) kinship, (2) neighborhood, and (3) friendship as definite and meaningful derivations of these original categories, [Toennies, 1957, p. 42].

It is apparent that Toennies was not speaking of any one group. He had certain relationships in mind: the relation of the acting out of natural will among groups of people over long periods of time. However, people act according to rational will as well as natural will. There are, thus, numerous groups which are *like* Gemeinschaft, but the Gemeinschaft is never fully realized. But as far as any group *could* develop a Gemeinschaft form, the village came closest to this development; that is, the village came closest in all three forms of development, in kinship, neighborhood, *and* friendship (for example, with mutual aid). In some respects, other groups can develop other aspects of Gemeinschaft, such as the family in the Gemeinschaft of kinship, or the town in Gemeinschaft of friendship. But the fullest development of all three is found in the village.

There is an extremely close linkage of Toennies' notion of the village with the concept of the folk village developed in this book. The linkage is not exact. We speak of families in folk villages, not kinship per se; of spatial relationships, not neighborhood; and of status cooperation (mutual aid), not friendship. The conclusion seems warranted that the present writer saw the same thing in the folk village that Toennies saw in the Germanic village (the villages are probably identical), but the observations were made from different perspectives. The folk village is described from an inductive examination of ten villages; Toennies viewed the village as illustrating certain basic, essential concepts, the interaction of natural will in social relations. The differences in shades of meaning are probably to be interpreted as products of these different perspectives, and we may conclude that the folk village would be as Gemeinschaft-like as anything Toennies could choose from his own experience.

But if Gemeinschaft overlaps so closely with the folk village, the same correspondence cannot be made between the city and Gesellschaft. Such an identification is attempted quite often in the literature, and indeed, there is room in *Gemeinschaft und Gesellschaft* to make such an interpretation. Toward the end of his book, Toennies makes such statements as "The city is typical of Gesellschaft in general" (1957, p. 227). Of course, Gesellschaft-like relations are found more often in the city, but to associate the two in as close a manner as the association between Gemeinschaft and the folk village is to miss the essential nature of the type. Although it must be admitted that Toennies did make the identification, his own concept does not correspond to the model of the city as developed in this book.

It is best to return to Toennies' basic theory. Just as Gemeinschaft is produced by the interaction of natural will in social situations, so is Gesellschaft the product of interaction of rational will in social situations. Toennies does not become this specific, but a few quotations will show the essential accuracy of this interpretation: "The concord of will at each exchange, inasmuch as the exchange is regarded as taking place in the Gesellschaft, we call a contract" (p. 71). ". . . Gesellschaft . . . is called a society, an association or special-interest group, a corporation, or any such name" (p. 75). The second quotation is especially important because it shows the wide range of groups which can be called Gesellschaft-like—not the city alone and, one may argue, not the city exactly.

"The more extensive the area, the more completely it becomes an area of the Gesellschaft, for the more widespread and freer trade becomes. Also, the more extensive the trade area, the more probable it is that the pure laws of exchange trade prevail and that those other noncommercial qualities which relate men and things may be ignored. Trade tends, finally, to concentrate in one main market, the world market, upon which all other markets become dependent" (p. 79). In other words, the world market is more Gesellschaft-like than the city.

"In a fully developed Gesellschaft, however, every commodity would be produced in adequate quantities and sold for its value by a single capitalistic person possessed of a perfect knowledge of existing normal demand. Such a concept cannot be realized. It is in the approximating of this goal that the respectability of capitalist production distinguishes itself from that of common trade" (p. 91).

In comparison with the theory of the vill, the important point is that Gesellschaft is simply interpreted as rational will manifested in social conditions. There is no *complex* of foci such as has been found necessary to an understanding of the vill. Thus, Gesellschaft becomes qualitatively different from the vill (and in a sense from Gemeinschaft) in the theoretical "elimination" of kinship and space from its consideration as a social entity.

Toennies is actually trying to divide all social behavior into Gemeinschaft and Gesellschaft. The vill on the other hand, explicitly does *not* apply to all social systems. It is intended to describe only one general social type. Thus, Toennies' theory matches with the theory of vills at the point where Gemeinschaft and the folk village overlap. It leaves the theory of the vills as one approaches Gesellschaft, because the theory of vills is based on a complex of the traits of space, family, and cooperation, while Gesellschaft is based solely on rational behavior, a type of behavior found only to some degree in certain types of cooperation.

Probably the most important contribution which Gesellschaft offers to the theory of vills is its abstract quality. Gesellschaft is less attached to any specific person, place, or thing than is Gemeinschaft. When it is remembered that Gesellschaft is found, according to Toennies, particularly in the city, then the possibility arises that the city may be less oriented to particular persons, places, or things than the folk village (although the essential dependence of the cities on these foci must be recognized). There is evidence from the model of the city developed in this book that this deduction has validity. Cities are less isolated and more cosmopolitan in their base of operations than folk villages.

For the vill, this means that the city must be understood more in relation to its hinterland than the folk village. In other words, to understand the city, one must place more emphasis on entities outside of the city than is true of folk villages. Neither social system is isolated, but the difference in isolation is the point a study of the difference between Gemeinschaft and Gesellschaft brings out most clearly.

The further implications of Toennies' theory of *Gemeinschaft und Gesellschaft* must await a later chapter when our sociological exploration extends outside of the theory of vills.

## EMILE DURKHEIM

Durkheim, like Maine and Toennies, was essentially oriented toward a historical problem. But Durkheim consistently stands closer to Maine than he does to Toennies. Both Maine and Durkheim differ from Toennies in the data used, in methodology, and especially in the nature of their problem. The similarity of these scholars exists in their historical orientation to change in modes of human behavior and in a dualistic conception of this change. But as important as this similarity is, it should not mislead one into thinking that all three were speaking of the same thing.

"Social life," Durkheim maintained, "comes from a double source, the likeness of consciences and the division of social labor" (1933, p. 226). The first type of society he called mechanical, the second type he called organic.

The individual is socialized in the first case, because, not having any real individuality, he becomes, with those whom he resembles, part of the same collective type; in the second case, because, while having a physiognomy and a personal activity which distinguishes him from others, he depends upon them . . . and consequently upon the society which results from their union [Durkheim, 1933, p. 226].

There has been, further, an evolution of societies from those based on mechanical solidarity to those based on organic solidarity.

Although Durkheim published *The Division of Labor* (1893) six years after Toennies published *Gemeinschaft und Gesellschaft* (1887), the two works should be viewed as different attacks on two related but analytically separate problems. Durkheim was trying to trace the development of selected social conditions, as was Maine. Toennies was attempting to deduce the consequences of certain psychological forces as they were acted out in social situations.

The two writers differ especially in the type of data they employed. Durkheim, as did Maine, relied much more heavily on information drawn from existing and historical societies— specific, indentifiable groups figure prominently and even dominantly in his writings. Toennies, on the other hand, seldom employed concrete data. He talked, instead, of communities in general, without naming specific communities, and so for all the other social types.

When the differences in the approach of these writers is correctly interpreted, the apparent contradictory usage of the term "organic" becomes resolved. Durkheim was employing an analogy between society and organisms. It follows that the more complex society (from Durkheim's point of view) would be more like an organism than it would be like a mechanism. Toennies, on the other hand, was postulating a kind of will (or motivation) that had its origin, its genesis, in the organism. This was natural will, and it was opposed to a will which lacked such a genesis—rational will. This latter he often described as artificial. But, as is apparent, this concept of "artificial" is not used in anything remotely approaching Durkheim's concept of "mechanical."

Probably the most significant feature of Durkheim's writing is in his repeated attempts to match his theories with data. This was the approach used by Maine, but Maine confined himself only to data provided by (statute) laws. Durkheim ranges over a wider field, including not only law but data from preliterates, from the Bible, from biology, and from modern Europe. Unfortunately, the use of data is a two-edged sword. When one commits a scientific postulate in writing, it stays there. If he is successful in making himself clear, his errors stay, also. And if he is one of the first to have so conducted himself, he must expect to make mistakes. But even with his mistakes, the beauty of Durkheim's effort is that it is possible to "get at him." More than is true of his predecessors, his reasoning is presented in empirically testable forms. And thus he appears more often wrong than many earlier writers when he is actually closer to the truth—at least to scientific truth.

Consequently, it is not surprising that of all the three scholars considered so far, Durkheim figures most strongly in the development of the theory of the vill. The analysis in this book has not been historical, and the data give little if any justification to infer a historical trend (see Goldenweiser, 1945, pp. 507–21). Nevertheless, the differentiation between folk villages and cities in respect to increasing heterogeneity, particularly in respect to an increase in the division of labor, has been clear. Further, that some solidarity accompanies this variation in heterogeneity is obvious in several ways, particularly in the integration which the various social systems display, both spatially and socially, and in the fact that they are entities, both in terms of the viewpoint of their members and in terms of the usefulness of treating them as entities for analytical purposes.

The argument of this book has not followed Durkheim completely, to be sure, especially in that no firm support could be found for making the conceptual leap from the data on heterogeneity to the conclusion that heterogeneity was responsible for (or represented) solidarity (see Appendix A, Fig. 3 and Table 12). Certainly, solidarity is an accompaniment of these social systems, and equally certainly it is useful to treat the data *as if* the solidarity is a product of homogeneity, on the one hand, and contracts based on a division of labor, on the other. But a firm linkage cannot be established at present. The inability to provide such a linkage is probably a result of the fact that the data for this book were used more systematically than that employed by Durkheim. Durkheim's sources were scarce; the late nineteenth century saw relatively few ethnographic studies. Thus, where the present analysis is able to proceed on careful documentation, Durkheim was limited to a few examples which could be used to do no more than illustrate a point. But while the system employed in developing the theory of the vill has excluded many types of data because they were incomplete, Durkheim's lack of systematic data freed him to utilize more data and direct them where they would cast the most light. Paradoxically, then, we cannot proceed as far because our data are better. Because they are better, we are able to employ a system, but the system necessarily limits. Explorations beyond the system, of course, are always in order, but explorations within the system come first.

A mere description of Durkheim's types of solidarity does not completely describe the affinity which his thesis has with the theory of the vill. The argument can be advanced that Durkheim had in mind precisely such systems as we have called vills, and that he came very close—if imperfectly—to describing the full complexity of their organization. In fact, a satisfactory interpretation of the relationship between Durkheim's thesis and the theory of vills may be explained by reference to: (1) Durkheim's lack of complete data; and (2) his development of a more extensive theory than has been attempted thus far for vills.

The range of societies in Durkheim's theory is so extensive because he is attempting to show the evolution of society from its most extreme beginnings to its most extreme end. On the one hand are hypothetical and ideal types of primitive hordes; on the other, pure occupational societies. Between these are numerous other types, arranging themselves on a continuum:

1. Hordes;
2. Segmental societies with a clan base;
3. Segmental societies with classes and castes;
4. Segmental societies based on family and territory;
5. Territorial organizations losing their significance;
6. City specialization on the basis of occupation;
7. Societies organized purely on the basis of occupation.

(Durkheim, 1933, pp. 174–5, 185–90.)

Note that these are not stages—the notion of a continuum is strong with Durkheim.

It is on the fourth and fifth points of Durkheim's continuum that the correspondence with the theory of the vills is clearest. On the sixth point, cities are specifically discussed, and the cities per se correspond (as far as they are described) to the model of the cities presented in Chapter 3 of this book. Thus, where Durkheim speaks of cities (his points 5 and 6), and to some extent where he speaks of villages (his point 4), the three foci are all present. Durkheim, however, sees villages as existing more completely toward the organic end of the (our) continua. The occupational, territorial, and familial environments noted by Durkheim clearly have their counterparts in the foci of the vill. But Durkheim neglects the cooperative aspect in villages. Concerning the segmental societies just prior to the village level, he notes that "The relations of a barbarous despot with his subjects, as that of a master with his slaves, of a father of a Roman family with his children, is not to be distinguished from the relations of an owner with the object he possesses. In these relations there is none of the reciprocity which the division of labor produces. They have with good reason been called uni-lateral" (1933, p. 180). The extent to which Durkheim would find such a relationship in later stages of social evolution is not known, but the relation is obviously a far cry from that of mutual aid. Durkheim, further, does not cast any light on the nature of cooperative relationships which would correspond to mutual aid. In fact, cooperation for him exists only in the contractual realm—or he only speaks of it in that connection.

Nevertheless, if one looks at cooperation from Durkheim's point of view, it is easy to interpret mutual aid as a relatively undeveloped form of cooperation; his logic in following his bias must be admitted.

Of course Durkheim treats these types of solidarity primarily as evolutionary types. His admission that the types can exist at the same period of time is not intended as a denial of this evolutionary condition. And the theory of the vill, as noted, is ahistorical.

Durkheim's contribution to the theory of the vill is in providing broader vistas in which the theory may be placed. He furnishes a context which raises the possibility that vills *may* exist as parts of more extensive continua—or even a single but generalized continuum. He also raises the possibility of the continua of the vill being historical at the same time that they are contemporaneously descriptive.

## HOWARD BECKER

The theories of Becker are directly in the tradition of Maine, Toennies, and Durkheim. For the purposes of this analysis, Becker is important chiefly in that he carries his ideal types logically, significantly, and systematically farther than the others. He also makes an attempt to integrate his theory with other theories, and he thus provides an avenue for those who wish to proceed farther in the study of dualistic concepts of society (1950, pp. 258–60; Becker's first publications in this area appeared between 1931 and 1933—cf. Becker, 1950, pp. 248–49 n).

Though Becker's typology is related to those of his predecessors, it is also different. "Sacred and secular are not synonymous with holy and profane, folk and urban," etc. (1950, pp. 249–50). A sacred society is simply one that develops among its members a high degree of resistance to change. What is changed—that is, what is new—is new as defined by the members in terms of the society's existing culture. A secular society is one that develops among its members a willingness and ability to change. Put another way, sacred societies in their most extreme form are isolated "vicinally" (locally), socially, and mentally, whereas the most extreme secular societies are accessible in all of these ways.

On this basis Becker develops eight types of sacred societies and twenty-two types of secular societies. These types are not meant to be complete descriptions of reality. They are ideal types or, as Becker called them, constructed types. All of these types are not completely described, however, even as ideal types. The "small book" which Becker said would be needed to depict them never appeared (1950, p. 275). Perhaps the lack of such a development is just as well. One can build logical types ad infinitum.

Becker's contribution to the theory of the vill rests in his emphasis on the quality of the permeability of the value system as this permeability is measured by the degree of isolation, on the one hand, and accessibility, on the other. It was this emphasis which gave rise to Zimmerman's localistic-cosmopolitan dualism which figures so prominently in the models for the vills (Zimmerman, 1939, pp. 80–81—see Appendixes A and B).

MAX WEBER

The contribution of Max Weber is more specifically to the model of the city than to the vill. He represents one of the pioneers in the development of urban sociology, especially in being one of the first to give his analysis a specific focus (the city), to tie it to specific data, and to do so within an essentially sociological context. In spite of the fact that there are limitations to his theory, he offers important insights concerning the nature of the city.

Weber's method of analysis is ideal typical, a method which he largely developed. (See Chap. 7 for a discussion of ideal types.) The essentials of the ideal type for the city are as follows:

To constitute a full urban community a settlement must display a relative predominance of trade-commercial relations with the settlement as a whole displaying the following features: 1. a fortification; 2. a market; 3. a court of its own and at least partially autonomous law;

4. a related form of association; and 5. at least partial autonomy and autocephaly, thus also an administration by authorities in the election of whom the burghers participated [1958, pp. 80–81; first published, 1921].

To understand how Weber arrived at this picture, one must have in view all of the wealth of his historical detail, particularly for the Western world. Nevertheless, the picture Weber gives is distorted. The necessity of fortification is undoubtedly a historical peculiarity (no matter how widespread) and is not pertinent to the existence of the city, itself.

The remaining points in the ideal type are essentially that the city is based on market relations and that it has at least partial autonomy. That these features are essential is not disputed. However, the model developed in Chapter 3 indicates that the city also has other features, and Weber ignores these, without giving a reason for ignoring them. The family is unmentioned, except as it influences formal organizations. Spatial components are similarly ignored. Thus, no matter how valuable the material Weber presents, one should read it with the realization that he omits many or even most of the things that cities contain and that cities have used in the course of history.

In his discussion of autonomy, Weber first maintains that partial autonomy is permissible for the development of a true city. Then he maintains that Oriental cities are not true cities because of a "relative absence of autonomous administration" (1958, p. 81). The difficulty is that we have no criteria for knowing how partial the autonomy can be. But, more important, Weber clearly shows that full autonomy was a historically peculiar thing. (Cf. 1958, p. 181.) In the Occident, it appeared neither in antiquity nor in modern times but in a "transitional" period. It might follow that, in Weber's terms, the tremendous urbanization that has occurred in modern times is not urbanization at all! Perhaps so. But then, there are other things that need to be understood, such as the things we have called cities in this book.

Accordingly, Weber's argument for autonomy as an essential component of the city—even partial autonomy—does not help us to understand modern urbanization. But if one shifts from autonomy to conditions necessary for the full development of contracts, the picture changes. Cities—at least Occidental cities

—had to become autonomous at one period in their history if they were to break from traditional restraint against the fuller utilization of contracts. When the rest of society developed a more contractual orientation, then the cities could be (and were) reintegrated into the larger society; that is, they relinquished their autonomy.

Parenthetically, we must not confuse autonomy and identity —cities are entities. Further, we are not arguing that cities are not partially autonomous. Each of the five cities in the model were. The argument is one of emphasis. Weber uses autonomy as a central element of his ideal type when more realistically it should be relegated to a minor role. It is not autonomy which is so important to the city but the development of contracts. Autonomy is important only as it contributes to that end.

Weber also discusses another component of the Occidental city, one that is related to autonomy—that of democracy. An underlying theme in the models of both the folk village and the city in this book is the importance of freedom, a theme that will become particularly crucial in distinguishing the models so far developed from others. Weber thus suggests an important point in community theory: community is sui generis. It cannot be imposed from without (or it has not been, typically). Its essence is freedom, and though this freedom may be organized, it cannot be organized too closely.

When one considers Weber's evolutionary approach, the implication is strong that democracy evolved as did the city— that is, as did contracts. Note, however, that there is a basic village democracy, too. What the city provides is a new kind of democracy—one based on differences rather than similarities. The implications for Durkheim's thesis are obvious.

Weber's translators, Martindale and Neuwirth, pose an interesting question. The most fundamental of oppositions in the city, they maintain, is that which occurs between market and household economies. If there is such an opposition, perhaps it is the reason for the city's freedom—the market never becomes so important that it becomes the key to the city (in spite of Weber's contention to the contrary). The family provides a fundamental check to the market, and where the family is subverted—as in totalitarian societies—then the essence of community is also subverted.

Reasoning from his ideal type, Weber concludes that "An urban 'community,' in the full meaning of the word, appears as a general phenomenon only in the Occident" (1958, p. 80). If we are careful, and do not conclude that only in the West did cities appear, then the conclusion is an interesting one. It says, in essence, that only in the West was the contract allowed to develop to its fullest extent. And this development was made possible by the independence of the city. The development, in turn, permitted the flowering of industrialization, which is a further development of the system of contracts.

The development of the system is not finished. Contracts must yet be extended into the vacuums now existing in the interrelations between cities and nations. Other deficiencies probably also exist. But the fact remains that only in the West has the contract been allowed to permeate so extensive a segment of city life. We thus can see the power of Weber's ideal type. Distorted as it is (and all ideal types are distorted), it yields fruitful hypotheses.

Although Weber was by no means the first to write about the city, he was one of the first (if not *the* first) to systematically develop one of its most significant foci: that of contracts. Most important, Weber focuses on the city and carries his analysis of contractual relationships *in the city* (as opposed to the society) to greater detail than do others. Weber's main contribution, then, is that of providing evidence for the probable evolution of contractual relations in cities. He thus did for the city what Maine and his followers did for society in general. And if we see the seat of contractualism in society as resting in the city, Weber's contribution is the more important.

# 6

# The Theoretical Position
# of Human Ecology

The study of human ecology is indispensable to the study of vills.
The following discussion, however, is not an attempt to review
the entire field.[1] The most pertinent ecological principles have
been treated in earlier chapters (and are further treated in the
appendices), especially in the consideration of the element of
space and in the treatment of mobility and the vill as a base of
operations. The intent here is to provide an overview of the
position of human ecology in the study of vills and to consider
selected theories of most immediate importance to this interest.
Four topics are considered: human ecology as conceived by its
founder; the discipline as it is today; its relation to social morphology; and the theory with greatest specific relevance to vills,
social area analysis.

### ROBERT E. PARK

No one has been more instrumental in developing the field of
human ecology than Robert Park. Although Park by no means

[1] For a detailed consideration, two sources are especially valuable: Theodorson (1961) and the series of reprints on ecology in The Bobbs-Merrill Reprint
Series in the Social Sciences.

intended that human ecology be limited exclusively to the city, his writings clearly emphasize it, and our discussion maintains a similar emphasis. Ecology provided an entirely new perspective on the study of the human community. With this new perspective, the scope of social investigation was broadened to include everything that could conceivably be related to the city's social existence, including colonies, segregated areas, vocational classes and types, news, the mobility of the social group, the church, the school, the family, courts, advertising, social control, temperament and the urban environment (Park, 1925).

But the emphasis that Park placed on the study of the city was in its spatial organization. In one of his more extreme statements, he maintained, "It is only as social and psychical facts can be reduced to, or correlated with, spacial facts that they can be measured at all" (1926, p. 18). To the family he gave no more than passing attention. As will be shown, Park by no means claimed that the city *was* its spatial organization, or that spatial organization was the most important part of the city. He recognized also the existence of a moral order which he linked closely to the division of labor. But he believed that the opening attack on his own program of study of the city could best be coordinated through the study of its spatial organization.

Park's initial conception of human ecology was much broader than that followed in practice by his students. First, he assumed the essential validity of the definition of ecology: the study of the relation of the organism to its environment. Thus, he did not restrict the term to the study of cities (although this has been the general result in practice). He recognized, further, that the human environment was distinguished by the addition of a fundamentally different quality from that of other animals: the quality of culture. This addition meant, in effect, that at least two factors differentiate human from plant or animal ecology: (1) man's decreasing dependence on the physical environment; (2) man's increasing capacity for reacting upon and remaking his habitat and his world. In other words, man has established upon the basis of the biotic community an institutional structure inextricably intertwined with custom and tradition. Human society, then, as Park saw it, is organized on both the biotic and the cultural levels, and both exist in mutual dependence (Park, 1936).

But there is more than just a biotic-cultural dichotomy. The social order seems to arrange itself in a hierarchy of levels, the ecological order forming the base of the pyramid. The individual finds himself more completely incorporated into and subordinated by the social order on each of the successive economic, political, and moral levels, the last forming the apex of the pyramid. The function of society is everywhere to restrict competition (as found on the purely biological level) and so bring about a more effective cooperation of the organic units of which society is composed. Thus,

Human ecology is, fundamentally, an attempt to investigate the processes by which the biotic balance and the social equilibrium (1) are maintained once they are achieved and (2) the processes by which, when the biotic balance and the social equilibrium are disturbed, the transition is made from one relatively stable order to another [Park, 1936, p. 15].

## HUMAN ECOLOGY

The essential contribution of Park, however, is not in his theory as much as in his students. Park left a dynasty that was to effectively establish the study of human ecology in a position of such strength that it could withstand its major failure. This failure consisted in attempting to study human ecology as a discipline in its own right rather than as a means—and only one of many—for understanding the cultural level. Park clearly saw the cultural and biotic orders as intertwined. At least some of his more prominent students ignored the intertwining. (For a notable exception, see Hawley, 1950; Hawley is also discussed in Chap. 4.) Park regarded the cultural order as composed both of a body of customs and beliefs and a corresponding body of artifacts and technological devices. His followers separated the material from the non-material aspects of culture, at the expense of the non-material, and proceeded to study the distribution of things in space as an end in itself.

The reaction was severe and prolonged. In the face of critics, chief of whom was Alihan (1938), two kinds of corrections have developed: (1) to reject the practice of excluding culture from ecology and to emphasize the tracing of interconnections between the cultural and biotic levels (Firey, 1947); or (2) to recognize the impossibility of separating the levels but still to retain an emphasis on the biotic level (Hawley, 1950; Quinn, 1950). These Theodorson (1961) has called the sociocultural and neo-orthodox approaches, respectively. The result has been an extensive literature probing deeply into the spatial and material aspects of city life. The probings have sometimes been of a widely different nature, for example, Fleming's study (1954) of the relation between city size and per capita sales as contrasted with Firey's investigation of the relation between sentiments and land use (1947). But, as Theodorson maintains, these approaches are to be viewed as complementary rather than contradictory.

What contribution can the model of the vill developed in Chapter 4 make to the study of human ecology? For the most part, it encourages a development along lines now being followed. Its major criticism is of the classical school. Thus, the current recognition that human ecology is only one means toward understanding the city is supported by the finding that the vill is essentially composed of three focal components—space, cooperation, and families, rather than space alone.

The model of the vill also supports the shift in ecological theory that has moved away from attempting to freeze the city into any one spatial pattern or even any single type of evolution. For example, the *inverse* correlation between status and distance from the center of the city, a correlation which occurred at some time in the history of all five cities, shows clearly that the classic Burgess theory is a cultural and historical peculiarity (see Appendix B). Burgess (1925) claimed, as is now well known, that there was a positive and direct relation between status and distance from the city's center.

The importance of the model of the vill, then, is that it forces attention on the dynamic aspects of human ecology. Note, especially, in this connection, that *processes* of human ecology, such as centralization and (in cities) segregation, were clearly evident in the vills used to build the model. The presence in each of the vills of fluctuating, changing, or conflicting (that is, vague) boundaries also strengthens this dynamic viewpoint.

A further contribution of the model of the vill is found in its support of another current finding. Though ecological processes are found in all vills, the values associated with and probably "motivating" the processes can be expected to differ from culture to culture. Thus, centralization can occur variously around economic, political, or religious institutions. Accordingly, as studies by such writers as Benyon (1943) and Caplow (1952) have indicated, we have no right to assume the industrial hegemony in ecological processes as was assumed by Park's followers.

The major criticism that the model of the vill has to offer the field of human ecology is that ecology has not found its proper place in the study of the community. Hawley (1950, p. 179) attempts to set bounds on human ecology explicitly excluding motivations and attitudes. Gibbs and Martin are perhaps more precise in referring to human ecology as the study of sustenance organization (1959). Duncan, however (1959, 1961), goes to the opposite position, advancing ecology as the key to integrating all sciences concerned with man. He does this through studying the interrelations among categories of the "ecosystem"— population, organization, technology, and environment. This choice of categories he admits is arbitrary, and obviously it does not correspond with the components of the vill. However, the vill's focal components are identifiable things around which other things are organized; the foci do not *include* these other things. Duncan's categories, on the other hand, are conceptual boxes into which other things are placed.

The place of ecology in the study of community thus inevitably depends on whether one views ecology as a general or a specific system of relationships. As a system of relationships between the organism and its environment, it is all-encompassing. As a study of sustenance relationships, it is only one part of the study of human behavior. Perhaps it is both, and if so, the two aspects should receive different names. If Duncan's concept of ecosystem is broadly encompassing, then human ecology in the narrower sense may be viewed as synonymous with social morphology. But if this is done, it will probably mean a more restricted view of human ecology than is usually accepted. In order to understand this point of view, we must examine the meaning of social morphology.

SOCIAL MORPHOLOGY

The concept was first suggested by Durkheim, although it has received perhaps its most extensive development by one of his students, Maurice Halbwachs (1960). As used here, social morphology refers to the study of all material factors that have an influence on society, that is, those factors that Durkheim called the "material substratum." However, Durkheim did not make himself entirely clear about how far one should go in what is to be included in the material substratum. Whatever was meant by the French school,[2] we are employing the concept to include everything material that has social relevance: population, technology, and environment (cf. Durkheim, 1960, and Schnore, 1958).

The implication in the definition, however, is that social morphology is not a complete study, in itself. It exists for another purpose: the understanding of society. This counterpart of social morphology Durkheim labeled social physiology, but we shall refer to it more simply as sociology. Social morphology, then, is the study of the material accompaniments of society.

It will be helpful also to define two other terms which have been used in discussing human ecology: *society* and *culture*. Society may be defined as the consequence of interaction, culture as the consequence of the use of symbols. (Interaction, in turn, is the mutual influencing of two or more organisms; symbols are those things which can have more than one meaning, or whose meaning is arbitrary.) It follows from these definitions, that there are both animal and human societies, but that there is *only* human culture. Animal societies, whether they are of bees or beavers, are more the consequence of biological interaction, whereas human society operates primarily by means of symbols. It is inseparable from culture (except analytically). Thus, artifacts are both cultural and social consequences. Accordingly, the attempt of the classical ecologists to study society apart from culture can now be seen as pointless, and this is generally recognized.[3]

Two implications follow: (1) social morphology is also cultural morphology; and (2) social morphology is to be regarded

[2] For a more complete treatment, see Halbwachs, 1960, pp. 7–21.

[3] Although there is still unnecessary confusion between these concepts. See Kroeber and Parsons (1958) and Ogles, Levy, and Parsons (1959).

largely as a consequence of society rather than its effect. We say "largely" because the physical environment sets varying limits on the nature of social organizations, and one of these limits is imposed by space.

With this conception of social morphology, one which attempts to retain as much as possible the spirit of Durkheim, let us see what the concept has to offer toward an understanding of human ecology and the theory of the vill. Consider human ecology first as synonymous with social morphology. From this point of view, human ecology exists to help in understanding sociology. It follows, therefore, that although the investigation of morphology is logically prior to sociology, morphology is theoretically less important. The study of sociology becomes the end, an end for which morphology serves only as a necessary stepping stone.

On the other hand, taking ecology in its broadest sense—as the relation of organism to environment, or, as Duncan puts it, as the study of the ecosystem—the study of ecology is an end in itself, though here "ecosystem" is not ecology considered as morphology. For insofar as we are trying to study the position of social organization relative to population, technology, and environment, we turn our attention away from the study of the structure and function of the organization, per se, away from the internal system, as Homans has phrased it (1950), and emphasize the external system (see also Warren, 1963, Chap. 5).

Such an approach may not help us to understand the functioning of a classroom, an industrial shop, or the decision-making process in a community, nor will it explain the operations of contractual systems as these influence and limit familial organizations, but it does offer promise of showing how vills are interrelated with their environment. For this reason it is a justifiable pursuit, even though we must realize that when we study the ecosystem we are operating on a level that will tell us little about sociology—that is, we largely ignore the internal system. (Note that the internal system is not synonymous with social psychology.)

We have thus identified three levels of investigation, each of which is relevant to an understanding of man as a social being.

These levels can be shown as:

$$\text{Ecosystem} \begin{cases} \left. \begin{array}{c} \text{Social} \\ \text{Organization} \end{array} \right\} \text{Sociology} \\ \\ \left. \begin{array}{cc} \text{Population} & \text{Technology} \\ \text{Environment} \end{array} \right\} \begin{array}{l} \text{Social} \\ \text{morphology} \end{array} \end{cases}$$

The ecosystem is the most inclusive, although it is concerned only with the external system of a human group. Concentration on the human group is reserved for sociology, which discipline, in turn, depends heavily on social morphology for its data. The dependence, however, is not an exclusive dependence, since much of sociology comes directly from a study of symbolic systems, themselves (for example, laws, diaries, questionnaires, etc.).

But whether ecology is identified as ecosystem or social morphology, it is not synonymous with sociology. And in either case it is important that the ecologist understand which perspective he is adopting. As a student of ecosystems (ecosystemist?), his outlook is broader than sociology. As a social morphologist, he is a student of the social substratum. Of course, he can study the morphological level for its own sake (witness the demographer or the human geographer), but relative to sociology his work is essentially that of providing it with a certain type of social fact.

Duncan has provided a promising perspective for ecology as a frame of reference integrating several disciplines concerned with the study of man, addressing himself, in effect, to a problem even larger than that seen by Park. He has thus provided ecologists with an important challenge.

For most of ecology as it has been practiced, however, social morphology is the more meaningful perspective in which the sociologist can place human ecology, and social morphology, therefore, is the more meaningful perspective for this study. Its most basic assumption is that no society exists without its material structure. Furthermore, it assumes that this material existence is relevant to social existence. But it also assumes that the interest of the sociologists is not so much in material things as it is in society itself. Thus, the study of social morphology is an attempt to obtain clues to the social order by studying the material things accompanying it.

Social morphology, accordingly, does one of the things Park was trying to do in his original formulation (1925) of a program for the study of the city—it broadens the perspective. On a more general level, it serves as a warning and a reminder that nothing can be ignored in an attempt to know the vill as a society. Above all, societies are not only symbolic systems; they are composed of people, their technology, and the natural (and transformed) physical environment.

It can be seen, then, that the consideration of space in the model of the vill has actually been a discussion of social morphology. The most significant topics that are absent (or relatively so) are those of population and technology. As noted, population appears to have none but the grossest relation to life in vills. (A revealing analogy may be made between the population of a vill and the physical size of a man.) Technology will be discussed in the next chapter in connection with the pre-industrial city.

## SOCIAL AREA ANALYSIS

This technique is an attempt to describe the social characteristics of large cities with a minimum of statistical measures (Shevky and Bell, 1955; see Theodorson, 1961, for further references). Thus, social area analysis has much the same general task as this book, especially in its emphasis on parsimony of descriptive devices for "communities." If such a goal is realistic and if each approach is valid, one would expect similar answers, an expectation confirmed for all practical purposes.

The similarities between the two approaches will be indicated below. For the present, it is important to stress the differences. The analysis of social areas has a fundamentally different method, uses different data, and was initially studied with a somewhat different type of social entity. The method of social area analysis has been essentially deductive; the comparative method is inductive. The data in social area analysis have been exclusively statistical, that is, quantitative; the comparative method has been essentially qualitative. And the city that was first subjected to social area analysis—Los Angeles—was many times larger than the largest city used in this study. (In 1950, the urbanized area of New Orleans contained 659,768 persons;

that of Los Angeles contained 3,996,946 persons.) In view of these differences, the convergence between the comparative method and social area analysis is all the more significant.

The method by means of which the specific indexes were constructed is summarized in Table 5. The authors began by conceiving of the city as a product of the society as a whole. Then they postulated "some statements descriptive of modern society as compared with traditional societies, or of a particular modern society compared at two points in time" (Shevky and Bell, 1955, p. 227). The next steps consisted of progressively becoming more specific in describing functions related to these postulates, bringing the descriptions ever closer to the modern city as an entity, and finally developing the specific measures that could be drawn from available data. (The reasoning involved is given in detail in Shevky and Bell, 1955.)

These progressive steps are indicated by the six columns in Table 5, the arrows representing the direction of the reasoning. The final indexes are designated as social rank (or economic status), urbanization (or family status), and segregation (or ethnic status).

Independent work by Tryon and his associates (1955) and by Schmid and his associates (1958) have given practical verification to the validity of this method. Results differ only in minor details. In other words, these authors have agreed with Shevky and Bell that the three indexes of social area analysis provide essentially the most parsimonious description of urban areas. Such verification is especially important since it has come about through factor analysis, one of the most elaborate techniques for showing statistical interrelationships among variables.

The convergence between social area analysis and the comparative method used in this study is quite marked. In fact, two of the indexes—economic status and family status—are simply particular applications of the foci of contractual relations and the family. This convergence is all the more important when it is recalled that the foci of the city were derived from the foci of the folk village, each focus being only an extension of a continuum. Thus, one of the criticisms of social area analysis made by Van Arsdol, Camilleri, and Schmid (1958) is refuted: "Presumably the dimensions become differentiated in a process of urban development and would not be found in folk society"

Table 5. Steps used by Shevky and Bell in construct formation and index construction

| Postulates concerning industrial society (aspects of increasing scale) (1) | Statistics of trends (2) | Changes in the structure of a given social system (3) | Constructs (4) | Sample statistics (Related to the constructs) (5) | Derived measures (from col. 5) (6) |
|---|---|---|---|---|---|
| Change in the range and intensity of relations | Changing distribution of skills: Lessening importance of manual productive operations—growing importance of clerical, supervisory, management operations | Changes in the arrangement of occupations based on function | Social rank (economic status) | Years of schooling, Employment status, Class of worker, Major occupation group, Value of home, Rent by dwelling unit, Plumbing and repair, Persons per room, Heating and refrigeration | Occupation, Schooling, Rent } Index I |
| Differentiation of function / Complexity of organization | Changing structure of productive activity: Lessening importance of primary production—growing importance of relations centered in cities—lessening importance of the household as economic unit | Changes in the ways of living—movement of women into urban occupations—spread of alternative family patterns | Urbanization (family status) | Age and sex, Owner or tenant, House structure, Persons in household | Fertility, Women at work, Single-family dwelling units } Index II |
| | Changing composition of population: Increasing movement—alterations in age and sex distribution—increasing diversity | Redistribution in space—changes in the proportion of supporting and dependent population—isolation and segregation of groups | Segregation (ethnic status) | Race and nativity, Country of birth, Citizenship | Racial and national groups in relative isolation } Index III |

SOURCE: Eshref Shevky and Wendell Bell, *Social Area Analysis* (Stanford: Stanford University Press, 1955).

(p. 283). They *are* found in folk society, but as folk rather than urban developments; that is, at the opposing ends of continua.

The index of ethnic segregation presents a different case. It specifically measures the proportion of persons of different ethnic groups living in given areas. Comparing this index with the focus of spatial differentiation in the model of the city, it is apparent that ethnic segregation in effect does tap a dimension of spatial differentiation, but that it is only one dimension. This is especially evident when one considers such a city as Ch'u, where there are no ethnic groups. Segregation obviously cannot be the more general concept. Furthermore, it is significant that this index comes into the most serious criticism of any of the three indexes (cf. Udry, 1964; for other criticisms, see also Bell and Greer, 1962).

There are other limitations to social area analysis. Its indexes have been devised primarily for use on large U.S. cities and for U.S. census data. But insofar as social area analysis can be taken as a special case of the comparative method developed here, then the way is open to remove such limitations. The work of McElrath in applying social area analysis to Rome (1962) lends support to this conclusion.

On a more positive side, social area analysis offers strong confirmation that the urban model (as well as the model for the folk village and the more general model of the vill) can be expressed in more precise terms—that is, statistically. It also shows that the model of the city developed through the comparative method is widely represented among American cities (see especially Van Arsdol, Camilleri, and Schmid, 1958). Equally interesting, the fact that social area analysis was developed for the metropolis of Los Angeles and has also been applied to San Francisco, indicates that population size is no effective barrier to the theory of vills.

CONCLUSION

Ecological considerations are of significance to the theory of the vill since this theory is concerned with a kind of group that is in part defined by non-social conditions. In this sense, vills share a trait with families, but while families are defined in part by biological needs and consequences, vills, are defined (in part) by the fact that certain kinds of human groups are located some-*where*, in some particular place. Spatial considerations, as previous chapters have shown, are considerations with which all vills must deal. The economic aspect of ecology is more variable. In the folk village, the physical environment is more important to the economy; in cities, the economy is influenced more heavily by the social division of labor. Spatial limitations, however, are confronted by both types.

Vills then may be defined in one sense as social systems in an ecological setting. But in such a description there is also a warning to those ecologists who would confine the study of community to their branch of investigation. Although ecology is very important to vills, the ecologist is a student of vills only to the extent that he is considering a *social* system, and this he must do from a sociological perspective.

# 7

# An Evaluation of
# the Work of Redfield
# and His Successors

## ROBERT REDFIELD

Of all the theories discussed in this book, those advanced by Redfield are the most relevant. Not that further developments have not been made by others, but in a very real sense, the theory of the vill may be regarded as an extension of Redfield's work. This extension was made possible by two conditions: (1) more data are now available than were available to Redfield when he did most of the development of his theory; (2) Redfield's theories themselves provide a basis on which to build.

Two of Redfield's works are particularly significant to a discussion of vills: His theory of the folk society and his empirical findings relative to the culture of Yucatán. Although the folk society was a later formulation, it is discussed first because it concerns only one aspect of the theory of vills, the folk village.

*The folk society.* Redfield's emphasis throughout his work is on the folk rather than the urban society. His concept of the folk society represents one of the more significant attempts to integrate the theories of such writers as Maine, Toennies, Durkheim, and Becker.

The agreement between the model of the folk village constructed in this book and Redfield's ideal type is especially important. Folk villages and folk societies are small, the villages ranging from slightly more than 100 to approximately 3500 persons. Both are relatively isolated, though the folk village is probably less isolated than the folk society. The same can be said for homogeneity. Group solidarity is strong in both systems, as witnessed particularly by the universal ethnocentrism of the folk village, and in reference to kinship, Redfield's words apply equally to either case: "Its relationships and institutions, are the type categories of experience and the familial group is the unit of action" (1947, p. 293).

Redfield also depicts the folk society as "traditional, spontaneous, uncritical, and personal" (1947). It is difficult to evaluate the extent to which the folk villages were traditional, since the studies used as sources did not often permit an adequate historical appraisal. But it is known that more than half of the villages have existed for a century or more, and thus a traditional orientation is highly probable.

Neither can one say whether behavior in the folk villages is uncritical and spontaneous, since no way is known by means of which these attributes or variables can be measured precisely. Impressionistically, one would be inclined to agree that these traits are present in the folk village, but it would be very difficult to document this impression.

There are grounds for describing behavior in folk villages as personal, and insofar as spontaneous behavior is a concomitant of personal behavior, then the description applies there as well. The chief basis for such a conclusion is to be found in the traits of familism, mutual aid, and even in the importance of religion in these social systems. If personal behavior is a function of such traits, then one would expect to find this behavior in folk villages as well as in folk societies.

There are also differences between the two concepts. Most significant is the nature of the theory upon which each concept is based. The folk society is an ideal type; the folk village should more properly be called an "empirical abstraction." The folk village is intended as a working model, so constructed that it depends on each and on all of the villages which it uses as data. Any item not common to all of the villages is discarded. Redfield's ideal type, on the other hand, is not intended to correspond precisely with any known society (Redfield, 1947, p. 294) but to emphasize those features believed to be inherent in a given object in its pure state. Thus, an ideal type is in a sense a set of hypotheses, and such is particularly true of Redfield's description of the folk society. In contrast, an empirical abstraction is an inductively derived construct which abstracts selected evidence from the empirical world according to a given method. It is first and foremost subject to its data, the "evidence from the empirical world." The folk village, from this point of view, constitutes in part a test of the folk society, a measure of its applicability to concrete situations.

There are four other areas of special interest where the folk village diverges from the folk society. First, while the folk society is non-literate, some degree of literacy—from minimal to extensive—characterizes all of the folk villages. Second, organic solidarity is universal among the folk villages, whereas among the folk, in Redfield's sense, "all the tools and ways of production are shared by everybody" (Redfield, 1947, p. 297). Third, the folk society is not a market economy, whereas a significant degree of market consciousness occurs in more than half of the folk villages. Fourth, the folk village is *localized*, whereas the folk society is an ideal type of much broader generality, referring to non-localized social systems as well as localized ones. Examples would be tribes and bands, social systems which can range over wide territorial expanses.

If the assumption is made that the similarities to the folk society are valid and that the differences point to the opposite end of the continuum (that is, to an urban rather than a folk society), then the differences increase in theoretical significance. The increased literacy, the presence of organic solidarity, and the enhancement (though hardly the dominance) of the market place are those influences which could be expected from the impact of urbanizing forces on the traditional folk society.

There is an interesting theoretical possibility raised by the presence of space in the folk village and the absence of this element in the folk society. It may be that the peculiar emphasis on space displayed by all of the villages has much to do with their departure from the ideal type. (Of course, not to be overlooked is the possibility that a village form of existence has social peculiarities which stand in contrast to the social structure of a tribe or band.)

In any case, each construct should be used for a different purpose: *the folk society as a theoretical extreme, the folk village as a picture of existing social systems*. Thus, the model of the folk village is limited with respect to the types of social systems to which it will apply. But, on the other hand, generalizations concerning the folk village apply to each of the ten social systems employed in building the model. Therefore, one is not required, as is true with Redfield's ideal type, to make allowances for the fact that no society fits the description. There *are* societies which fit the description of the folk village. Such an empirical abstraction thus permits one to maximize the sensitivity of theory to data, a condition not always possible to realize when one works with the folk society.

The model of the folk village and the ideal type of the folk society, then, contribute substantially to each other. Since the folk village clearly stands on the same continua as those represented by the folk society, the folk village becomes the first point to be empirically identified on these continua. And, similarly, the folk village demonstrates that Redfield's hypothesis of the folk society represents a meaningful extreme, unattainable, perhaps, but nevertheless a useful reference point.

Alone, the folk village is mainly a description of a type of social system and the folk society is merely a collection of hypotheses. Together, the two theories provide one basis for a theory of community. Thus, the empirical abstraction is not intended to replace the ideal type. Instead, the descriptive theory furnished by the model of the folk village is an empirical approximation to the ideal type, a theory of a higher level of abstraction. A chain of links is established, from raw data to case study to theoretical model (empirical abstraction) to ideal type. The model of the folk village provides a necessary link from raw data to a relatively highly generalized theoretical formulation—the ideal-typical folk society. To the extent that such linkages are completed, the study of community is afforded a more stable foundation.

*The continuum in Yucatán.* Though Redfield's work in Yucatán is on a lower level of abstraction than is his theory of the folk society, the study of the Yucatecan communities is more relevant for the theory of vills because it attempts to treat the entire folk-city continuum. The basic concern of Redfield in this earlier study (1941) was the relation among the variables of isolation, homogeneity, disorganization, secularization, and individualization. No one of these variables was assumed to be the sole cause of the others. For the purposes of the investigation he was making,

the isolation and homogeneity of the community are taken together as an independent variable. Organization or disorganization of culture, secularization, and individualization are regarded as dependent variables. The choice of isolation and homogeneity as independent variables implies the hypothesis that loss of isolation and increasing heterogeneity are causes of disorganization, secularization, and individualization. Even if this should be established, it would not follow that these are the only causes of these effects ... [Redfield, 1941, p. 344].

Redfield's main theoretical concern, however, is with the dependent variables. The bulk of his argument is based on "the approximately simultaneous investigation of a series of contemporary communities," all taken from the same culture—that of the Yucatán peninsula. The cultures are arranged according to their variation with respect to the independent variable: Tusik, the tribal village is the most isolated and homogeneous; Merida, the city, is least isolated and homogeneous. Ranging between are Chan Kom, the peasant village, and Dzitas, the town; the peasant village is closer on the continuum to the tribal village, the town is closer to the city.

The dependent variables follow suit. Tusik shows the highest degree of cultural organization, the most extensive sacred orientation, and the greatest importance of the family. Chan Kom and Dzitas each show less evidence of these traits. Finally, Merida shows the most cultural disorganization, the most extensive secular organization, and the greatest importance of the individual.

These theoretical relationships, unlike those of the folk society (1947), constitute not an ideal type but an organization of existing data. Thus, the theory is quite comparable to the theory of the vill. The independent and dependent variables can be likened to the foci. There are numerous other components of these four communities, including all of the components of the model of the vill (Chan Kom and Merida were, of course, used in constructing that model). But while the vill treats the remaining components as integrated around the foci, Redfield used these components to demonstrate the existence and variation among his independent and dependent variables. The two approaches are merely two different ways of solving the same problem.

The difference between the vill and the folk-urban continuum lies in those variables which are considered to be most important in each case. These differences are, for the most part, reconcilable. The choice of relevant independent variables, Redfield recognized, is heavily influenced by the given culture. Accordingly, he proposed "that increase of contacts, bringing about heterogeneity and disorganization of culture, constitutes one sufficient cause of secularization and individualization." Upon examining the data supplied by Sol Tax for Guatemala, as well as studying the history of his own society, Redfield also suggested that the development of important commerce and a money economy may be another such sufficient cause (Redfield, 1941, p. 369).

He implies, therefore, that the causes of change along the folk-urban continua are culturally variable. Thus, a cross-cultural study would necessarily have to posit different causes for the change. Redfield's observations should serve as a clear warning that universal causal factors are perhaps not to be obtained. It is thus not surprising that although all of the supposedly causal factors are present in all of the vills, there is as yet no way to untangle causal priorities among them. Redfield's data no doubt permitted him observations which cannot be made with the vills used in this study. If we had an array of vills for each of the approximately one dozen cultures comparable to that which Redfield had for Yucatán (that is, involving sixty systems instead of fifteen), more light could be shed on the problem of cause.

The matter of dependent variables is another question. The folk-urban continuum of individualization is, of course, largely another way of describing the continuum in vills that is associated with the focus of the family. Redfield's definition of individualization is to the point here: "We may understand a society to be individualistic to the extent that the socially

approved behavior of any of its members does not involve
family, clan, neighborhood, village, or other primary group"
(Redfield, 1941, pp. 355–56).

Another quotation is equally revealing: "In the villages it is
relatively easy to say 'the family did this' or 'the community did
that'; in Merida it is not so easy" (1941, p. 356). Here the
implication seems to be that the family and community are
more often entities towards the folk end of the continua. The
data on vills, however do not offer support to this position. The
theory of the vill would retranslate Redfield's conclusion to say
that in folk villages it is families which become the more basic
principle of community organization, while in cities contracts
become the principal institution and families are only one of
several other institutions. As was noted in the chapter on the
city, to claim a greater importance of the individual in cities is
to miss the significant point that seldom if ever can one speak of
an individual—he is always a part of some group. Redfield
recognized this point, but his emphasis on the individual
obscures it.

The conclusion, therefore, is that the continuum of individualization and the continuum of familism in each case is
identical but that it is seen from a different point of view.
According to this interpretation, one of the chief variables of the
folk-urban continuum also agrees significantly with one of the
chief variables of the vill's continua.

The vill, however, offers little confirmation for Redfield's
use of the sacred-secular distinction, especially given his interpretation that sacred refers to religious activities, secular to the
activities of the market place. Although one may say that folk
villages generally are more "sacred" and less "secular" and
that the reverse is true of cities, this distinction does not remain
for all vills if examined on a rigorous basis. It is difficult, for
example, to speak of Romonom as a religiously oriented community—religion there was of very little importance. But
Romonom is very much a folk village. Similarly, Timbuctoo is a
city, but religion is a chief determinant of individual behavior—
certainly more so than is true of the folk village of Romonom.

The argument may be advanced that we are interpreting
"sacred" too narrowly, but it should be borne in mind that this
is Redfield's interpretation, not that of Becker. If, instead, we

regard the continuum Redfield was describing as simply one of an increasing secularization rather than viewing secularization as necessarily the antithesis of religion, then the folk-urban continuum matches the cooperative continuum of vills. All of which is not to deny the accuracy of Redfield's observation for Yucatán but only to note that on a more general level—that is, from a cross-cultural perspective—Redfield's opposition of sacred and secular does not seem to be useful. In this sense, Becker's interpretation agrees more with the theory of the vill. "Sacred," it will be recalled, was interpreted by Becker to mean "isolated," whereas "secular" meant "accessible." (There is also some confirmation from Weber. See especially *The Protestant Ethic and the Spirit of Capitalism* [1930] and *General Economic History* [1950], wherein religion is seen as a chief motivation for a more secular orientation.) It is interesting in this connection that Redfield does not cite Becker's work in *The Folk Culture of Yucatán*, but in his later writings he places Becker on a level with Maine, Toennies, and Durkheim. More important, he specifically mentions Becker in connection with the sacred secular dichotomy (1950, p. 143). It would seem that, in later years, Redfield came to accept Becker's concepts.

The point at which the folk-urban continuum departs most radically from the theory of the vill is in respect to the concept of disorganization. The question considered by Redfield to be most basic in this connection is: "To what extent may each of these four communities be described in terms of an organized body of conventional understandings?" (1941, p. 345). Redfield spends considerable effort on this question, but only two major points need concern us. First, his basic question necessarily emphasizes mechanical rather than organic solidarity; that is, those societies organized on the basis of common understanding as opposed to societies so organized that *common* understanding is incidental (for example, where the division of labor is the organizing principle). In other words, Redfield so framed his basic question that folk societies would appear more organized than cities.

Probably the most serious point which Redfield's thesis of disorganization overlooks is the stability and success of city life. Cities have been with us for thousands of years. Furthermore, the proportion of persons living in cities has been increasing throughout most of this century in such diverse corners of the world as New Zealand, the United States, the Union of South Africa, Japan, Finland, and Algeria (Anderson, 1959, p. 133; see also International Urban Research, 1959). If city life is characterized by disorganization, then "disorganization" is an old method of social adjustment and an increasingly successful one. The contradiction is too apparent. Unless one holds to a theory of a golden age, he is forced to the rather anomalous conclusion that "disorganized" social systems may be relatively permanent and quite successful. If disorganization does vary as Redfield suggests, perhaps it is not important, at least from the point of view of the survival of the vill.

But, having said that, one final point must be admitted: Cities *are* disorganized from the point of view of folk villages: families recede in their position in the system, mutual aid virtually disappears as an institution, and spatial patterns become more diversified. The point is, of course, that what is disorganization for the folk village is organization for the city. Families are still significant units of urban organization, but they share their position with systems organized on a contractual basis. And cooperation in the form of contracts supplants cooperation on the basis of mutual aid. Space, finally, becomes integrated on the basis of interdependence rather than through relative homogeneity. The criticism of the thesis of disorganization, then, is directed mainly at its one-sided view. A better description of the transition from folk village to city would be to call it a reorganization. (The work of Oscar Lewis [1953] has raised the quite interesting suggestion that folk villages are not without their own forms of disorganization. This subject will be discussed in the next section.)

Redfield's contribution, in summary, has been two-fold: the ideal type of the folk society and the tracing of the folk-urban continuum through four social systems in a single culture. These are two contributions, though interrelated. The folk-urban continuum is examined in reference to the theory of the folk society which, in turn, is shown to be useful by the data gathered in Yucatán. The folk society, on the other hand, is a theory on a quite abstract and general level.

Redfield attempted to show the manner in which certain series of data arranged themselves, and his observations on the folk-urban continuum were based on these data. Thus, all critics of Redfield's work had to meet him on the grounds of showing discrepancies in his Yucatán data (which almost none have done), or in producing new data which would cause a modification of the theory. Thus, Redfield continues in the tradition of Durkheim. It is often overlooked by Redfield's critics that he stated his work in such terms that it could be corrected. No longer is it possible merely to present another theory of society. If any theory about the nature of folk or urban communities (vills) does not reconcile itself to Redfield's data or correct his interpretations, it is simply not as useful as Redfield's formulation. If Redfield is interpreted correctly, he can be seen as marking the end of an era, an era wherein speculation could suffice.

## CRITIQUES OF REDFIELD

The impact of Redfield's work can be gauged both by the discussion it has engendered and by the fact that it has prompted further work. Advances have been both critical and substantive. Two of the most important critiques of Redfield's theories have been offered by Oscar Lewis and Horace Miner. They are discussed here because they help to clarify the nature of Redfield's theory and the nature of the vill. Examples of substantive contributions are found in Miner's *The Primitive City of Timbuctoo* (1953), one of the vills studied in this book, and the work of Gideon Sjoberg, to be discussed in a later section.

*Oscar Lewis*. Of the two critiques, Lewis' is the most negative and apparently the most often misinterpreted. Lewis' comments were based on a restudy of Redfield's pioneering work on Tepoztlán (1930). The specific findings in this restudy, made seventeen years after Redfield's original effort, are not of major concern. Tepoztlán appears to fit the model of the vill according to the data gathered by both investigators. In the main, Redfield and Lewis disagree on relatively minor details and emphases (a point not generally recognized).

The most important of these differences, from the point of view of the present study, rests in the observations concerning cooperation. Redfield emphasized cooperative and unifying factors in Tepoztecan society. Lewis' "findings, on the other hand, would emphasize the underlaying individualism of Tepoztecan institutions and character, the lack of cooperation, the tensions between villages within the *municipio*, the schisms within the village, the pervading quality of fear, envy, and distrust in interpersonal relations" (Lewis, 1953, p. 123).

An essential point in interpreting these differences is that Redfield was not looking for these traits, whereas Lewis was. The discrepancy is thus to be expected, and we are indebted to Lewis for developing it. But the two sets of findings should not be used to invalidate each other. Rather, in large measure, the findings are complementary. Lewis would hardly say that the people of Tepoztlán remained together *because* of fear, envy, distrust, and lack of cooperation. The disagreement he raises with Redfield is that conflict is a very significant part of Tepoztecan life. The findings for the vills confirm Lewis' observations—but they also confirm Redfield's. Societies can be both cooperative and conflictful at the same time. The question remains, which is more important to the existence of the social system? And, which is more important in distinguishing it from other systems?

The differences which Lewis encountered in reexamining the site of Redfield's data could be expected for many reasons, as Lewis, himself, points out. The village had changed to some extent during the seventeen years; Lewis' study was of broader scope, including many more resources (it had Redfield's work with which to begin); and the two men differed markedly in their theoretical orientation. Redfield was just beginning to develop his folk-urban theory when he studied Tepoztlán, and this village furnished a major role in that development. Lewis, on the other hand, was more concerned with "a combined historical-functional approach, in which the categories for analysis of change grow out of the historical data from a given situation" (Lewis, 1953, p. 133). On this point, incidently, it should be noted that to some extent Redfield pushes his theory beyond his data. The question remains as to whether he is justified in doing so.

In examining Lewis' criticism, the reader must remember that Lewis does not dwell on the similarities between the studies. Unless Lewis' critique is read carefully, one is apt to believe that there are more differences than similarities. A close examination of the two studies yields the opposite conclusion: the data are more often in agreement than in disagreement. In this connection, a comment of Lewis is especially pertinent: "On the whole, many of our findings for Tepoztlán might be interpreted as confirming Redfield's more general finding for Yucatán, particularly with regard to the trend toward secularization and individualization, perhaps less so with regard to disorganization" (Lewis, 1953, p. 130). And such was generally the conclusion reached earlier in this chapter when the folk-urban continuum was compared with the foci of the vill.

*Horace Miner.* Lewis raises additional criticisms, but these have been effectively treated by Horace Miner (1952). Miner, himself, has three other criticisms which in fact point up the value of the theory of the vill. First is the problem of lack of fit between particular societies and ideal types, whether of the folk society or the implied ideal type of an urban society. Of course, to a large extent Redfield obviates such criticism by taking four existing social systems and showing how they in fact fit on the folk-urban continuum. Further, in constructing an ideal type of the folk society, Redfield was purposely dealing with a pure type, one which was not expected to fit any real case. Nevertheless, the deficiency is there—we need some theory which will correspond more closely with the data. As mentioned earlier, the theory of the vill corrects this difficulty by means of models which are empirical abstractions, these having been constructed entirely from the records of living societies.

Related to the "lack of fit" is the lack of evidence that societies change in all three of the variables as Redfield predicted; that is, changes in disorganization, secularization, and individualization were supposed to occur together. In the concept of structural free-wheeling, the theory of the vill again offers a corrective. Parts of societies are not linked together as is a machine or even as an organism. The connection is much more tenuous, relying primarily on symbolic communication. In consequence, such things as culture lag take place, and such developments as contractual orientations in a familistic environment can occur. Redfield recognized this principle: ". . . the societies of the world do not range themselves in the same order with regard to the degree to which they realize all of the characteristics of the ideal folk society" (1947, p. 306). But he failed to integrate the concept satisfactorily into his theory.

Miner's second criticism is of special interest in that the theory of the vill does not clearly offer a solution: "The weight of evidence seems to be that, irrespective of the merits of the folk-urban continuum for theory building, the characteristics of the ideal type must be operationalized before relevant theory can be reliably tested cross-culturally" (1952, p. 537). Of course, the theory of the vill emphasizes qualitative data, in spite of the desirability of quantification. The point has been stressed that, so far, comparisons between vills can be accomplished only on an ordinal scale, that is, relatively. The data we have do not permit cardinal measures. And yet, there are indications that quantification is feasible. Within North American culture, the work of Shevky and his associates is of great value in this regard (see Chap. 6). The data for the vills, themselves, also suggest measures, especially in relation to the two principal foci: family and cooperation. The importance of the family can be measured by such means as the percentage of persons living in extended families and the number of non-familial groups in the system. Cooperation can probably best be measured by such things as the extent of monetary economy (as opposed to an economy of use) and the number of specialities in the given vill.[1]

Admittedly, these are suggestions. They have been used as guides in developing the theory of the vill, but ongoing research projects are needed which will attempt to apply these and other measures on a cross-cultural basis, Miner's chief criticism has not yet been completely met. (But see Aurbach, 1955, 1960, and Mayhew, 1963.)

The last of the three major criticisms must remain largely unanswered in this chapter. Miner notes that the folk-urban continuum has limited theoretical insight. Of course no theory is unlimited, but Miner is attempting to express a dissatisfaction with the folk-urban hypothesis which is rather widespread in sociology and anthropology. The problem is that, limited or not, no one has anything better or even as good. The social scientists are caught in the uncomfortable position of being dissatisfied with the theory but being unable to discard it. Improvement seems the only alternative.

In reality, the theory of the vill, like the folk-urban con-

---

[1] For further discussion of the operationalization of Redfield's continua as they relate to the vill, see Mayhew, 1963.

tinuum, is equally limited as long as it remains undistinguished from other theories. Only when a theory discriminates between what it does and does not do can it become useful. We will return to this criticism at the conclusion of this chapter.

### GIDEON SJOBERG

The nature of the folk-urban continuum has received significant development by Sjoberg. Recognizing the value of Redfield's work, Sjoberg nevertheless points out the discrepancies between the ideal type of the folk society and complex societies in Asia, Europe, and Latin America. These are not accurately folk societies—and neither are they urban. To fill this gap, Sjoberg offers a constructed type of the feudal society and the pre-industrial city. The relevance of Sjoberg's efforts to the vill is quite broad, extending to method, purpose, specific comparison with the model of the city, and general relevance to the theory of vills.

*Methods.* Sjoberg's major effort that is pertinent to this book is contained in *The Preindustrial City* (1960a; cf. also 1952 and 1955). His aim in this work is to describe and analyze the city prior to its transformation through industrialization. "Our principal hypothesis is that in their structure, or form, pre-industrial cities . . . resemble one another closely and in turn differ markedly from modern industrial-urban centers. . . . We seek to isolate for preindustrial cities structural universals, those elements that transcend cultural boundaries" (1960a, pp. 4–5).

The method that Sjoberg uses overlaps the one used in this study, but there are differences. The most important similarity is the cross-cultural approach. Here, Sjoberg's position is firm: "If sociology is to justify its self-concept as a 'science of society,' it must establish propositions that have cross-cultural validity" (1960a, p. 2). But Sjoberg also relies heavily on historical data, and thus his analysis provides an important supplement to that employed here.

His basic analytical tool is the constructed type. The ideal type, employed by Redfield, is a purer model—and thus one not as likely to be found in reality (see Chap. 1). The constructed type, on the other hand, is more objectively probable in that in some sense certain aspects of it can be found in the "real" world. "No claim is made that every preindustrial city displays each one of the traits delineated in the preceding chapters. . . . We have introduced into our 'constructed type' only those traits for which empirical evidence is at hand for cities in at least several divergent cultural systems" (Sjoberg, 1960a, p. 321).

There are thus several important differences between Sjoberg's method and the empirical abstraction used here. Particularly, the elements in the empirical abstraction must be found in all cities—even pre-industrial ones. Consequently, on the one hand, Sjoberg is permitted a wider range of data than is available to the empirical abstraction, including incomplete sources. On the other hand, the constructed type is not as systematic. Nevertheless, in view of the kind of data available for the pre-industrial city, one can argue that the distinctions Sjoberg draws between the pre-industrial and the industrial city could have been made in no other way.

There is, however, a fundamental similarity between the two methods in that data are raised to the position of limiting the theory. One is permitted to interpolate in a constructed type— to fill in the gaps *between* known data—but he is not permitted to extrapolate. He is not permitted to construct an imaginary picture of what the pure situation would be, as is done in the ideal type. The elements in the type must be found somewhere.

There is a difference also in the purpose for which Sjoberg's type was constructed. Sjoberg is essentially interested in a causal analysis in the historical sense; that is, in how preindustrial cities have come to be. In contrast, the empirical abstraction is concerned with an entirely different kind of question: How does the city operate? How does it function?

Thus, technology for Sjoberg becomes the main variable in delineating folk, feudal, and industrial societies, since only with a superior technology can cities arise in otherwise folk societies. Additional variables are also pertinent, however, especially social power. "In the earliest cities a political structure had to exist to obtain, through taxation or tribute, a food surplus from the peasantry to support the urban non-agriculturalists, most particularly the power elite itself. For peasants have not always willingly produced surpluses and relinquished them to the urbanities" (1960a, p. 31). Also of importance are cultural values and the city itself, but primarily insofar as they can explain *why* cities (pre-industrial cities) ever existed in the first place.

The empirical abstraction, in contrast, is essentially limited to existing conditions. Under such a model, the city is a place where families and individuals engage in contractual relations. How does it come to be? Probably as Sjoberg contends, but his is another question.

*A comparison with the model of the city.* In spite of particular differences, there is a high degree of agreement between the two sets of findings, especially on a more general level. The three foci contained in the model of the city are all given extensive attention by Sjoberg, if not always with the same terms. Ecology and the family are mentioned explicitly. Contractual relations, on the other hand, are treated with other topics, particularly under economics. The remaining components of the model are mentioned either by implication or directly, except possibly ethnocentrism and the city as a base of operations.

This is not to maintain that Sjoberg sees all cities as identical. In fact, one of the primary theses of his study is that "pre-industrial and industrial cities are fundamentally distinctive entities" (1960a, p. 330). But "fundamentally" does not mean "qualitatively." When industrial cities are compared with folk villages, pre-industrial cities are seen to occupy a point approximately midway between them. Indeed, in some respects, pre-industrial cities may well be farther from folk villages than they are from industrial cities. Sjoberg's position, however, is somewhat different. He claims, and with justification, that there are important differences between the two kinds of cities when compared with each other, differences that are systematic, significant, and extensive.

The fundamental distinction between pre-industrial and industrial cities appears whether the perspective is that of Sjoberg or that of the urban model in this book. From Sjoberg's point of view, technology is vastly more developed in the industrial city, and here none can disagree. And, to a large extent as a consequence of technology, social power is no longer openly concentrated in the hands of a few ruling families. It is diffused further down the social hierarchy. The hierarchy, in turn, is much more of an open-class system than in the pre-industrial city. The values of the city members, further, as a general rule, work to support this increase in technology and the open-class system; in the pre-industrial city they oppose such things. Finally, given the growth of cities and the increased dependence of the greater society upon cities, cities breed cities in the industrial society, just as the lack of cities tends to impede the growth of cities in the pre-industrial or feudal world.

Similarly, in terms of the foci, the two types of cities differ markedly (although still quantitatively rather than qualitatively; that is, more and less rather than either-or). Spatial patterning is much less differentiated in pre-industrial cities. The delineation of natural areas is seldom sharp, even in industrial cities, but it is easier to find numerous areas devoted to fairly specialized land use: commercial, industrial, recreation, residential, education, etc. In the pre-industrial city, spatial differentiation is not nearly as complete.

In industrial cities, the family must participate much more on an equal level with other institutions than in pre-industrial cities. To be sure, the family still has a central position, but no longer can an individual expect to obtain a job in a certain plant merely because his uncle works there; no longer must an individual expect to remain illiterate merely because his father is; no longer need he marry someone chosen by his parents, and so on. Each of these changes represents a type of change experienced as one moves from pre-industrial to industrial cities, And the difference is fundamental, with the qualification noted.

Contracts receive extensive development in the industrial city, becoming norms which govern social relations in their own right. In pre-industrial cities, the guild mediates between the family and the contract. In industrial cities, the nuclear family and the individual are the chief bargaining units; in the pre-industrial city, the family is integrated into the contractual structure through the guilds, and the family exerts a significant force on the operation of guilds.

Accordingly, a brief analysis should be given to the operation of guilds in pre-industrial cities. First, "Guild membership is a prerequisite to the practice of any occupation, and among the qualifications, for membership, kinship ranks paramount" (Sjoberg, 1960a, p. 191.) The functions of guilds, furthermore, are extensive: they operate to maintain a monopoly over their occupation, they select personnel into the occupation, train the personnel, regulate the occupation, and in addition have political, welfare, and ceremonial functions over and above their economic functions. Thus, the guild assumes to a considerable degree some of the areas of control which are the province of the family in the folk village. However, we must repeat, one cannot *contrast* guilds and families in pre-industrial cities, for the two work together.

Another quotation from Sjoberg is relevant: ". . . the guild serves as a social security agency on the local level, ranking next to the family as a haven for the worker in time of crisis." (1960a, p. 194.) Thus, contractual and familial agencies are those on which the city-dwellers' life is fundamentally based—fundamental in that these are the institutions to which the worker returns and the ones around which he orients his other activities. The use of the phrase, "on the local level," is even more significant from the point of view of the urban model.

One of the problems in describing contracts in the pre-industrial city are the imperfections in contract formation. Slaves, for example, are not completely pertinent to the system. Price haggling is a marked deviation from true contractual relationships. Even in the industrial city, contract evasion is everywhere in evidence. Perhaps we can say that contractual relationships have not yet developed to their purest or most extreme form in either the pre-industrial or the industrial city. Contracts have evolved further in industrial cities, but their application still leaves much to be desired. In both types of cities, however, contracts may still be looked upon as a normative relationship, a norm *from which* deviations occur.

All of which means that the pre-industrial city, though it has existed for millenia, was nevertheless an unstable thing. And the same must be said for modern cities. Human societies are still evolving from mutual aid to contract.

A few comments are necessary concerning Sjoberg's discussion of extended families. His basic position is as follows: "The large extended family, . . . erroneously assumed by many writers to be rural, is achievable in its full-blown form only by the literate urban elite." (1960a, p. 111.) To fully understand this position, one must also realize that Sjoberg does *not* say that extended families are not found in rural areas. We have seen them, of course, in the folk village. Rather, they are found in "full-blown form" only in urban areas. This position is probably generally accurate, since, as Sjoberg indicates, cities are much more likely to provide the economic surplus necessary to sustain large kinship units.

Second, Sjoberg does not say that the extended family is characteristic of the city in general. Rather, it is the product of the urban elite. "Rural families and those of the urban lower-class and out-caste groups are much less able to maintain large households, and, consequently, close family ties, though they seek to do so wherever possible" (1960a, p. 158).

We may, in fact, regard the extended family as the culmination of a trend which is initiated in the folk society (though here we take an opposing view from Sjoberg). Sjoberg himself maintains that "The extended family, where it can be achieved, is a much more effective mechanism for mutual aid than is the simple conjugal unit. Whereas the incapacity of one or two breadwinners can be disastrous to the small nuclear unit, the extended organization, wherein economic cooperation is the rule, can more readily adjust to adversity . . ." (1960a, p. 160). The city thus makes it possible for mutual aid to produce larger extended families and, thus, for a folk trait to be brought to greater fruition. The irony is that the industrial city, which permits the extended family to develop, also nourishes the contract and thereby takes a significant step toward reducing the importance of the family.

The origin of the extended family, then, is probably in the folk society, its culmination in the city. But more important is the central position of the family in the pre-industrial city. (This is, of course, a main tenet of the urban model, also.) The family is not as important in the pre-industrial city as it is in the folk village (though for upper-class families an exception must be noted), and not as important in the industrial city as in the pre-industrial city; but even under industrialization, one cannot understand the urbanite unless one also has an understanding of the urban family.

In conclusion, the analysis of Sjoberg's pre-industrial city considerably strengthens the city model: it not only supports it in some of its most central features, but it clarifies and supplements it as well. Sjoberg clarifies the city model in showing what it does not do. But in using a method which taps a wider range of data, Sjoberg shows a more extensive and thus more detailed picture of an important type of city.

*Relevance to the vill.* The primary contributions which Sjoberg's work has for the theory of the vill are two: (1) a basis for additional sub-classification of vills is suggested; (2) the manner in which vills are integrated into the larger society is examined, especially the manner in which several vills at different points on the continua may be found in a net of functional interdependence.

Only two subtypes of vills have been developed in this book, folk villages and cities. Upon reexamining the fifteen vills in the light of Sjoberg's analysis, it is clear that at least the villages of Suye Mura, Kaihsienkung, Dragalevtsy, Silwa, and Sharmirpet fall within the range of feudal peasant societies, whereas Timbuctoo and Ch'u are pre-industrial cities.

Sjoberg would argue, then, that the theory of vills confuses types which have important differences. When industrial and feudal cities are compared, though they are logically parts of the same continua, the differences appear great, indeed (as great as the differences, say, between Caucasoids and Negroids—if one forgets about the cross-breeds). But the point made by the theory of the vill is that logically both feudal and industrial societies contain vills which can be placed at various positions on the continua of family dominance, spatial differentiation, and cooperation. The family in industrial cities is only *less* dominant than is true of feudal cities; the division of labor is only *more* completely developed; spatial use is only *more* highly differentiated. In other words, the differences in each focus are differences of degree. And this type of difference, according to the method used in this book, denotes an important relationship. Thus, we may agree with Sjoberg: Feudal societies—whether more folk- or more city-like—should not be "lumped" together, *except as their common elements form a more general theory.*

The value of the vill, therefore, lies precisely in its broadness, in its capacity to show the similarities in a number of otherwise different things. This argument does not deny that the vill accounts for differences: it accounts for them by means of the concept of continua, but such an accounting does not provide the elaboration which Sjoberg is able to achieve.

Sjoberg also places great stress on the integration of feudal peasant and city populations. His point is that vills are not complete social systems because they are always dependent upon a larger society. To be completely understood, a folk village must be looked upon as interrelated with the type of society in which it occurs, whether folk or feudal, and the same reasoning applies to cities. Again, we meet an important limitation of the theory of vills. To be completely understood, one must also understand what the vill is not.

By implication, Sjoberg raises another problem. The range of vills in feudal societies necessarily overlaps with the range of vills in folk and in industrial societies. Conceive of four societies: a folk society with tribal societies and folk villages, a feudal society as described by Sjoberg with folk villages and feudal cities, an industrial society with industrial-agricultural villages and industrial cities, and a society such as Yucatán which includes the whole range. The questions then arise, can a folk village in the folk society be compared with a folk village in the feudal society? Or can a folk village in Yucatán be compared with either? The implicit assumption in this book is yes—the comparisons can be made. And yet, it is now obvious in the light of Sjoberg's work that such comparison does some violence to the cultural context in which these villages and cities appear.

The only satisfactory answer to these questions lies in a different set of answers for different purposes. Previous chapters demonstrate that proceeding on the assumption that comparisons can be made is a quite valuable strategy. The models constructed for vills have isolated cultural consistencies from the cultural variations. The components of the models do occur, of that there can be no doubt. For example, the families in Yucatecan Chan Kom occupy as important a place in Chan Kom as do the families in Egyptian Silwa in respect to its village. However, if one wishes to understand Yucatán villages on the one hand, and Egyptian villages on the other, he must examine the villages in these respective cultures—and the cities, too. There is no substitute for understanding a particular culture by studying that culture, not even the help given by viewing the culture from a cross-cultural perspective.

The answer, then, is that cross-cultural comparisons are valid, but only on certain levels. Everything is not amenable to a cross-cultural explanation, just as everything is not amenable to a psychological explanation. An investigator must pursue the problem in which he is interested and resist the temptation to stray because his problem does not deal with others.

ADDITIONAL THEORIES

In the preceding discussion, the observations of those students whose work is most relevant to the theory of vills has been presented. The work of others has been mentioned at numerous places throughout this book—Zimmerman, MacIver, Wirth, Sorokin, Steward, Parsons, etc. Additional observations, such as those of Arensberg (1955); Hiller (1941); Nelson, Ramsey, and Verner (1960); Reiss (1959); Sanders (1958); and Sutton and Kolaja (1960) remain undiscussed because many do not bear directly on the theory of the vill and, in other cases, their work is essentially accounted for in the theories discussed. Also, for some, it is difficult to present a critique because they are still in the process of development.[2]

Some observations remain unmentioned because, although they deal directly with concepts raised here, they do not do so according to the method employed here. The work of Sorokin provides an important example. Sorokin offers the interesting theory of a continuum between cooperation and conflict, giving rise to his three systems of interaction: familistic, mixed (contractual), and compulsory (1947, p. 93). But he offers no test of the usefulness of this dichotomy, and especially no systematic and empirical application. Sorokin necessarily stands in a position different from that of Becker and earlier theorists. Their theories are germane to this work because they provided the basis for further development. When Redfield, however, offered a detailed empirical application of the concepts employed in his folk society in connection with the folk-urban continuum in Yucatán, the work of future theories of community necessarily had to assume a fundamentally different complexion. *Either subsequent works had to show their relevance for the work of Redfield* (implicitly or otherwise) *or they had to take the course of a more purely conceptual development.* The latter course is of value, but it

___

[2] See the reference list, pp. 347–56, for works by these scholars. For additional comments concerning the convergence between the work of Conrad Arensberg, Oscar Lewis, Irving Spaulding, and myself, see Seymour (1963).

represents an approach so different from that employed in this book that it cannot be treated without necessarily turning the discussion in a different direction.

Many of the theorists mentioned, however, become relevant in another context. That is, unless the theory of the vill is articulated with other theories, it remains a rather limited theory. Obviously, vills are only partial systems, and they are found in more inclusive societies. A full exploration of the nature of these more inclusive social systems is an undertaking which cannot be completed within this book, but we must at least attempt a beginning. This is an important task, and one which can no longer be postponed.

# 8

# The Contrast of
# Total Institutions

Prisons and mental institutions are called "total institutions," following the suggestions of Erving Goffman (1957). This type of system is examined in order, first, to discover whether the total institution is similar to either the city or the folk village. And are the differences qualitative or quantitative? Second, the total institution affords an opportunity to elaborate on the nature of community. Some investigators regard them as communities, others do not.

Some scholars dismiss consideration of total institutions as communities on a priori grounds. But it should be stressed that the list of those who have considered total institutions to *be* communities is a long one, and seldom if ever have the two—total institutions and communities—been conceptually distinguished.[1] The lack of such a distinction leads to a second point. Theories of community are notoriously deficient in distinguishing community adequately from non-community. But since we cannot know a thing unless we know also what it is not, it

[1] For references in each case, consult Hillery, 1963, from which parts of this chapter are taken.

follows that the theory of vills will be significantly incomplete until we know at least one social system which differs from it and why.

## GOFFMAN'S HYPOTHESIS

As a type of denotative definition, Goffman indicates five rough groupings of total institutions: (1) those that care for persons considered to be both incapable and harmless (for example, orphanages); (2) those that care for the incapable who are some sort of threat to the larger society (tuberculosis sanitoriums, mental hospitals, and leprosoriums); (3) those organized to protect the society against persons thought to be intentional dangers (prisons); (4) those organized for technical tasks (such as army barracks, ships, boarding schools); and (5) those established for religious purposes (monasteries and other cloisters). The basic characteristic of these organizations is found in their encompassing tendencies. All social systems have such tendencies, but "when we review the different institutions in our Western society we find a class of them which seems to be encompassing to a degree discontinuously greater than the ones next in line. Their encompassing or total character is symbolized by the barrier to social intercourse with the outside that is often built right into the physical plant: locked doors, high walls, barbed wire, cliffs and water, open terrain, and so forth" (Goffman, 1957, pp. 43–44).

This attempt to control the total life of its inmates in Goffman's view is a defining characteristic, and hence the name of this social system. There are several consequences of this total character. The first is a basic split between inmates and staff such that they form separate worlds, each significantly antagonistic to the other. A second consequence is that these institutions are incompatible with the work-payment structure of our society. Labor takes on punitive features, therapeutic features, or it may become simply an escape from boredom. More important for the purpose of this book, labor in total institutions lacks certain of the essential elements of the contract. A third consequence is that these institutions are incompatible to the establishment of the family, for in the family as it appears in the models of the folk village and the city there arises avenues of escape from the total control. An additional development (whether it is a consequence is hard to say) is that these establish-ments have become "the forcing houses for changing persons in our society. Each is a natural experiment, typically harsh, on what can be done to the self" (Goffman, 1957, p. 48).

If Goffman is correct in his analysis, then the total institution will differ qualitatively and sharply in certain important re-spects from the folk village and the city, and the model of the folk village (or the vill) will not be useful for describing total institutions, though the folk village will remain the necessary device for comparison (given the assumptions of this book).

One indication of the nature of the difference between total institution and vill is found in the comparability of the cate-gories in the models. In some cases, although the same labels can be used, they refer to clearly different things. For example, the emphasis on custody that total control necessitates may be treated as a type of government, the staff-inmate split is dis-cussed under stratification, etc. But one set of factors, in par-ticular, may be classed as a new organization of norms: the institution of maintenance. Within this category may be placed recruitment, discharge, custody, and treatment.

A cross-cultural criterion has been used for the vills. This criterion has not been met for prisons and mental asylums, and thus one must constantly bear in mind that he is studying accounts of Western institutions—and, in this instance, institu-tions confined to England and the United States. A study was catalogued for use in this book of a Dutch prison—Thorsten Sellin's Rasphuis (1944), but probably because his investiga-tion was limited to historical data, information on many points which are important to this analysis was omitted, specifically: interaction, ethnocentrism, awareness, and the prison as a base of operations. Nevertheless, Rasphuis is important for providing certain historical soundings.

In the following discussion, "asylum" is used in its literal sense as a sanctuary or place of refuge. The term still seems appropriate and under some conditions is preferable to "hospi-tal" when speaking of organizations caring for the mentally disorganized. Goffman's label of "total institution" is quite descriptive for certain points he wishes to emphasize, but be-cause an analysis becomes confused when speaking of institutions within total institutions, and because the term "total" is sometimes misleading, total institutions will also be referred to here as "custodial systems" or "custodial institutions." The word "custodial" refers to "The care afforded in institutions to socially incompetent persons who need close supervision or require personal assistance in performing elemental human functions" (Fairchild, 1944, p. 84).

## A COMPARISON OF MODELS

The components of a model of the total institution are compared with those of the vill in Table 7. (The specific total institutions are described in Table 6, more fully in Appendix C.) The same method is used for the model of total institutions as is used for

*Table 6.* Selected identifying characteristics of the five total institutions

| Name | Inmates | Staff | Types of inmates | Time of study | Investigators |
|---|---|---|---|---|---|
| Belmont | 100 | 35 | Chronic unemployed neurotics | 1947–50 | Jones *et al.*, 1953 |
| Caudill's hospital | 35 | 35 | Severe neurotics, character disorders, psychotics of recent origin | 1951–52 | Caudill, 1958 |
| Southern Hospital | 2,960 | 610 | Quite diverse but mainly various types of psychotics (including senile) | 1951–52 | Belknap, 1956 |
| Clemmer's prison | 2,300 | 200 | Maximum security prisoners and others | 1931–34 | Clemmer, 1940 |
| Trenton Prison | 1,200 | 300 | Maximum security prisoners | c. 1954 | Sykes, 1958 |

all models in this book; that is, every component described in the trait list is found in each of the five custodial systems, and the integrating construct of the model refers to all five cases.

The general nature of both the models of the total institution and of the vill must be stressed. We are working with simplified pictures, obtained by seeking only traits common to a number of phenomena. To understand any specific total institution, more detail would be necessary. The reader must thus distinguish between what *may* happen in a given vill or total institution and what is found in these *types* as types, generally and systematically. What is important to an understanding on a specific level is often irrelevant to an understanding on a more general level.

The total institution possesses qualities contrasting with each of the foci of the vill. As the "integrating construct" for its model, the total institution may be described as *a system in which a bureaucratic staff compels a localized collectivity to act for certain ends.* The localized collectivity is the population of inmates, whether these be patients or prisoners. Between inmates and staff, there is a basic and essentially antagonistic split that permeates the entire total institution, and its nature must be understood if the structure and function of these systems are to be grasped.

Three traits reveal no essential differences between vills and custodial systems: Personal contact, awareness, and continuance (Table 7). They are the only traits among the nineteen to be discussed which are not qualitatively dissimilar when the two systems are compared. In all probability, these traits are those which both types of systems share with most other human groups, including those which are more different from each other than are these two. Interestingly, the trait of awareness (that is, awareness of the system as some type of unit) was originally hypothesized as a possible "crucial" factor in testing whether prisons and mental asylums were the same kinds of things as folk villages. However none of the systems studied, including cities, lack the trait. Probably the more correct interpretation is that awareness is essential to any type of social system, as is personal contact and continuance, in the sense that all three are basic components of social interaction.

Note especially that these three traits are not foci of the vill. It is to the foci that attention is now turned.

*Localization.* The localized nature of the vill contrasts strongly with that of the custodial system. Most apparent is the presence of sharp boundaries around total institutions. Although the inhabitants of the vill may recognize boundaries for certain purposes, they do not always do so, and even the boundaries which they distinguish are ignored in many aspects of their lives. For example, political boundaries may be rigidly drawn (though this is not always so), but economic boundaries always show a different configuration, and the vill residents move in and out

Table 7. Components for a model of the vill and a model of the total institution

| Component | Vill (folk village and city) | Total institution (prison and mental asylum) |
|---|---|---|
| **1.0 Interaction** | | |
| 1.1 Personal contact | Interaction varies from an emphasis on direct interaction (in folk villages) to less of such an emphasis (in cities); practically everyone knew everyone else (folk villages) or strangers could be integral parts (cities). | Both direct and indirect interaction operates in a system-wide network of contacts. Staff is isolated from inmates and various inmates are isolated from others. |
| 1.2 Social processes | Cooperation is most in evidence, though competition and conflict are also described. | A basic hostility (conflict) exists between staff and inmates; contractual cooperation is found among staff; both mutual aid and conflict occur among inmates, though neither is institutionalized. |
| **2.0 Space** | | |
| 2.1 Spatial integration | Space in folk villages is integrated politically or by common recognition (mechanically) or both; in cities, integration is political, economic, and organic. Ecological centralization occurs in both types. | Space is integrated according to the custodial or treatment goals of staff in reference to inmates. |
| 2.2 Spatial patterning | | No common pattern visible. |
| 2.3 Boundaries | Boundaries are vague. | Boundaries are "pathologically" sharp and are part of and symbolic of staff's control over inmates. |
| **3.0 Activities** | | |
| 3.1 Base of operations | Vills are bases of operations for both localistic and cosmopolitan activities. | Staff does not necessarily use the total system as a base of operations in either sense; inmates use the system in both senses, but only with staff's permission. |

| | | |
|---|---|---|
| 3.2 Mobility | Mobility varies from low in folk villages to high in cities. | Though generally high, the degree of mobility varies for staff. Inmates pass through three discrete stages of mobility: admission, confinement or residence, and discharge. Residence is a period of sharply limited mobility: territorially, horizontally, and vertically. |
| 3.3 Continuance | All cities were more than a century old; six of the ten villages were more than a century old and two of the remainder might also be included with the majority. | Two of the five systems were more than a century old. |

**4.0 Sentiment**

| | | |
|---|---|---|
| 4.1 Ethnocentrism | All vills reveal ethnocentric values directed toward parts of the system and the system as a whole (complete data not given in two studies). | Ethnocentrism is not a general sentiment in all of the systems; all systems reveal hostility between staff and inmates. |
| 4.2 Awareness | Inhabitants of both types of vills showed awareness of the vill as a whole (with the exception of infants). | Both staff and inmates are aware of the total systems as an entity, though the degree of awareness was sharply reduced among a minority of inmates in some systems. |
| 4.3 Solidarity | Mechanical solidarity is more developed in folk villages, organic solidarity in cities, though each type displays some evidence of both forms. | Mechanical solidarity occurs among inmates, organic solidarity among staff, and antagonism or absence of solidarity appears between staff and inmates. |

**5.0 Institutions**

| | | |
|---|---|---|
| 5.1.1 Family | Family ties are found for most residents of all vills. | None of the inmates live with their families in the system, and family connections in the system are generally absent among the staff. |
| 5.1.2 Maintenance | No comparable institutions. | Each system has or is associated with institutionalized practices of recruitment, custody, treatment, and discharge of inmates. |

Table 7. (cont.)

| Component | Vill (folk village and city) | Total institution (prison and mental asylum) |
|---|---|---|
| 5.2 Economics | Economic institutions occupy a dominant place in the social systems of vills, whether they concern primary production (folk villages) or secondary production, distribution, and service industries (cities). | Staff positions constitute occupations in service industries. Total systems, however, are not necessarily organized for economic ends and are seldom economically profitable. |
| 5.3 Religion | All vills have religious and magical institutions and beliefs. | Religion was only of minor interest to the investigators of custodial systems and apparently of minor importance. |
| 5.4 Government | Increased specialization occurs in governmental activities in cities as contrasted with folk villages. | Government is highly specialized. Four of the five systems rely on power rather than authority and all employ force in regulating inmates. |
| 5.5 Cooperation | Mutual aid characterizes economic and other institutional behavior in folk villages; contract supersedes mutual aid in cities. | Staff cooperation is contractual and heavily institutionalized. Inmate cooperation, when it occurs, is mutual aid and is not institutionalized. Cooperation was supplanted by staff dominance in staff-inmate relations. |
| 5.6 Stratification | Stratification is always dependent in part on family ties; cities add achievement and possessions (though some folk villages have these also). | Stratification is based primarily on power and authority accompanied by a caste-like split between staff and inmates. Family ties are irrelevant. |
| 5.7 Socialization | Socialization is achieved both in families and formal schools. | Socialization is directed toward inmates by both staff and inmates. |
| 5.8 Recreation | Feasts and festivals, games and music are institutionalized and occur at least in part through cooperative activities. | Only games are consistently mentioned, though music, feasts, and festivals can be inferred. Some of these activities occur in spite of staff proscription. |

of both of these boundaries as suits their purpose. In custodial systems, the staff sets sharp limits beyond which none of the inmates may go without special permission.

The spatial patterning of each of the fifteen vills displays a process of ecological centralization of various institutionalized services. Total institutions segregate staff and inmates to some degree, but centralization is not a common practice. (No one would maintain, of course, that custodial systems could not centralize their activities. The various prisons modeled after the panopticon stand as classic examples, and one of the cases studied—Sykes' Trenton Prison—approached some of these features. But centralization did not play an important part in most of the total institutions discussed here.)

The dissimilarity in spatial patterns can be attributed to the different methods of spatial integration employed in each system. The vills integrate their space by economic and political means and according to the type of solidarity in the subtypes. That is, folk villages are relatively mechanical in their use of space, while cities integrate their space in part organically by allotting different portions to different status groups. Custodial systems, on the other hand, integrate their space on the basis of the various needs of the staff. Prison space is oriented primarily around needs of custody, whereas asylums employ space more frequently for treatment purposes.

Differences in localization are also apparent in the element of activities. Vills are bases of operations for all their members; custodial systems are consistently localized only for the inmates. The staff of the total institution may or may not use the system as a base of operations. The system may be and often is one of the places to which staff travel *from* their homes. (They may live within the system, but do not necessarily do so.) Inmates on the other hand, remain *inside* the boundaries of the system. They cannot cross the boundaries if staff chooses not to permit them to; thus they do not use the system as a base of operations in the same way that inhabitants of vills do the vill.

Mobility in folk villages is generally low, that in cities higher, whether this mobility is territorial, vertical, or horizontal. This description applies to the general populations of vills, not to any single population segment. In custodial systems, the *staff* generally exhibits each of the three types of mobility to a high degree. *Inmates*, on the other hand, experience three separate periods of mobility with reference to the system. As an adult, each inmate is "recruited" into the system, held in custody, and discharged. All inmates (except those who die) necessarily experience these phases, and thus—from the point of view of the inmate—one cannot speak of high or low mobility. Mobility of vill members is qualitatively different; this applies not only to the spatial aspect of the system but to group membership and status structure as well.

Thus, a major difference between total institutions and vills is that vills occupy some *particular* space, and this localization pertains equally to all members,[2] while custodial systems are localized only in part, in reference to the inmates. They may or may not be localized in reference to staff. In addition, the localization comes about through the dominance of staff. A comparable operation of forces is not observed in vills.

*Cooperation and conflict.* Cooperation is institutionalized in vills in the forms of contract (in cities) and mutual aid (in folk villages). Conflict is very much in evidence in both types of vills but it is not always institutionalized. In the custodial systems, on the other hand, conflict is institutionalized in that an organization of norms is employed by the staff to control hostile or potentially hostile inmates. The institution is characterized by a basic split dividing the system into at least two discrete groups: the controllers and the controlled. Various adjustments are made to this conflict, but these are technically forms of accommodation, not cooperation. The distinction rests in the prior history of conflict or its expectation in the case of accommodation, whereas neither mutual aid nor contract presuppose hostility. Prolonged accommodation may develop true cooperation in individual cases, but such exceptions do not suspend the rule: staff cannot afford to ignore the *potential* hostility of inmates as a class.

There are "institutional dependents," persons who become better adjusted to institutional life than to the "outside," and even prefer it to the outside (although the sources do not clearly indicate the presence of such cases in the five custodial systems considered here). These persons accommodate to the conflict by

---

[2] For example, New York is equally New York both to the bank clerk who works in the city and to the traveling salesman who has his home there.

accepting a subordinate position. Should total institutions change so as to facilitate such an accommodation, the basic custodial orientation might well be drastically altered. (Note that we do not contend that custodial systems necessarily have to be organized in the manner depicted here. The five systems studied *are* so organized, and they appear to be representative to some extent of other custodial systems.)

Of course, cooperation does occur in custodial systems but, as noted below in the discussion of sentiments, it occurs primarily *within* the opposing factions rather than between them. Jones' account of Belmont is instructive in this connection since the staff places special stress on friendliness and helpfulness towards inmates. Yet even at Belmont the inmates frequently express hostility toward staff and the staff-inmate distinction is clearly institutionalized.

The two types of systems differ markedly in their sentiments. Ethnocentrism is as conspicuously absent in total institutions as it is present in vills. Admittedly, all vills do not display equal degrees of ethnocentrism, but even for the two for which data are not available (Timbuctoo and Ch'u), the people stay, and their stay is not contingent upon the use of force. The closest approach to ethnocentrism recorded in the prisons were the "center men" described by Sykes, that is, prisoners who identified with staff. Such loyalty is regarded as treason by the inmates, however, and is not typical of prisoners. In mental hospitals, the patients display ambivalence at best; positive feelings toward the program, hostility toward the doctors. In fact, a manifest function of staff usually consists of minimizing consequences of inmate hostility.

Solidarity in vills may be regarded as a function of the relationship between degrees of heterogeneity and types of cooperation. Thus, folk villagers cooperate according to norms of status (mutual aid) and by means of the basic similarity of social units. Division of labor based upon heterogeneous roles, though universal, is minimal. In the city, solidarity occurs through the operation of contracts in a social environment of extensive heterogeneity. The heterogeneity is mainly the result of a division of labor which, in turn, functions by means of contractual ties.

Where it exists in total institutions, solidarity is found within the two opposing factions, not between them. Interestingly, the solidarity in staff is organic, that among inmates is mechanical. But the line between the factions is one of antagonism. Of the custodial systems comprising the model, the English hospital (Belmont) probably does most to modify this antagonism. Yet even there antagonism is very much in evidence.

*The family*. Of each of the three foci of vills—space, cooperation, and family—it is probably the family that provides the sharpest contrast between vills and total institutions. Although there is variation between cities and folk villages in the position of families in the vills' structure, the family is always present and always involves a majority of the members in each system. But families are, at best, incidental to the functioning of total institutions. True, Belknap notes that the ward attendants at Southern Hospital were relatives and even maintained family members in certain positions in the system through several generations. (Rasphuis also at one time apparently had a work supervisor whose family was part of the prison staff.) But these attendants were in the minority, even at Southern, and the other total institutions functioned equally well without such kinship ties (probably better, in many ways). Conceivably, inmates could exist as family members in the system. Most important, none of the inmates lived with their families in the total institutions under consideration.

The family fulfills certain requirements that must be met if vills are to continue in operation, not the least of which is the provision of new "recruits"—children. These requirements are satisfied in an entirely different manner in total institutions, and with them other requirements are met which are peculiar to these types of system. This is accomplished through what may be called "institutions of maintenance." These are recruitment, custody, treatment, and discharge. (1) Recruitment may not be a direct part of the custodial system, as when new members are received from the courts through legal processes, but the custodial system is nonetheless entirely dependent on the institution of recruitment for new members. (2) Once the inmates are within the boundaries of the system, measures must be taken to insure their continued presence, that is, their custody. At the very minimum, the custodial task consists of warnings that failure to adhere to the institutional demands means either confinement or discharge. At the maximum, it means death. (3) Whether the inmate receives treatment depends on the nature of the system. Treatment in prisons tends to occur only as it contributes to custodial requirements. In mental institutions, treatment is apt to be more fully developed as a specialized goal. (4) Finally, there is always some procedure whereby most of the inmates are discharged (even if this "discharge" is by means of execution).

In the institutions of maintenance, a complex of practices is encountered which are as foreign to the vill as the family is to the custodial system. But vills and custodial systems differ not only in that one has the family and the other does not. They differ also in that vills are structured in reference to the family and custodial systems are structured in reference to an entirely different set of practices, the institutions of maintenance.

The remaining institutions found in the model of vills may be treated in reference to the manner in which they revolve around the three foci of space, family, and cooperation. In custodial systems the same institutions (if present at all) function according to requirements stemming from staff dominance over inmates. Industries, if any exist, are operated because of the dictates of the staff (and staff is, basically, operating because of the dictates of the larger society), not because of any economic needs of the inmates. A similar description may be applied to religion. Governmental institutions operate in reference to the institutions of maintenance, and these institutions in turn exist as a consequence of the staff-inmate split.

"Stratification" is similarly oriented around the opposing factions, and in this same sense "stratification" is a "caste" system—though the absence of the family renders the term "stratification" metaphorical according to prevalent theories. Most attempts at socialization take place both because of staff dictates and in terms of the dichotomy which these dictates produce. Thus, the inmates have their own system of socialization, but the institution revolves largely around the structure and function of staff. Institutionalized recreation is largely· organized by the staff—or prohibited by them. (The success of these efforts varies.)

## THE MEANING FOR COMMUNITY

If the differences between the folk village and the city are taken as a standard of comparison, then the total institution differs more from the vills than either type of vill differs from the other. All differences between folk villages and cities are differences of degree and may be expressed by means of continua. Examples can be found in the greater spatial differentiation, greater importance of the individual, and greater frequency of contractual relations found in moving from the folk village to the city. It is the nature of this kind of difference which prompts the more general name given here to both types: the vill.

Differences between the vill and the custodial system, however, are almost always qualitative. Only in three of nineteen comparisons can a quantitative difference be argued. Even more important, the qualitative differences are found between the total institution and the *focal* components of the vills: space, family, and cooperation. Spatial use is controlled in a sharply different manner in custodial systems than it is in vills. The family is absent among the inmates of total institutions and is generally absent among the staff. Finally, cooperation occurs *within* the staff and inmate segments of custodial systems rather than between them. The chief implication is clear: if vills are to be considered communities and if community is to have any distinctive meaning, then total institutions are not communities.

Before the distinction between total institutions and vills can be fully understood, we must know the objects to which each of the phenomena in question are related. And, to reach that point, we must understand the objects themselves. Considerable attention has been given to this subject in the case of vills, but the question remains for total institutions: If the total institution is not a vill, then what is it?

In one sense, it is something in its own right, as Goffman's theory indicates. In a more general sense, the total institution may be studied as a type of complex or formal organization. Practically all theories of complex organizations are based on the theories of Max Weber and Chester I. Barnard (cf. Etzioni, 1961). One of the most comprehensive syntheses of these theories (as well as being a contribution in its own right) is Talcott Parsons' (1960). His theory of organizations provides a more general setting within which Goffman's concepts may be placed.

The defining characteristic of an organization, according to Parsons, is the *"primacy of orientation to the attainment of a specific goal"* (Parsons, 1960, p. 17). This feature distinguishes organizations from such a group as the family, which "is only partly an organization; most other kinship groups are even less so. The same is certainly true of local communities, regional subsocieties, and of a society as a whole conceived, for example, as a nation" (Parsons, 1960, p. 16). In our terminology, the "local community" is the vill, which has anything but a specific goal. From Parsons' view, one might even say that the vill is twice removed from the total institution—once in its own right and once through the families which make it up.

With the total institution identified as a formal organization, we are in a better position to ascertain the meaning that total institutions have for community. There are three contributions. First, the study of the total institution enables us to substantiate one of the hypotheses advanced in Chapter 1 and thus delineate some major dimensions of community. Second, with this delineation, we are in a better position to assess community theories. Third, total institutions are taxonomically useful, for they reveal the distinguishing features of two specific kinds of human groups and, by extension, the groups to which each of these is related.

It will be recalled that of the original eight hypotheses advanced concerning the possible relation between folk villages, cities, and total institutions, only hypothesis 5 has been demonstrated: folk villages and cities are connected by continua, and total institutions differ qualitatively from both folk villages and cities. Thus, total institutions systematically lack certain things that are found universally in vills (both folk villages and cities) and vice versa. Vills have families and are based on cooperation, localization being functional for these two things. Total institutions lack these foci. On the other hand, total institutions have the staff-inmate split, dominance of staff over inmates, and a primacy of orientation to specific goals. Vills lack these foci. Consequently, we argue that each type of vill is distinguished from total institutions by means of discrete and qualitative differences. This is the condition depicted by hypothesis five, except that vills have more than one continuum.

This distinction can be used as a limiting case, in the same sense in which the various models that have been developed in this book have been used. With this distinction, we are able to throw the phenomenon of community into considerably sharper focus, simply by weeding out the extraneous. We can now correct the identification of these systems that has become part of the literature, both classic and modern. (For a partial list of students who have identified the two systems, see Hillery, 1963.) To include total institutions under the heading of community destroys any precision that may be attached to either term. Although we cannot yet define community, we *can* now indicate some of the things that it does not include and some of the things that it does.

For those who now limit community, in effect, to vills, the distinction may appear obvious. But the fact that total institutions have by some been considered as communities attests to their failure to recognize the differences. Reference to correctional or therapeutic communities may represent an effort to call attention to the pervasiveness of these kinds of social organizations, but it raises too many questions about both concepts. No matter how attractive it may have been to relate these systems in terms of the relatively wide satisfaction of needs, the findings of this study reveal that the *way* in which needs are satisfied is more important. Thus, whatever value there may once have been in referring to total institutions as communities is now outweighed by the greater value of regarding them as complex or formal organizations.

If communities are seen as generally composed of conformists, and if total institutions are generally composed of deviants, then it is not surprising that total institutions are really anti-communities. Whatever justification the concept of total institutions may have, therefore, it at least has the value of suggesting the most extreme form of non-community.

A further value of the distinction is taxonomic; that is, the distinction helps in classifying or placing these (and, indeed, other) systems in relation to one another. Although taxonomy is very poorly developed in sociology, there are some rather well-established types, such as the family, associations (churches, businesses, and schools), as well as dyads, primary groups, etc.

A taxonomy has numerous advantages. Most obviously,

classifications are useful because they present an efficient way of describing objects. Second, a taxonomy that is also closely linked with its data permits recognition of variables and attributes in the objects that are typed. In this way such qualities can be controlled or otherwise accounted for in further studies. Should one wish to study the rate of diffusion in several communities, for example, then the researcher would do well to search for those communities with similar ecological, cooperative, and familial structures (that is, with similar vill foci). Otherwise, he will inadvertently study not diffusion but the effects of differences in those kinds of structures.

The distinction between vills and total institutions will not of itself provide a systematic typology, but it does provide a way to organize large quantities of data into meaningful categories, and it is on this basis that any taxonomy is built.

A GENERAL TYPOLOGY OF HUMAN GROUPS

In closing this chapter, we now proceed by means of an entirely different method of investigation. Instead of using data to limit theory, we shall use data to suggest theory. One of the most important taxonomic contributions which a comparison between vills and total institutions can make is a distinction between various kinds of organizations. To see the distinction, we must relate each of these systems to some larger class of systems and thus consider them within a more general theory of social organization. For total institutions, the larger class of systems has been extensively developed as the theory of formal organizations. And although the lack of uniformity in community theory prevents such a similar identification for vills, we can reach such a goal by comparing vills with formal organizations.

The question now arises, what is the simplest and most extensive way of separating vills and formal organizations? Most apparent is the kind of goals for which the group members strive, as group members. The goals of formal organizations are sharp and recognizable: profit, or custody of dangerous people, or recreation, or education, or so on. The vill, on the other hand, has no goal, as a vill. It may be described, instead, as the consequence of cooperation among families in a given location. Of course vills contain systems with specific goals, but these must

be distinguished from any goals which would be pertinent to the
vill as a whole. Also, vills may follow specific goals, such as occur
in a community chest drive, but these goals are either temporary
or they are peculiar to specific vills rather than being common
to vills in general.

This distinction suggests that one way of classifying groups
is in terms of whether the system as a whole possesses goals.
Accordingly, groups may be viewed as being defined by specific
goals, on the one hand, or merely being a result of following
other goals. We are thus distinguishing between groups which
come into existence because they are purposely created to do
certain things, and groups which are seldom if ever specifically
created but which evolve because other groups bring them into
being. To express this distinction in another way, some groups
are brought into being merely through the process of human
living.

As important as this distinction is, it includes entirely too
many unlike things. Crowds are not formal organizations, but
in part they are defined in terms of specific goals (rioting crowd,
lynch mob, spectator crowd, etc.) and, similarly, cliques and
ethnic groups are not vills, but they need not give primacy to
specific goals. Obviously, there must be further subdivision.

Two questions will show the nature of the needed division:
(1) How are crowds different from formal organizations?
(2) How are cliques different from vills? Note that the first pair
of these groups is defined by specific goals, the second pair is not.
Within each of these pairs, a further distinction may be drawn
in terms of the degree of their institutionalization. One member
of each pair is structured by means of an extensive pattern of
norms—that is, it is institutionalized—whereas the other member of each pair is much less institutionalized.

On the basis of the reasoning thus far, a preliminary typology
may be constructed as shown in Figure 2. There are numerous
groups yet to be placed within this scheme, but there are several
questions to be asked before the typology can serve as a working
tool for future discussion.

The first question concerns the manner in which one distinguishes systems with specific goals. Following Parsons (1960,
pp. 17–18), we may describe a specific goal as having at least
three characteristics: (1) the product of the goal is identifiable,

such as automobiles, academic degrees, etc; (2) the product can be used by another system—that is, the output of one system is an input for another system; and (3) the output is amenable to a contract, it can be bought and sold. An organization *has* specific goals if its members recognize the possession of specific goals and if its norms are so organized that they contribute to the attainment of those goals.

The System Is:

|  | Defined by specific goals | Not defined by specific goals |
|---|---|---|
| Structured (institutionalized) | Formal organizations | Vills |
| Relatively unstructured (uninstitutionalized) | Crowds | Cliques |

Norms:

*Fig. 2*—Preliminary Typology of Human Groups.

At this point, goals must be carefully distinguished from functions (Davis, 1949, pp. 124–25). The latter may be defined as a contribution to the existence of a given system. The attainment of the goal is virtually always functional for such groups as formal organizations, of course, but there are other functions besides goal attainment, as well as dysfunctions.

In formal organizations, both the goals and the structures are intentionally (manifestly) functional for each other. The organization *may* achieve latent or unintended results, but the latent consequences cannot be so important that they prohibit the attainment of the manifest goals in the eyes of the members of the organization. For example, a latent dysfunction of prisons is that inmates are taught to be more efficient criminals. This dysfunction *impedes* the attainment of the manifest goal, that of custody, but it does not *prohibit* the attainment of that goal.

The situation is almost exactly reversed in structured systems without goals. Vills, for example, have no specific raison d'être. At least in the vills studied here, no specific goal they were created to attain is ever overtly stated. Indeed, none of them were purposely created to do what they do (at least within the memories of their inhabitants): to promote living and cooperation among a collection of families who reside in a given place.

One of the basic identifying features of such groups as vills and cliques, therefore, is the absence of specific "defining" goals, that is, those goals for which the system exists. In this sense, one might say that such systems are ends in themselves, though such a statement leaves too many questions unanswered, not the least of which is the number of people that must feel this way before the criterion applies. Further, there is little evidence on the point: all that we know is that people are ethnocentric about vills; but they are ethnocentric about other groups, too. Thus, in the absence of better data, we will say that the vill and similar types must be identified by a negative criterion: There are no specific goals which define the system, there is no specific goal to which the members give top priority or "primacy of orientation," in Parsons' terms (1960).

It is possible for vills to have specific goals, but only insofar as these goals are not intentionally harmful, that is, manifestly dysfunctional, to the goals of living and cooperating together. Thus, the same condition prevails as in systems with specific goals, except that the presence of the goal varies. In one case, the system is a consequence of recognized goals without which the systems will not exist. In the other case, the system is a consequence of the goals of other systems and has no goals of its own.

The second question concerning the typology develops from the first: Is the distinction between the cells discrete or continuous? A first answer can be obtained by considering the distinction between institutionalized and relatively uninstitutionalized systems. Obviously, prisons are heavily institutionalized, whereas crowds are practically uninstitutionalized. But as one considers other types of systems, the distinction is not always so clear. The best example would be a political party. Its goal is the attainment of political power. In its infancy, it can hardly be called institutionalized—it may not even follow (may. even oppose) the norms established for it by the larger society. As parties mature, however, they become institutionalized.

The same argument can be made for ethnic groups: Negroes

widely scattered over a city are an ethnic group but not a vill. Gathered into a ghetto, they begin to assume some of the attributes of a vill. It is conceivable that either of two things could happen eventually: the ghetto will become institutionalized to such an extent that it matches the model of the vill, or it will expand in size sufficiently to the point where the city would, in effect, be a Negro city (and this again would be a vill).

Social systems, then, are regarded as *more or less* institutionalized rather than as either institutionalized or not. The same, however, does not hold true with reference to goals. There is hardly a continuum between systems with specific and those with no goals. A system either has goals or it does not, as of a given point in time. In fact, the very nature of groups defined by specific goals makes impossible any continuum between such groups and systems without such goals. Whenever a group becomes so organized that its existence depends on the continued striving for a specific goal, then that group, by its very nature, can no longer be said to be the same kind of a thing as a vill. It is possible for a group to be two things at once, as when a boys' gang (which has no specific goal) engages in a riot, but the distinction remains.

This possibility of a group having a "double identity" is brought about in part because groups change from cell to cell in the typology. Formal organizations can produce social movements which can establish vills (for example, "utopian" communities), vills can produce ethnic groups, etc. In fact, a basic principle of the typology is that *groups in any cell can produce types that appear in any other cell*. The number of types that can participate in this process seems endless: families operating a business concern, social movements operating hospitals, vills operating businesses, etc. To the extent that the principle is valid, then one will expect "in-between" types.

The typology also has another dimension, a systematic variation which appears in each of the cells of the typology: the systems will be found to vary from those which include all of the other systems in its class to those which include none of the others. Thus, nations include vills which include neighborhoods, etc., but not vice versa (at least normally). Similarly, ethnic groups may include cliques, but not vice versa, and social movements may include crowds, but not vice versa. Formal organizations are more difficult to describe, because in order to classify them we must also consider the segment of society which benefits from the formal organization (Blau and Scott, 1962). With this principle in mind, we may distinguish between organizations which serve the entire society, or commonweal organizations; those which serve some limited segment of it (either service organizations or business concerns); and those which serve only themselves (mutual benefit associations). This principle will be referred to as the principle of inclusiveness.

Thus, three principles or criteria have been identified which may be used in classifying human groups: The quality of working for a specific goal or of having no goal, the degree of institutionalization, and the degree of inclusiveness. The application of these three principles produces the categories found in Figure 3. The groups have been distributed within each of the

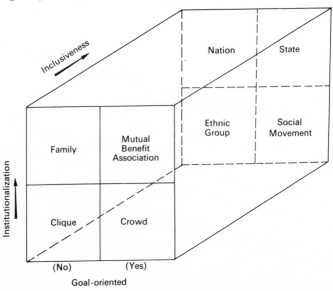

*Fig. 3*—Schematic for a General Typology of Human Groups

four cells of the preliminary typology according to the criteria of inclusiveness. Accordingly, at the upper end of each of the lists of groups are the most inclusive systems: nations, ethnic groups, social movements, and commonweal organizations (for example, states). At the lower end of each list are the most limited systems: families, cliques, crowds, and mutual-benefit associations.

The concepts of "formal" organizations and "informal" groups are of course well-established in the literature in the general sense in which they are used here (although unanimity has by no means been reached). The distinction between "group" and "organization" is intended merely to emphasize the greater complexity in organizations. "Expressive group"

*Table 8.* A general typology of human groups

| | The system has primacy of orientation to specific goals: | | Inclusiveness relative to the smaller systems: |
| --- | --- | --- | --- |
| | *Yes* | *No* | |
| Institutionalized | (Formal Organizations)* | (Communal Organizations) | |
| | Commonweal organizations (e.g., police) | Nations | Maximum |
| | Service organizations (e.g., hospitals) | Vills | |
| | Business concerns | Neighborhoods | |
| | Mutual-benefit associations | Families | Minimum |
| Relatively un-institutionalized† | (Expressive Groups) | (Informal Groups) | |
| | Social movements | Ethnic groups | Maximum |
| | Crowds | Cliques | Minimum |

Principles: 1. Any group can be formed from any cell. 2. Some types in any cell can contain types in other cells.

* The typology for formal organizations is that of Blau and Scott (1962), pp. 42 ff.
† As noted in the text, no group is ever completely uninstitutionalized. The distinction is relative.

is a term borrowed from Hawley (1962). It refers to forms of collective behavior. Hawley's general term appears preferable, especially since the term "collectivity" has recently been used to refer to groups in general.

The most troublesome name is that of "communal organization." "Community" has been used in so many contradictory ways as to render it almost useless for describing a specific system. "Communal organization" is used because it connotes a range of specific things. "Communal" associates the term with a broad collection of related groups, and "organizations" gives the collection some specificity.

There are numerous groups which do not appear in the typology. Their absence is due, first, to the fact that their existence as social systems with a relatively distinct membership may be in question (for example, publics or social classes). Second, their distribution may be too limited to warrant including them in a general typology (for example, the Hindu caste). Or, third, they may be in-between types, such as city-states. Only those types are described which would most clearly be a product of the various forces that have been mentioned: goal attainment (or its lack), institutionalization, and inclusiveness. Human groupings are inherently things of change. The types we have described are thus not immutable objects. They are, rather, the product of innumerable social forces which may at times even be contradictory. As such, the types that have been described are only those coalescences of forces which emerge clearly.

The distinction between vills and total institutions, then, has relevance for community in two ways. First, the distinction is relevant in its own right as a means of discarding phenomena which should not be considered with folk villages and cities. Second, the distinction provides a basis for showing what other groups are related to vills and total institutions. The typology that results suggests at least two group types that have so far received little attention in this book and yet which are proper objects of study for those interested in communal organizations: the nation and the neighborhood. A consideration of these and other types is given in the next chapter.

# 9

# A Survey of
# Communal Organizations

Each of the groups discussed in this chapter has a close relationship to the vill or to some other communal organization.
Thus, for example, a consideration of the *state* is necessary to an
understanding of nations. In addition, such a consideration
focuses on a system devoted essentially to conflict or conflict
regulation and thus, by contrast, emphasizes the significance of
cooperation in vills. The *nation* poses different problems: What
is the relation of the vill to the larger system which often includes
it? The *neighborhood* directs attention to types which match the
model of the vill in its more important components but which
lacks certain minor or secondary characteristics. On the other
hand, a study of the *kibbutz* leads to an examination of the importance of the family. The kibbutz has shorn the family of as
many of its functions as has ever been done by any group for any
considerable length of time.

It is important to realize that we are still proceeding on the
same strategy as adopted in the last section of the preceding
chapter. We are using single cases to suggest theory rather than
to establish theory.

THE NATION, THE STATE, AND RELATED SYSTEMS

These systems do not belong in the same cell of the general typology, but they present similar problems in an attempt to understand the nature of the vill, and they are considered together for that reason.[1] This is especially true of the United States, which is the main case used for illustrative purposes. The distinction between the nation and the state is simple but crucial to a proper understanding both of the nation and the vill. The state is a political association organized to maintain a monopoly  of power. Power is interpreted in its limited meaning as the ability to use force. Since the power of the state is in most cases a legitimate ability, we speak of authority, and thus, practically speaking, states become the ultimate sources of authority (Bierstedt, 1950). Nations, on the other hand, are comprised of all social systems which are subject to a given state. In terms of these distinctions, the state is a formal organization, that is, a highly structured system with a specific goal, whereas a nation is a communal organization, that is, a highly structured system without goals. We will consider the state first.

*The state.* All states have at least one specific goal: they seek to monopolize the use of force. Indeed, a state is truly successful only when it has attained this monopoly. If the monopoly is challenged and the state does not meet the challenge, then ipso facto the state has capitulated to the challenger, if only informally. The state thus constitutes the ultimate enforcement agency. All parts of vills, from this point of view, are subject to the state, but as will be shown, they are not in the same sense a *part* of the state.

States do more than monopolize power. They also regulate, whether commerce, the distribution of booty acquired through conquest, or the welfare of orphans. From this point of view, the goal of the state is to issue regulations, and regulations fulfill all of the requirements of goals in Parsons' sense (1960, pp. 17–18): they are identifiable, they are outputs which are inputs for other systems, and they are subject to a set of terms or conditions. In the U.S., the terms are set forth in the Constitution. More ulti-

[1] The following discussion depends heavily on the work of Toennies (1957, pp. 208–10, 216–18), MacIver (1947), and Williams (1960). For a somewhat similar treatment but one which emphasizes historical analysis, see Martindale 1960, Chap. 9.

mately, as MacIver has said, the terms are set by the will of the people (1947).

There may seem here a contradiction with Weber, who claims that the state cannot be defined in terms of its ends (1946, Chap. 4). We are, of course, using "goal" in a more restricted sense. Weber further says that the use of physical force is the specific *means* peculiar to the state. Again, our emphasis is different: logically, the first goal any organization must attain in order to become a state is the attainment of a monopoly of power. The use of force is the means, the monopoly the goal. Once attained, this monopoly must be maintained. And the chief manifestation of this goal is the issuing of regulations, which may itself be termed a type of goal, as we have seen.

Because of the multiplicity of different things which the state regulates, states appear to fall in the categories of both formal and communal organizations. But because all states necessarily have a specific goal—no matter what other goals they have— they are thus different from all vills. States, therefore, may do some of the same things that vills do (and as we shall see, vice versa), but they are to be distinguished because of their specific goal of the acquisition and monopoly of power.

Thus, the important thing about the state's multitudinous activities are not the activities themselves, but the regulations. These regulations, in turn, are a consequence of the state's monopoly of power. If the state were to engage in a private business completely divorced from taxes or from state authority, then we would truly have a non-political activity and one, thus, not part of the state's system. For example, if private individuals could operate a postal service in competition with the government, if there were no taxes supporting this service, and if the government could not protect this service any more than it protects any other service, then the government would be engaged in a type of activity which would not involve its power.

Of course, this specific goal has consequences which can carry the state into numerous areas to such an extent that the state becomes totalitarian. But merely because the state may grow in number of functions, one should not lose sight of its essential goal. This conclusion is the same kind that was developed for the total institution: the state is not a vill merely because it may do some of the things that a vill does.

The city-state raises important points in this connection. Undeniably, such systems have existed in both meanings of the word: cities which were also states. But this possibility should not confuse the distinction. Cities are diffuse organizations capable of assuming many functions. They can act as states, they can also contain and operate total institutions, but they are not necessarily either. Analogously, it is possible to conceive of a folk village in which all persons are kin, but that would not make the village and the family synonymous.

*The nation.* Nations, almost by definition, are much more complex than states, since they are composed of parts drawn from each of the four cells of the general typology. (1) The nation is a communal organization and is also made up of vills and those types which are probably closely related, such as open-country neighborhoods. Furthermore, just as the individual's immediate family generally is a means of binding him to a given vill, so his larger kinship group, if it is found outside of his vill, can operate as a force binding him to the nation as a whole. (2) Formal organizations are at the same time parts of the nation and provide it with some of its main integrative forces. Most important are the various political associations, particularly the state. But almost equally important are the economic associations. After these come the religious, educational, scientific, recreational, and other systems. All of these associations—state, economic, and other—join vill to vill, open country to vill, and individual to individual. (3) Social movements are probably one of the more important forms of expressive groups comprising a nation. However, they generally do not last with sufficient tenacity to provide more than sporadic binding power—at times they are actually divisive. Movements are designed to "bring about fundamental changes in the social order" (Heberle, 1951, p. 6). As such an aim is realized, the nature of the movement necessarily changes. It either retains its relatively low degree of institutionalization and becomes an informal group (as, for example, an ethnic group), or it becomes incorporated into the larger society as a formal organization (such as a political party or, at the height of its success, as the state itself). (4) Ethnic groups perhaps most frequently integrate nations either through the family or through social movements.

As is true of the vill, the nation is not purposively organized by these types of groups. Even though the nation is integrated (at least in part) by the state, this does not make the nation a formal organization. The nation has no specific goal. It is the state which has an objective—the monopoly of power. Nations are not set up to do anything—states are. Nations develop in the process of living and are products of the particular culture a people has. But the nation is nonetheless an entity and the things mentioned are its essential parts, the fabric and weave of the system as a whole.

The nation therefore differs from vills in at least two ways. First, the nation *contains* vills *and* other things, and thus it is as different from a vill as an organism would be different from any of its constituent parts, though these parts themselves may be organisms. Second, while vills are integrated by three discernible foci—space, cooperation and families—the nation is integrated primarily by one—the state. The only focus of the vill that in any way approximates the state focus of the nation is cooperation. But precisely because the state assumes a monopoly of power, it is a *conflict*-regulating system.

Space is possessed by nations, but it is not space which is the integrative factor, it is the state. Should the state give up part of its territory, then the territory is lost to the nation, and, conversely, a physically separate space may become part of the nation *if the state claims it.* The loss of Alaska by Russia is an instance of the first point, its acquisition by the U.S. illustrates the second.

Nations also differ from vills relative to other components in the model of the vill. Most different are base of operations, space, and awareness.

The vill is different from the nation in the quality the vill has of serving as a base of operations for the routine activities of its members. For the lives of most citizens, the nation (or some part of it) becomes one of the objects of this base; that is, it is the area to which the vill members go when traveling from their base (the vill). The nation is not *a* base of operations, nor is it even a collection of bases, as is the city. More simply, a nation is not a vill as much as it is a collection of vills. Of course, there must be more than vills—there must be the organizations binding vills together, of which the most important is the state. Otherwise, one does not have a nation but a collection of vills with a common culture. (In this connection, see the discussion of regions in the next section.)

It is apparent, then, that vills are spatially integrated in a different way than nations. Furthermore, vills are generally much smaller, and thus their spatial integration is more readily perceived when the members physically move over the area of the vill during the course of a day.

The boundaries enclosing the territory of nations and vills are also different. Boundaries around vills are vague; those around nations are sharp. Even though a citizen retains his nationality when he crosses the national boundary, he is subject to the laws of his nation only insofar as the host nation permits. This fact more than any other places ethnic enclaves in a different category from nations, and so they have been treated in the general typology.

This difference brings us to the last of the differences in components between the two systems: the quality of awareness. It is important to recall the conclusion concerning awareness that was reached in the study of total institutions—that it is probably a quality common to all social systems. Thus, any distinction would not be found in the presence or absence of the quality itself as much as it would in the nature of the quality; that is, of what are the nation's citizens aware as opposed to vill members? Since the nation differs from the vill in the components of co-operation, as a base of operations, and as a locality group, one would expect that the nature of the awareness would differ also.

If a citizen is aware of his nation at all, he is aware of it primarily as a symbol and as a conflict-regulator. In each case, the principal *source* of awareness is the state rather than the nation. The hypothesis can be offered that awareness of the nation as a symbol is chiefly in ceremonial occasions, such as national "birthdays," celebration of famous battles or victories, or inaugural ceremonies. As a conflict-regulator, the citizen thinks of the nation when he pays taxes, goes to war, or otherwise comes into contact with national laws and their enforcement. Rarely does one think of the nation when his attention is turned individually to any of the numerous special-interest groups which bind it together: the labor union, the supermarket chain store, the gasoline companies, the mass media of communication, etc. Thus, the chief awareness that the citizen has of the nation would not be of the numerous interlocking complex organizations and vills that form it but of the aspect of it that we have called the state.

The awareness of the vill member of his vill probably originates from an entirely different source: that part of the vill that he perceives as he moves over his base of operations. There is a personal contact that occurs in vills that does not occur in nations (except perhaps for the minority who travel extensively). Since awareness is conditioned by perceptions, awareness will accordingly differ in the two types of systems.

Even with these differences in view, the essential distinction between nations and vills is, for the most part, not found in the traits the two systems contain but in the way in which the components are organized; that is, the focus (or foci) of integration is different, depending on which system is being examined. With few exceptions, nations contain and are composed of the elements of interaction, space, activities, sentiment, and institutions, just as are vills. They differ in that nations are more inclusive and are integrated on a different basis. What few differences there are in the components of each system are essentially consequences of the two major differences.

The difference between the two systems may be briefly summarized by noting two major points. First, nations contain vills, and second, nations are integrated in a different manner. Since nations contain vills, it follows that everything in vills are found in nations, also. However, because of this inclusiveness and because the two systems are organized differently, certain qualitative differences occur in the components of the respective systems. The most significant of these differences are (1) the integrating force for nations is conflict-regulation rather than cooperation, families, and space; (2) the nation is not a base of operations; (3) spatial boundaries of nations are precise instead of vague; and (4) the awareness of the nation differs from that of the vill.

The question follows: Are nations more different from vills than total institutions are different from vills? This question must be answered on several levels. On the most specific level, nations have all the traits that vills do, whereas total institutions lack some of the traits in vills, and vice versa. On a second level, all three systems have different foci. But on the most general level used in this discussion, nations are most similar to vills in the lack of specific "defining" goals. (All three systems, it will be remembered, are highly structured.)

The classification introduced by the general typology, therefore, assumes that the difference between groups with specific goals and those without them is more significant than are the differences in the foci. One justification for giving more importance to the criteria in the typology is found in the nature of the foci. These are merely the fewest traits which are integrated with all other traits in the system. As such, foci are inherently oriented to a given type of system. When the analysis shifts to more inclusive categories, we must necessarily speak in terms that include more than certain specific systems, that is, the concepts must be more general. The typology provides such general concepts, especially in the concepts of structure and goals. These concepts, therefore, do two things: they separate things that should be separated (for example, total institutions and vills) and they allow specific systems to be related to other systems.

*The world, the region, and the county.* If one of the conditions of a social system is an awareness of the existence of such a system on the part of its members, then there is no social system corresponding to the world as a whole, and on this basis the world cannot be a communal organization. Whether there ever will be, whether MacIver's speculation of the possibility of a world community will ever materialize (MacIver and Page, 1949), will probably depend on the emergence of some sort of world government.

For much the same reason, it is not feasible to compare regions and vills. Regions vary from statistical abstractions to actual coalescences of a given number of traits which are recognized by the inhabitants. The West South Central geographic division of the U.S. Bureau of the Census would be an example of a statistical abstraction. An example of a region which is a social entity cannot be given in unambiguous form. There are such things as multi-factor regions, as, for example, the Southeastern U.S. But the conflicting attempts to devise such regions (compare Odum and Moore, 1938; Mangus, 1940; and Bogue and Beale, 1961) provide ample warning that there is as yet no entirely satisfactory scheme for objectively describing such areas. One might speculate that a social region would be similar to a nation without a state, but since the state is an essential integrating factor of a nation, there is little left to compare.

The concept of a metropolitan region includes numerous different things. In the narrowest sense, there is the metropolis proper; that is, the city together with its built-up fringe (the "urbanized area," as defined by the U.S. Bureau of the Census). The data in this book indicate that this concept is essentially that of the vill, especially in that the same foci are observable in such diverse metropolitan areas as New Orleans, San Francisco, Los Angeles, and even Rome (see Chap. 6). Nevertheless, special attention needs to be given to the extensive conurbations of New York, Tokyo, London, etc. These will no doubt present special problems that have not been taken into consideration here.

The question remains, where to draw the line around the metropolis? The fact that it is a vill means that its boundaries will be vague. Should the satellite cities be included? The area of economic dominance? Of communication dominance? Because of this uncertainty, the metropolitan region presents essentially the same problems as those for regions in general. Whenever one goes beyond the city and its recognized suburbs, no matter how logical his criteria, he risks the danger (with a high degree of probability) of studying an academic abstraction instead of a social entity. The abstraction may be highly useful —such as the metropolitan region delineated on the basis of newspaper circulation—but its relation to communal organizations in general and to vills in particular remains to be demonstrated in each case.

The world and region have been mentioned because they have been considered as communities (see MacIver and Page, 1949). Theoretically, they may be compared with vills in much the same manner as the nation. Another comparison may be made between vills and the political components of the nation: states and counties. (Since "states" in this sense may be confused with the state as a system for the monopoly of power, we will limit our remarks to the county, realizing that state-as-a-national-subdivision is also included.)

Three possibilities arise in considering the nature of counties: (1) They may exist as purely administrative units, somewhat arbitrarily superimposed over a part of a cultural area or over several cultural areas. (2) They may be miniature nations, social systems subject to an organization which has a monopoly of power (delegated or left to it by the state); these would contain, for example, several vills. Finally, (3) counties might exist as vills. In this last case, the vill and the monopolistic power of the state would coincide in a single administrative unit.

Thus, attempts to treat counties as communities (cf. Jonassen, 1949) can be successful only in certain cases. Wherever counties exist purely as administrative units (which is probably generally the case), then they have a unity that exists essentially on a political basis and are, therefore, complex organizations in the same sense that states are. Accordingly, they are to be contrasted with vills, rather than equated with them.

THE NEIGHBORHOOD: BEECH CREEK

The main questions before this section are: (1) In what ways can a neighborhood differ from a vill and still remains a viable system? (2) What does the neighborhood reveal about vills?

The neighborhood selected has been carefully observed for approximately twenty years. It has been given the fictitious name of "Beech Creek" (Brown, 1950, 1951, 1952a, 1952b, 1952c; Brown, Schwarzweller, and Mangalam, 1963). For the purposes of the present discussion, a neighborhood is defined as a system containing the foci of a vill but lacking certain other components. It is not yet possible to identify the specific components that can be lacking and still accompany an existing system, although the investigation of total institutions of course indicates that neighborhoods should contain the components of personal contact, continuance, and awareness.

It seems likely that neighborhoods will be most deficient in that they lack certain institutions. By definition, the foci of family, cooperation, and space have to be present. But systems which could probably be classed as neighborhoods have been observed in the course of this investigation which lacked one or more of the following institutions: economic, religious, governmental, stratification, socialization, or recreation ("Lack" in the sense of something deficient, rather than absent. City neighborhoods of the "dormitory" type, for example, "lack" the economic institution in that a major share of a breadwinner's economic activities is performed outside the neighborhood; however, some economic functions are carried on within the household, if only the function of consumption. Therefore, residents will probably engage in the behavior associated with these institutions but they will do so to a significant extent outside of the neighborhood.) Beech Creek conforms to the definition in that it lacks its own governmental and religious organizations. (Later, as we shall see, it came to lack other things, but by then it was visibly disintegrating.)

*The rise and decline of a partial system.* Beech Creek is in the mountainous portion of eastern Kentucky. At the time of its initial study in 1942, it was " enough unchanged to be known as 'backward' and 'retarded' by outsiders and as 'old-fashioned' even by its own citizens" (Brown, 1951, p. 232). In this respect, it was like many other farming areas in the southern Appalachians (Ford, 1962). The neighborhood was probably settled around 1800, most of its first members being native-born Americans from Virginia, Tennessee, and North Carolina. Their culture was primarily English and they apparently were Baptists. The present population of Beech Creek derives mainly from the descendants of the first settlers.

Beech Creek has always been composed of self-sufficient, subsistence, family farms. The families lived along the bottomland of the creek and its forks and branches, virtually surrounded by steep hills rising 300 to 500 feet above the valley floor. Among the factors which helped bind the families into a group with some sense of unity and solidarity were topography and geography, travel and mail routes, economic and informal social ties, common kinship and history, and cultural homogeneity.

Isolated geographically and culturally, Beech Creek has understandably been set off from wider currents of change. Its isolation, however, was relative. Major events from the outside world have made a difference in Beech Creek life. The Civil War saw Beechers in the Union Army and it saw them suffer from Confederate raids. Veteran's pensions were to come later, and the consequent Republican loyalty is still evident. Lumbering came in the 1870's and 1880's and has had an intensive and continuing impact. It reduced the holdings of the Beechers (through the use of more accurate surveys than the people had been accustomed to) and rendered them suspicious of outsiders. But it also provided jobs and income, and in this way it lessened their self-sufficiency.

Both World Wars influenced the Creek by means of work opportunities in war plants, especially in the industrial areas of southern Ohio. Army experiences of the men further reduced isolation, and pensions continue to influence the economy. Even the Great Depression was not without its effects, since it was at this time that WPA work came to the area, an event which not only offered another source of cash income but which supplanted one of the last remaining vestiges of the institution of mutual aid in the Creek: county road work.

A comparison of Beech Creek with the folk village would show that, technically speaking, it contains all of the components as well as the foci of the model—with the exception of government and religious organizations. But such a statement tells only part of the story. A more complete picture can be shown in two ways: by an examination of certain components in the structure of the Beech Creek system, itself, and by a comparison with an adjacent neighborhood.

What are the significant ways in which Beech Creek approached the model of the vill, particularly the model of the folk village? First, the family was the most important single social group. Economic roles on the farm could not be separated, except analytically, from familial roles. The division of labor by age and sex was functional both for economic effort and for the assumption by each immature family member of his adult role in a conjugal family of his (or her) own. Most children were able to assume full adult work status by the age of fifteen or sixteen. Virtually everybody in the area married, and the few who remained single were regarded as "quare" (odd or unusual).

Spatially, also, Beech Creekers approximated a folk village. The boundaries separating the Creek from other areas were not precise. The isolating effect of the topography, however, forced the people into close association. Since the most important type of economic endeavor was farming, and since the familial and farming roles were indistinguishable, the area understandably was relatively homogeneous in spatial patterning. There was, however, a tendency toward nucleation in that houses were built in the creek bottoms, forming a pattern of settlement resembling the line-village (Smith, 1953).

Beech Creek could also be described as a localized system of cooperating families, but there are enough qualifications to this cooperation that we really meet a divergence from the model. In the early days, an extensive institution of mutual aid had developed.

There were the usual log-rollings, barn- and house-raisings, quiltings, "bees" of all sorts. Churches were few and far between but in the summer Beech people, and especially young men, went far and near to every "meeting" held. Graveyard cleanings and memorial meetings (belated funeral services, postponed usually to the fall of the year when streams were low and farm work was not so pressing) afforded favorite opportunities for great crowds of people from miles around to get together to visit and talk and incidentally listen to as many preachers as could be mustered. Stir-off's (making sorghum molasses) and "workings" of all kinds were much more common than now [Brown, 1950, p. 60].

Some participants in these affairs are still living. According to one informant, about fifty years of age in 1960, as a boy he could expect to attend three or four such "get-togethers" a year. People would be invited from miles around for what would be an all-day affair. After the work, the women would prepare a meal, and then a dance and a party would follow. These "workings" would also be given for someone who was sick, or a man would give a "working" if he got too far behind in his farm operations.

These customs, however, had begun to die out at the time the informant married. By 1942, when Brown's study was originally made, there were few inter-familial economic relationships. Tools and implements were loaned and borrowed, there was some exchange of labor, and there were even a few instances where two families, not kin, cooperated in raising a crop. But none of these practices was widespread. In fact, there were no organized parties, bees, dances, or "workings" on Beech Creek during 1942–43. There are none today.

Thus, in terms of the theory of the vill, one of the vill's foci was visibly deteriorating by 1942, and Beech Creek was on the verge of not being a neighborhood at all, as neighborhoods are defined in this discussion. We may correctly say that the entire social system of Beech Creek was slowly melting away. Twenty years later, when the Creek was resurveyed, only one-third of the original families was left, and most of these were of the older generation.

Mutual aid was not the only component which deteriorated. There was no organized church on Beech Creek in 1942 and there had been none for years. Consequently, few adults went to church, and when they did they went outside the neighborhood. Still, the church (like mutual aid) was something the Beechers *had* had. Its absence could be designated as another sign of disintegration.

The absence of a governmental body must be viewed differently. The Beech Creek neighborhood never had one. The Creek was a part of the same magisterial district as many other neighborhoods, but this was not an important tie among its families. Further, though "Beech Creek people had great interest in politics, there was no indication that there was any special neighborhood political stand which set it off from other neighborhoods or tended to unite its families" (Brown, 1950, p. 152).

In one sense, the lack of a governmental body is to be expected in many neighborhoods. But it must be remembered that Beech Creek was effectively isolated from and thus not well integrated with other areas. It was a system in uneasy balance, its members trying to "make do" with what they had, and eventually lacking the resources to do that. Beech Creek was a neighborhood without a larger vill to which to belong. Judging from the surrounding neighborhoods, such systems can survive as long as they remain free of exceptionally devisive influences. Beech Creek did not so remain, and it is to these devisive influences that we now turn.

Beech Creek has long been jokingly known as "Wrangle Creek." Two families, the Johnsons and the Barnetts, became the center for much latent and overt hostility. The numerous and prolonged quarrels among the Johnsons themselves were common knowledge on the Creek. Being aggressive, the Barnetts lost no time making enemies, particularly among the Johnsons. Nancy Johnson

openly criticized the Barnetts' idleness, drinking, and gossiping and accused them of lying to keep their son out of the Army, of moonshining and bootlegging, of letting their girls "run loose," and of keeping an open house for sexual indulgence. Of course, Ed and Rachel Barnett never let Nancy's own supposedly cloudy past be forgotten. But back of all this antagonism was a struggle for power and prestige in the neighborhood. Nancy Johnson would not accept the Ed Barnetts as equals; to her they were inferior; they had records of "bad" behavior themselves as well as a background of "bad" families. The Ed Barnetts, however, were not meek and yielding or willing to accept an inferior place. They felt they were as "good as anybody" and Nancy's refusal to accept them made them all the more determined to outwit and berate the Johnsons [Brown, 1950, p. 83].

There was much hard feeling on both sides and an abundance of malicious gossip (though never any physical combat). Moreover, from the time the Barnetts came to the Creek, every significant neighborhood action was influenced by the struggle between the two families: elections of school trustees, choice of school teachers, and church and Sunday school affairs.

But this struggle was not as disruptive of neighborhood unity as that between the Barnetts and a third family, the Carters. In the eyes of many of the Beech Creek people, the Carters were the "lowest set of people in the country." They were accused of being sexually intemperate, of having great drunken orgies involving both men and women, of marrying close kin. Even more serious, they were not industrious, preferring to "lay around or hunt and fish." They were not clean and were continually stealing and fighting. To make matters worse, one of their sons courted one of the Barnett girls. In spite of vigorous protests from the girl's parents—and even blows—the couple eloped. Bitterness erupted openly in the form of property destruction and shooting. "For the whole Carter 'generation' united against the Barnetts" (Brown, 1950, p. 87). In 1942, hostilities still smoldered.

The adjustment between these families as well as within them is rated by Brown as "one of the most significant processes in the history of the neighborhood" (1950, p. 91). Considering that the Creek contained only thirty-nine households, the statement appears quite reasonable.

Conflict, of course, is nothing strange to vills. All those examined in this book have had significant dissension, and some have been destroyed by it. Apparently, increasing destruction is the tendency in Beech Creek.

Disruption, disintegration, "melting away"—these are all relative terms. Beech Creek is not yet gone. To a visitor, there seem few outward signs of decay. But we should remember from the experience of San Ildefonso, Hilltown, and Romonom that the disintegration of a vill can take a very long time.

Beech Creek is labeled as a disintegrating system for several reasons. First, relative to its comparison with vills, Beech Creek is disintegrating because it is losing certain very important components. In an even more basic sense, Beech Creek cannot possibly continue as it has. In 1942, the Creek had 191 persons; in 1961, only eighty-nine. At this rate, the neighborhood will disappear in less than three decades. Finally, Beech Creek is disintegrating because it is changing to another type of system: it is becoming increasingly more integrated with the county in which it lies at the same time that it is operating more and more as a migration system connected with the metropolitan areas of southern Ohio (Brown, Schwarzweller, and Mangalam, 1963).

Thus, disintegration is used in a relative sense: relative to the status of Beech Creek as a vill, relative to its population, and relative to its relation to other systems. In this sense, the "disintegration" of Beech Creek might be termed "change." But the change is fundamental.

Beech Creek can be understood more clearly by a brief reference to the Laurel neighborhood which lies adjacent. Laurel was much more tightly integrated and had more neighborhood spirit. Ten years after the first Beech Creek study, Laurel showed few if any signs of disintegration. (Later still, Laurel also declined, but the reasons for that would carry this discussion far astray.)

The two neighborhoods were different first in kinship relations between their families. About one-half of the total possible relations among Laurel families were first cousins or closer—in Beech Creek, only one-fifth. In addition, only two-thirds of the Beech Creek people—as contrasted with more than four-fifths of the Laurel population—had been born in their respective neighborhoods (at the time of the study). Finally, much of of the land on the Creek passed from the hands of the Johnsons to families from the outside who were no kin or at least not close kin. Many of these families, moreover, retained contact with their previous neighborhoods and were not fully absorbed into Beech Creek.

There were also other factors which worked to the disadvantage of Beech Creek. Laurel was much smaller in both territory and population, and the families there were much closer together. Also, Laurel families all sent their children to the same school. The Beech neighborhood was divided so that children on the lower part of the creek attended a different school than those on the upper part. Laurel had church services monthly and Sunday school weekly, gatherings which brought together most of the people; the Beechers had not had a church for several years. Similarly, as roads developed and as the stores and post office were located, the lower Beech Creek families tended to draw away from those on the upper part of the creek. Such changes did not occur sufficiently to divide the Laurel neighborhood.

Personalities undoubtedly entered in: both Mrs. Johnson and Mrs. Barnett, the principal antagonists, had reputations for being overbearing. Antagonisms were found in Laurel, too, but they never developed as intensely.

In considering all of the things which make a vill, organization is most easily overlooked. Thus, the lack of any central control emerges as an important factor in understanding the disintegration of the Creek. One could understand the lack of a government if there was one outside on which the Creek was dependent. Or such a lack could be feasible if some other institution assumed control (as happened in the Laurel neighborhood). But to lack all focus of control seems too much. Beech Creek once had such a focus in mutual aid, but mutual aid is based on family organizations, and two of the chief families on the Creek were at each other's throats, not to mention a side quarrel of one of these two families with still another. In addition, possible meeting places such as the church were either absent, or, as in the case of the school, store, or post office, so located that they tended to divide the people.

Accordingly, one should not look to the lack of neighborhood pride, to the decline in mutual aid, or even to quarrels in seeking the cause for disintegration. These were, actually, effects. Both Laurel and Beech Creek were potentially unstable in that they lacked any governmental institution. But Laurel was able to supplement something else (religious and school interests), chiefly, probably, because of the underlying solidarity prevailing among essentially close kin. In Durkheim's terms, their solidarity was truly mechanical. Beech Creek lacked this solidarity, due, probably, to the influx of families from the outside. And lacking a focus of control, disintegration is an understandable course. Idiosyncratic factors undoubtedly are to be considered when dealing with so few families: what if Mrs. Barnett had not been overbearing, if Ed Barnett had not been ambitious? Beech Creek would still be an unstable system, but it would probably be able to continue for a longer period.

Beech Creek was a poorly formed system in the beginning, then, and it remained so. The intrusion of outside forces and the changes in the spatial location of certain institutions required (apparently) more of an adjustment than the system could provide. The chief lesson to learn from Beech Creek is the nature of the instability which is associated with the absence of certain institutions in vills. We have seen this before in the case of some folk villages, especially San Ildefonso and Hilltown, but these systems lost institutions they once had. Beech Creek never had the institution of government. This deficiency can of course be filled by some outside agency. Neighborhoods can become stable to the extent that they associate with a more complete vill. Beech Creek is an example of a neighborhood which lacked such an association.

A system like Laurel can survive because of its mechanical solidarity. But when differences appear, something more is needed. Beech Creek had such differences in the families that came from the outside, and in the quarrels that followed, there was nothing to appeal to. As Brown observed:

> It is evident, for instance, that one reason why disputes among members of different family groups often developed and continued was the absence of any neighborhood mechanism for mediating these disputes. If there had been cliques of old men, such as Arensberg and Kimball [1940] describe in the Irish farm community, to talk over such disputes, reach common decisions, and then disperse and back up this group opinion in the neighborhood, there would have been much greater harmony [Brown, 1950, pp. 164–65].

In Beech Creek, then, is witnessed a need for a division of labor to accommodate the differences, a need which continued unmet. Consequently, the quarrels festered and other changes could find no institutional means through which to operate.

Although obviously not a complete vill, Beech Creek certainly approached one very closely. Further, the system had existed for more than a century, so there can be no charge that a system such as Beech Creek is not possible. Unstable, Beech Creek certainly is, but it does exist. Speaking in terms of the typology developed in the previous chapter, it is a more sensible procedure to compare Beech Creek to vills than to complex organizations, crowds, or ethnic groups; that is, Beech Creek is a system without specific goals and with institutionalized means (though not all of the means were completely institutionalized).

*A review of the typology.* Beech Creek permits an observation of one more type of system which diverges from the model of the vill in ways that can be specifically indicated. Four such systems have now been observed in some detail. The first type, the total institution, is so far removed from vills that it is best to classify it as a different kind of thing entirely. The state lends itself to a similar classification. The nation, on the other hand, is related closely enough to the vill to warrant calling it generally the same kind of thing but different in certain important respects— the same general type but a different subtype. This last phrase can also be applied to the neighborhood, except that it is more closely related to the vill than is the nation. Nations are organized in a manner qualitatively different than vills, as is shown by the different focus. Neighborhoods are organized in the same way as vills but lack certain secondary (that is, non-focal) components.

The underlying principle of this difference in organization has been identified as the principle of inclusiveness (Chap. 8). Nations are more socially inclusive than vills which in turn are socially more inclusive than neighborhoods. But before the validity of such a theme can be established, much more work needs to be done. Not only must various nations and neighborhoods be compared cross-culturally, but other types which approach the class of communal organizations need to be examined also, such as tribes or bands and castes.

One point seems fairly clear: nations, vills, and neighborhoods have more in common with each other than they do with states and total institutions (which in turn have more in common with each other than they do with communal organizations). In other words, there are various taxonomic or classificatory levels in terms of which human groups can be organized. Folk villages and cities differ, but on a more general level—the the level of the vill—they are related. Similarly, vills and nations differ, but on a more general level—the level of communal organizations—they are related. Finally, communal and formal organizations differ, but on a more general level—the level of the human group—they are related. The appearance of these levels prompts the present classification of groups.

## THE KIBBUTZ: KIRYAT YEDIDIM

*An urban village.* The Israeli kibbutz is the most recent development to have occurred in communal organization on so extensive a scale. Most simply, it can be called an urbanized, agricultural, communistic village. Relative to the questions it raises for the vill, the kibbutz is of interest chiefly for its treatment of the family and socialization. It serves as an instance of a vill that has experienced drastic attempts at modification, some of which have apparently been successful. As such, the kibbutz serves as a fitting case with which to pose some final problems.

With this orientation, then, it does not matter whether the kibbutz to be discussed is representative or not, either of the kibbutz or of the vill. We are purposely using the kibbutz as a case *in extremis* in order to learn something more about the vill and about communal organizations.

The thesis of this discussion is that the kibbutz is a vill which has been forced to move, or at least has moved, further along the folk-urban continua than is true of other vills. The kibbutz to be discussed here is given the fictitious name of Kiryat Yedidim. The observations are those of an anthropologist, Melford Spiro (1956, 1958), and the time period for the discussion refers to the time of study, 1951–52. Of his two works, the later one is the more valuable for present purposes, since it focuses on the *sabras* (those born in the kibbutz),[1] and thus it gives insight into the potentialities the system has for continuing.

Kiryat Yedidim was founded thirty years prior to its study by a small group of young, intellectual Jews from eastern Europe. They were motivated not only by the desire to escape

[1] Technically, *sabra* refers to a native-born Israeli. The usage here is for convenience.

anti-Semitic persecution but also by the idealistic sentiments (1) of Zionism, (2) of the nobility of labor (particularly agricultural labor), and (3) of the possibility of a society actively working in freedom and equality. In the eyes of its members, the village has today essentially realized these values. The kibbutz owns all capital goods, although individuals are permitted to possess some personal belongings. Labor is performed in work crews under a foreman who serves his tenure at the pleasure of the workers. With few exceptions, workers from the outside are not hired, since this would be considered exploitation. Thus, virtually all adults residing in the kibbutz are *chaverim* (members of the kibbutz; singular: *chaver*).

As is true of any vill, Kiryat Yedidim may be described as a localized system integrated around cooperation and families. But the kibbutz differs from other vills in that it has an unusual mixture of folk and urban qualities. Personal contact in the system is both extensive and intensive. Since there are only approximately 500 members, children as well as adults have numerous opportunities to interact with almost every member. One's life then becomes an open book to everyone else. Although cooperation is emphasized, conflict is frequently displayed. For example, open aggression among very young children is no less a problem than the "insolence" of the older. Group pressure, however, in the form of public opinion and the ultimate threat of expulsion, is an adequate means of social control. There is almost no deviation from kibbutz norms, and no criminal behavior among adult *sabras*, or juvenile delinquency among adolescents.

Probably again because of its size, the kibbutz is as tightly integrated as any folk village, if not more so. Living in the kibbutz involves also acceptance of collective ownership, perhaps the most important and characteristic feature of the kibbutz. Collective ownership is more than an ideal. In effect, it means that the kibbutz is integrated economically and politically through the action of all its members.

Most of the buildings are grouped in a nucleus, in spite of the high degree of spatial differentiation: nursery, toddler's house, grammar school, communal dining hall, parents' homes, etc. The one exception is the junior-senior high school, in which the children live in a relatively separate "community" just across the road from the kibbutz living area. (Thus, all of the kibbutz land is apparently not contiguous.) However, they visit their parents several times a week and are expected to take an active part in the labor of the kibbutz; accordingly, though the kibbutz is spatially integrated, its boundaries are somewhat vague.

The children experience at least three shifts in their bases of operations: from the kibbutz to the high school, residence outside the kibbutz (see below), and, when they become kibbutz members (as practically all do), back to the kibbutz again. As a parent, the *chaver* can still expect to journey from the kibbutz, since almost all parents have been absent from the kibbutz for at least a short time. A few fathers work outside, returning home only for weekends. For these, the cosmopolitan aspect of the kibbutz as a base of operations is high. Almost every father is away periodically for army service, although most of these also come home on weekends. Finally, both parents, but especially mothers, may be sent to the city to receive some type of training.

There is a basic minimum of horizontal mobility for all chaverin. Though born in the kibbutz, anyone wishing to become a chaver must apply for and undergo a year's probation. His membership is voted upon at a town meeting. In addition to this mobility, there are also the temporary leaves noted above, and there are in-migrants of varying kinds (for example, all sabras have married someone other than their fellow sabras, and these others must by definition be in-migrants). It is important to note that the sabras quite definitely engage in temporary mobility. Formerly upon graduation from high school, they were sent to the city where they worked for a year; now they are drafted into the army where they serve two years. They have invariably returned.

Thus, although all chaverim experience some social mobility (none can, by kibbutz norm, spend his entire life in the kibbutz), there is a relatively low degree of mobility once membership has been attained.

Kiryat Yedidim is essentially a society founded upon certain ideals, and these revolve largely around the value of work in particular and economic behavior in general. An understanding of kibbutz sentiment and institutions therefore must first begin with an understanding of kibbutz economics.

There is no money in Kiryat Yedidim. Goods are distributed in agreement with the principle, "from each according to his ability, to each according to his needs." The needs are largely ascertained by the entire membership through the biweekly town meeting, the ultimate authority on kibbutz matters. Elected officials implement policy determined by the meeting and administer the organization of the kibbutz. Tenure is never more than three years, to prevent concentration of power. Agriculture is highly diversified, rationalized, and mechanized. There are eight distinct branches: dairy, fodder, field crops, vegetable gardens, fruit orchards, fishery, flocks, and poultry.

There is a marked division of labor for so small a system: nurses, teachers of varying kinds, office workers, tractor drivers, field workers, seamstresses, cooks, etc. Yet, there is also an underlying homogeneity. First, Kiryat Yedidim has tenaciously opposed the introduction of industry in keeping with its emphasis on agriculture as a value in itself. And as would be expected in view of the ideological commitments of the chaverim and the intensity of their values, there is a basic homogeneity of sentiment. Most sabras, for example, are in general agreement with the party to which their kibbutz is attached and unanimously support it at the polls.

The members of Kiryat Yedidim perceive of their kibbutz "as the vanguard of man's quest for the ideal society" (Spiro, 1958, p. 5). It is understandable, therefore, that practically all sabras maintain that the kibbutz is the best form of social living. Perhaps their antagonism to immigrants from the Middle East and to strangers in general does not follow, but it is there and is further evidence of their ethnocentrism.

Two institutions are absent in Kiryat Yedidim: stratification and religion. Kiryat Yedidim is dedicated to establishing a classless society, and to a large degree the chaverim seem to have achieved that end. True, there is status consciousness, especially and evenly acutely among the sabras, concerning traits "which confer prestige within the kibbutz, such as proficiency in work or self-improvement through study" (Spiro, 1958, p. 360). But, according to Spiro, there is no visible linkage between the status of a sabra and his parent. Thus, Kiryat Yedidim has a society of statuses, even a stratified society, but not one which is perpetuated through the family.

Since Kiryat Yedidim is Marxist and pro-Soviet in orientation, it is not surprising that the chaverim attempt to raise atheistic sabras. The surprising feature, in view of the universality of religion, is the extent to which they have succeeded. All of the adult sabras, without exception, are opposed to religion. Their attitudes range from "I think it is all foolishness" to "Religion says nothing to me. Zero" (1958, p. 384). Some have argued (even Spiro) that they have substituted humanistic or socialistic ideals for their religion and thus that they are still religious. This argument is based on a difference in definition; regardless of definitions, the institutions focusing on worship of a supernatural deity and magical control of spirits has apparently vanished from this kibbutz. In the usual meaning of that term, there is no religion in Kiryat Yedidim. It has expelled its God.

Spiro described the members of Kiryat Yedidim as "not merely farmers" but as "a landed intelligentsia."

In the fields one hears discussions not only of crops and machinery, but of books and music, of politics and literature. At the end of the working day, the interest of a chaver may turn to . . . a lecture on genetics, a chamber-music concert, a discussion of politics, a dramatic performance. This is not to say that all chaverim turn their attention to such intellectual pursuits. . . . It is to say, however, that these activities are available, that they are valued by many, and that the kibbutz self-image demands at least lip-service devotion to them [1958, p. 5].

Recreation, then, is a significant part of the kibbutz structure, involving all of the constants found among vill recreation.

Most of the significant aspects of the kibbutz (as a vill) have now been mentioned. Two components are saved for last because they present the most important problems for this discussion: the family and socialization.

Spiro has claimed that the kibbutz "has already achieved a major internal revolution: it has revolutionized the structure of the family and the educational system" (1956, p. 6). This statement cannot be challenged, but it must be read carefully: these institutions have not been abandoned or eliminated in the same sense as have religion or class. Rather, the revolution has simply been one of bringing certain features of both the family and socialization to their logical conclusion.

The familial pattern found in both folk villages and cities is still present in Kiryat Yedidim: a sanctioned union of man and woman for sexual relations and for childrearing.[2] Each of these features will be discussed.

In the early days of the kibbutz, one might well wonder whether there was any sanction to the marital tie. Many of the original marriages were quite unstable. According to one chaver, "'There was really no such thing as a family'" (1958, p. 99). Whatever the situation originally, however, sanctions are very much in evidence at present. The kibbutz recognizes the marital relationship by granting a common room to the couple, and, although illegitimacy is not recognized in this kibbutz, the authorities are nevertheless opposed to sexual intercourse among unmarried students. The older chaver have a generally tolerant attitude toward sexual deviancy, but their sabras are more conservative, limiting their sexual experiences to only a few partners. Moreover, they marry early, tend to remain married, and are faithful to their spouses. Adultery, a term foreign to the vocabulary of the founders, has become an act of deviancy for the sabras, an act for which they request appropriate sanctions.

The woman's membership in the kibbutz is legally distinct from her husband's. She "changes neither her name nor her work when she marries" (Spiro, 1958, p. 6). "The marital bond is compounded of emotional, sexual, and social ties exclusively" (p. 7). Having a child poses no economic problems for the parents, since the kibbutz assumes responsibility for its economic welfare. Thus, the family is not cemented by economic ties. There are other ties, however. It is true that the infant enters the kibbutz educational system only four or five days after he and his mother return from the hospital, but parental influence remains an important feature of his socialization throughout his childhood. This is so in spite of the fact that the nurse also

---

[2] In his earlier book (1956, esp. pp. 110–23), Spiro has an extensive discussion of marriage and the family in the kibbutz in terms of Murdock's concepts. Essentially, according to Murdock (1949), there would be no marriage in Kiryat Yedidim since there is no economic bond between the partners, and there would be no family since the children have no common residence with their parents and are not socialized by them. Although it is more correct to argue that residence and socialization have been minimized rather than eliminated, the important point is that the kibbutz family agrees with the structural type of family that has been identified in the vills used in this book.

assumes the functions and duties normally assumed by the parent in Western society: she is responsible for the physical care and well-being of the children in her charge, gives affection and comfort, transmits the kibbutz values, and trains the children in the basic functions of feeding, toilet training, etc. Nevertheless, the parents are also regarded as partners in the task of childrearing. Insecure nurses may attempt to shut out the parent, but these attempts are generally ineffectual. Although the parents may doubt their own importance, this importance is not doubted by the chaverim as a whole. The role of the parent in childrearing shifts from that of a disciplinarian to that of an emotional nurturer, a provider of emotional support.

Quantitatively, the nurse, the nursery teacher, and later the teacher have greatest access to the child. The children are with the parents for two hours each day and on the sabbath. But these brief periods are devoted entirely to the children. The parents' responsibilities of the day are over, the children have been fed, and during the period before they return to the children's house for the night, they become the center of their parents' world.

Thus this overstimulating and highly satisfying two-hour period becomes terribly important for the child, and the parents, who are responsible for it, become strongly cathected. It is the intensity of this relationship that establishes the parent as the most important influence on the child's development [Spiro, 1958, p. 81].

It is important in this respect that the child's term for "my room" (and, as he grows older, "our room") refers almost exclusively to his parents' room, not the nursery. Another feature is significant: the parents stay with the child throughout the socialization period, whereas the children change from the nurse to the nursery teacher to the grammar-school teacher. The parents, then, compensate to some extent with their constancy for that which the nurse and teacher attain from temporary quantitative superiority.

One result of the reorganization of discipline is that the adult male, among all adult socializers, "stands out as an exclusively permissive and nurturant figure" (Spiro, 1958, p. 232 n). This consequence is in fact one of the aims of the kibbutz: to substitute for the authoritarian-submissive relation between the father and child one in which fathers and children are peers.

In discussing the kibbutz family, we have also discussed the socialization process. Of course, the family is not the exclusive socializing agent, but then neither is it in any of the vills we have considered. The difference is in the amount of time spent in socialization, the organization of that time, and the nature of the socialization (whether caretaking, training, or nurturance). The revolution mentioned by Spiro refers to the shift of these functions between the family and the nursery and school.

*Significance for the vill.* The kibbutz family may be most profitably interpreted as an institution that has been more fully developed than any of its predecessors. It may be correctly placed at the end of a continuum in which the family of the folk village stands at the other extreme. The kibbutz family is a logical development of the city family, particularly as the city family appears among the American middle class. The heritages from the rural family have apparently been completely severed among the chaverim. No longer are there economic ties, as is true of some urban families and as indeed is true to some extent of all five cities examined in this book. Further, the beginnings of the transfer of caretaking and training functions seen in the American grammar school are carried logically on their way in the communal nursery and schools of the kibbutz.

The question may arise, could the family be further deprived of its functions? Until we understand the family better, the answer to such a question is moot, but it is significant that the sabras have returned to a more stable family than their parents. It is as if the pruning yields a more sturdy social growth.

This suggested answer has serious consequences for the theoretical formulations of urban life that posit an ideal type wherein the family does not exist. Whether the type is implicit, as in the constructs of Redfield, Toennies, and others, or explicit as it is in Huxley's *Brave New World* is beside the point. The kibbutz family points strongly to the possibility of a limiting principle in human affairs. The functional consequences of the biologically induced intimacy generated between spouses and biological, social, and spatial intimacy generated between parents and children points to a kind of group which is more readily formulated on these bases than others. This sentence can be expressed in another (though less complete) way by noting that sexual relations induce a kind of intimacy, that prolonged companionship induces another, and that the combination is apparently something that humans everywhere will seek out. The family, as reduced to its minimum in the kibbutz, seems to be a type of group which can always be expected in human communal organizations.

The implication for the ideal types of urban life is that those types which posit no family have been operating on an erroneous assumption: that the familial component of the folk-urban continuum is linear. They have assumed that if in an ideal-typical folk society all persons will be engaged in familial relationships, then in the ideal type of urban society there will be no familial relationships. *All* of the evidence in this study, however, points not to a linear but to a curvilinear relation. Granted the supremacy of the family in an ideal-typical folk society, as one approaches the opposite urban type, there comes a point considerably short of the zero point where an irreducible minimum of familial relations exist and where the family is still very much present. No matter how urban the system becomes, it does not pass this minimum. The familial continuum in the vill, then, is more properly designated as one in which the family is the basic unit of action to one in which the family is one of the least important—not one in which the family does not exist.

This point brings us to the second: the validity of the foci that have been suggested for the vill. In the kibbutz, which has successfully shorn itself of class and religion (at least relative to all other societies), the family, contractualism, and spatial differentiation remain vital integration mechanisms. Here, we may seem to differ with Spiro:

By identifying with his parents and with their room, the child is, at the same time, emphasizing a social group whose structural significance in the kibbutz is minimal—the family [1958, p. 86 n].

This statement disagrees with our thesis only if "minimal" meant "unimportant." As the preceding description should show, however, the family is of inestimable importance to the kibbutz. Yet it is vastly overshadowed by the contractual institutions.

The contractual system of the kibbutz has not been developed to as extreme a condition as has the family, but the reason for this lack of development is not, paradoxically, because the chaverim have not changed the contractual system but because they have changed it at once too far and not enough. They are, in other words, involved in an incomplete experiment. This is most evident in the differential rewards attached to various positions, especially that of the teacher. The holder of this position in Kiryat Yedidim does not get the same prestige reward as other workers, especially laborers. Thus, few if any sabras want to be teachers, a condition extremely serious for Kiryat Yedidim. Any society which fails to solve its problems of socialization is in a state of crisis, and the problem of socialization has not been fully solved in this kibbutz. In effect, Kiryat Yedidim has assumed that the dictum "from each according to his ability, to each according to his need," is sufficient to motivate members to fill all positions.

It is logical to suppose, however, that filling positions in a highly differentiated society requires differential motivations. As Kingsley Davis has noted (1949, p. 367), if all positions were of equal importance and of equal pleasantness, then it would make no difference who filled which position, granted only a modicum of ability. But the opposite of such a condition is the situation in fact. In most of the world where contracts are used, one of the principal motivations for filling the more important and (or) more unpleasant positions has been monetary reward. In discarding money, the kibbutz has discarded a principal mechanism of contractual functioning. It can be safely assumed that if money is not used, the contractual relations of the kibbutz must be integrated by new mechanisms. In effect, this new integration means that the old capitalistic "planning" through use of money—instituted on an ad hoc basis and certainly capable of abuse—must now be substituted by new planning through the government of the kibbutz. Societal interest (necessary for any contract) is equally great in both cases. The difference is that instead of societal interest being extremely concerned with a *mechanism* for contract (that is, money), it becomes more directly concerned with the contract itself by focusing attention directly on the limited relationship (for example, teacher-parent-student), which is the essence of the contract.[3]

---

[3] For a similar example of dysfunctions in kibbutz clothing distribution, see Rosenfeld (1957).

Regardless of the problems which the chaverim may have in working with contracts, the fact that their contracts are generally functional and have produced a highly specialized division of labor is apparent. Even more important is the significance of contractual system relative to the familial one. One may, indeed, describe the kibbutz as a contractual system which has succeeded in supplementing the family and of paring down its functions to their minimum. We have thus moved perhaps the full length of Maine's continuum from status to contract, from the case in which the family is unquestionably the dominant institution to the case in which contracts are. But it should not be forgotten that the family maintains a basic position in the kibbutz, regardless of how minimal.

If the kibbutz shows the importance of the foci, it also shows the lack of importance of certain peripheral components. The absence of religion and family-based strata are two of the points that have already been noted. If the kibbutz is a vill, these cannot be foci of the vill since they do not exist in the kibbutz. The kibbutz also raises the point that perhaps these components are best relegated to a peripheral status.

In this connection, one other component should be discussed. It has long been thought that the chief trait of Gemeinschaft, folk, or status societies was the intimacy and personal knowledge inhabitants had of each other. But such a trait appears within the city also—for example, within families. The argument has been that this familial characteristic was an atavistic trait, an instance of a yet-remaining Gemeinschaft in Gesellschaft, of status in contract. And yet, Spiro shows quite clearly that the kibbutz, so rational in respect to the family, child-rearing, and economic behavior, still remains Gemeinschaft-like on the personal level. The explanation for this pseudo-atavism is that it is not atavism at all but a function both of population size and of an extended period of dwelling together. The functions of the vill continue to revolve around familial, cooperative, and spatial variables. The number of people with whom one can become intimate is a function of intensity of interaction, which in turn is limited by the amount of time available for the interaction and by the size of a population. Everyone can know every one else in a factory as well as a folk village, if conditions are right. Intimacy, then, is not a communal trait but a social trait; it is found in each cell of the general typology, just as is impersonalization.

Probably one of the kibbutz's most significant features is that its peculiarities arise from internal rather than external social demands. The shearing from the family of extraneous functions, the loss of religion and class, the intensification of the division of labor, and spatial differentiation—in an agricultural context —all these have been instituted by the chaverim. That these changes were inaugurated in conjunction with the larger federation to which this kibbutz belongs is beside the point. The changes in Kiryat Yedidim have been worked out by the members of Kiryat Yedidim; they have not been imposed by force.

A final problem remains, the problem of change. On the one hand, kibbutzim are not temporary phenomena. Some are approaching their jubilee, and Kiryat Yedidim is now operating with the second generation, its sabras, in leading administrative roles. And yet we cannot with certainty say that the kibbutzim prove anything until they have been in existence for a while longer—at least for several generations.

No one knows in just what direction changes will force the kibbutzim, but at least one factor to be considered is the social environment in which the kibbutz is found. Jerome Himmelhoch has said that "the Kibbutz, despite its limitations as a natural and uncontrolled experiment, enables us to probe the ultimate limits of cooperation and egalitarianism possible for a community within a larger urban, competitive, class-stratified society" (1957, p. 67). This statement has several implications. First, it may also be applied to the ultimate minimum limits of familial functions within a larger society in which the family has a more extensive role. But second, it is important that the kibbutzim are firmly bound to the state of Israel. The interrelations between these two systems have been imperfectly traced. One may not only wonder whether the kibbutzim could survive if the state had not tolerated them but how long the state will tolerate them, or at least tolerate certain of their practices. And, third, even without an explicit state policy, how long will the sabras continue to rate kibbutz life as superior to that in the city? How long will they continue to resist the rural-to-urban movement which has been so long a part of human history? Perhaps the answer lies in the fact that the kibbutzim are already urbanized.

Certainly, sabras in some places (Kiryat Yedidim, for example) have shown marked attachment to their kibbutz.

In general, however, interpretations of kibbutz future must consider the kibbutz's position as a social island in a larger social sea. Regardless of the aims of the kibbutz, it cannot go its way alone. The same statement, of course, applies to vills in general.

# 10

# Toward a Theory of
# Communal Organizations

In the theory to be suggested, we are not dealing with opinions but with principles that have been distilled from observation. It is hoped that this theory will be modified, corrected, and someday supplanted. But when that happens, it should only be because of the introduction of new data, because flaws are detected in the models that were built from the data, or because hypotheses deduced from these models fail to be substantiated.

THE THEORY

In providing first a brief overview, two points must be made. First, all communal organizations are not understood equally. Second, all statements about them have not been verified to the same degree. The latter .remark applies especially to theories formulated by others. They have been adopted because they showed a high degree of agreement with the models used here, but it is possible that some of their parts, though they may seem to blend logically with the context in which they are presented, may actually prove contrary to observation.

Communal organization, first, refers to a system of institutions formed by people who live together. The system has no specific goal. The reasons for living together are often no more than that of being born in the locality (for all communal organizations occupy a particular territory). And though specific reasons draw people to some communal organizations, the people always engage in activities unrelated to the initial attraction. Thus, the migrant may enter a city specifically for a job, but he also marries, plays, goes to church, etc.

It may be seen from these criteria that communal organizations include a wide range of social groups. For the most part, they can be divided into those that include vills and those that vills include. In the first category are nations and cultural regions. In the second appear neighborhoods and families (or, more appropriately, households). And communal organizations contain communal organizations. The nation may contain villages composed of neighborhoods, or it may also include cities comprised of other satellite cities, etc. The family, virtually always in its household, remains a basic building block.

Thus, communal organizations are often composed of communal organizations extending through level after level. But there are other differences. The importance of territory or locality differs markedly. For the larger organizations, such as nations or cultural regions, territory becomes the practical universe within which most people live out most of their lives. In this sense, then, MacIver's criterion is applicable (1937, p. 9), but we must modify it accordingly: A mark of *some* types of communal organizations is that one's life may be lived wholly within them. For smaller organizations (vills, neighborhoods, and households), the unit becomes more properly a base of operations from which people follow routine institutionalized activities.

Since the vill occupies a central position in the theory of communal organizations, it should be given particular attention. Whatever the type of vill, whether folk village or city, it functions in terms of three components—space, cooperation, and family. Invariably, vills have more components, but these provide the chief means by which vills are integrated.

Each focal component displays a clearly defined pattern of variation. Vills vary in the degree to which the family or kinship group is the dominant mode of organization, as it is in the folk village; they vary in the degree to which cooperation becomes separated from the family and becomes more contractual, as happens in the city. They vary, finally, in the manner of the organization of their space, whether loosely organized in a relatively homogeneous mass, as in folk villages, or intricately organized in highly specialized segments, as in cities.

The variations have a system—folk villages tend to consistently occupy one extreme, cities the other. However, change in the three foci is not always concurrent, as indicated in the theory of structural freewheeling. Contracts, for example, can develop without undermining families. Other variations are even less systematic. Communal organizations vary in the degree that status is important, from almost no visible status groupings to the extreme conditions of the Hindu caste. They also vary in population size. To some extent, this variation is part of the folk-city variation. But some villages are larger than some cities. The practice of emphasizing the family in the communal organization, to be sure, limits the size of the system, whereas emphasis on contracts permits fantastic growth (Los Angeles, for example, as one city which has been studied in accordance with the theory of the vill, contains almost seven million people in its metropolitan area). More must be learned of the feedback from population growth to the other components.

Finally, the integration of communal organizations varies tremendously. At one extreme are tightly integrated systems with relatively clearly delineated spatial patterns. The Israeli kibbutz and the Egyptian village of Silwa are examples. These types probably fill the literature in disproportion to their numerical importance precisely because they are so readily identifiable. At the other extreme are partially formed systems, disintegrating ones, and systems undergoing drastic reorganization. Beech Creek, Hilltown, and San Ildefonso are examples. These kinds of systems help to show the potential amorphous nature of some communal organizations.

The theory of communal organization includes only one type of social organization. Its principles do not refer to all social behavior, as shown by the general typology developed in Chapter 8. But it is important as an organizing principle, a frame of reference within which to place other theories and concepts.

The theory is an organizing principle in another way. Its central theory, the theory of the vill, places at least three fields of sociology in relation to each other: urban sociology, rural sociology, and human ecology. Communal organization in general also incorporates regional sociology, the sociology of the family, and what may be called the sociology of nations. (Political sociology, from this frame of reference, would be a bridge between the sociology of formal and communal organizations, though in practice it has emphasized formal systems.)

Communal organizations have a specific significance for sociology, since practically all social behavior still takes place within them. Because sociology is not as free to experiment as it might wish, this means that it is of the utmost importance to know the setting in which formal organizations, expressive groups, and informal groups can be found. The theory of communal organization also forces the sociologist to recognize social morphology. All groups have a morphology, but the morphology of most non-communal organizations is actually part of the morphology of communal organizations, and thus it is not always obvious. It can be taken for granted. The study of morphology, of course, is not the end of sociological investigation, but it does provide sociologists with an indispensable basis of measurement.

Communal organizations, then, being firmly grounded both morphologically and sociologically, stand as an excellent reminder of the nature of our being. Furthermore, the study of communal organizations provides an important link from sociology to other sciences, particularly anthropology, and human geography.

In terms of the evidence gathered to date, the theory of the vill must receive the main emphasis in a discussion of communal organizations. The significance of the vill is first that it identifies specific phenomena which must be considered communal organizations. In addition, the concept provides a basis for distinguishing communal from formal organizations.

The fact that the vill pertains to specific phenomena has an important theoretical significance. The field of community has been plagued heretofore by having numerous detailed studies with no systematic integration into the larger body of sociological theory. By means of the models of vills, the connection can be traced between particular human groupings and their position in general principles or concepts. Begin, for example, with the specific village of Chan Kom or the city of Timbuctoo. These are linked, respectively, with the models of the folk village and the city and these models, in turn, are integrated into the theory of the vill, which in turn takes its place in the general typology of human groups. At any one of these conceptual levels, a greater theoretical explanation can be found simply by referring to a given theorist or even a given field. For example, should one wish to know more about the kinds of things that Timbuctoo represents, then urban sociology is indicated as the area for further study and, more specifically, for example, the work of Sjoberg.

The vill thus serves as the primary reference point for both the nature of communal organizations and their variation. It is the vill upon which the data in this study are systematically based. Other types of systems are called vills to the extent that they significantly approach the vill. Of course, there is an arbitrary element in what one is willing to call "significant," but the most crucial test is the value of the vill in assigning border-line cases. We are able to provide the reasons why any system is a borderline case, not because it agrees or disagrees with some a priori theory but because it agrees or disagrees with the empirically established set of principles common to vills.

This type of significance leads to another. The vill becomes a criterion for critical evaluation of other theories. Thus we are able to single out the work of Redfield as probably most significant to the theory of communal organization because his work can be shown to be most relevant in terms of its relevance to the vill. There are numerous theories of community which have not been mentioned in this book because they are simply not relevant to the data that have been obtained.

Communal organizations, then, are heavily institutionalized systems which lack defining goals. They are related to each other principally in ever more inclusive levels, from households to neighborhoods to vills to regions to nations. The vills are understood best, especially in their village-city variation. What is less often noted is their lack of precise integration—a change in one aspect does not necessarily mean a predictable change in another. In part this is due to contradictory functional requirements of some aspects of the vill, in part to cultural lag, and in part to the symbolic nature of human interaction.

The theory is thus an organizing principle, relating not only various theories of a lower level of abstraction but more detailed work by other theorists and even other fields of investigation. Thus, in the most general sense, the theory is most important for what it integrates.

### THE TASK AHEAD

*Concepts.* This book attempts to solve the most serious problem in the field: the nature of communal organizations. But the very fact that such a problem exists indicates that there are probably other concepts which can be expected to be sources of trouble in the future. As Merton has observed, " *Too often, a single term has been used to symbolize different concepts, just as the same concept has been symbolized by different terms* " (1957, p. 20). Under the first heading, for example, is the lack of agreement on such terms as *family* and *stratification*. And as an example of the second condition, the urban sociologists speak of ecology whereas the rural sociologists speak of essentially the same thing under land use, land division, land tenure, etc.

Scientific concepts are essentially limited descriptions of the world around us. It follows that part of the problem in sociology is the youth of the discipline. There must be time for descriptive studies to accumulate, and for concepts to grow from the data and to grow again into the data as hypotheses are tested. The data-collection phase of sociology will, however, continue to be slow and involved. Nowhere is there better evidence for this point than in the case studies of communal organizations. Should one want 1,000 communities for statistical analysis, he would then need approximately 1,000 man-years of scientific investigation, to say nothing about the sampling problem. In consequence, the various .case studies that have been made become very precious indeed.

Of course, description alone is not enough. Descriptions must be combined and compared in the process of concept formation, and they must be integrated with hypotheses before they are of value. Two hypotheses raised by this book may be mentioned. Goffman has claimed that the family undermines the total control attempted in total institutions. Before this problem can be attacked, we must clearly understand the meaning of *family*, *control*, and *total institutions*. It makes a great deal of difference, for example, whether informal liaisons are considered families, and whether these liaisons are heterosexual or homosexual. And the concepts, whatever they are, must be observable in the empirical world, particularly in those areas which seem to contradict the hypothesis. In the present instance, for example, we need more careful study of systems containing slaves who live with their families. (It is significant in this respect that both New Orleans and Timbuctoo had slave populations.)

As a second hypothesis, vills have been described as not being created for the attainment of specific goals. Such a description requires a clear statement of the nature of vills and the nature of specific goals. The statement of such concepts, however, is only a first step toward their full development, for again observation of the consequences of their combination is a crucial step. If the concepts are valid and the proposition true, then studies of problem-solving in vills should help to show the validity of the position. It is here that work in community power and community action should prove of assistance, precisely because such studies have emphasized the consequences of communal organizations working for specific goals.

Thus, it is not agreement that is important. Rather, it is the working out of the relevance of concepts for the actions and things they purport to describe.

*The folk-urban continua.* These continua have been a consistent theme of this study. Most of the effort has been devoted to substantiating some principles and developing others. Thus, specific points on the continua have been identified : the extreme point of the folk society, the first measured point of the folk village, and the portions of the continua represented by the pre-industrial and the industrial city. Other points need to be investigated ; for example, the nature of systems closer to the folk society than the folk village. In other words, does the folk village really represent the closest empirical approximation to the folk society? I think not (consider especially the band), but the point remains to be demonstrated.

At the other end of the continua, we have not yet developed an acceptable ideal type of the city. From the evidence in this book, certain guiding principles can be mentioned, but they by no means give a complete picture. First, it is clear that one cannot simply describe the city as the opposite of the folk society.

The family, apparently, is here to stay and, in this sense, the change from the folk society to the ideal-typical urban society is curvilinear rather than linear: the decrease in the importance of the family never reaches the zero point. On the other hand, constant striving toward more effective contractual systems indicates that the ideal-typical city should represent some sort of integration of the perfect contract and the streamlined but vigorous family system (perhaps as in the kibbutz). If these types of systems turn out to be mutually incompatible, then we have Sjoberg's theory of contradictory functional requirements (1960b) which may serve as part of the picture. As far as considerations of space or territory are concerned, the situation is probably similar to that of the family. Space is an element which becomes increasingly more specialized and, with the development of technology, increasingly manipulated (witness, again, the increasing specialization), but always it is there to be considered.

Thus, in creating the ideal type, since we are considering a type of vill, we must consider its continua as revolving around space, family, and cooperation. In this sense, more work probably needs to be done on the spatial aspects of the ideal-typical folk society.

There is an important question to be raised, however, one which the taxonomy developed in Chapter 8 indicates. In view of the distinction between vills and nations, should the folk society be separated from the continua of vills? In other words, should we not differentiate between folk-urban and village-city continua? On the continua of vills would be placed folk villages, pre-industrial cities, and industrial cities, with their ideal types at the extreme ends. On the folk-urban continua would be placed the folk society of Redfield, empirical abstractions (or perhaps constructed types) of folk societies, Sjoberg's feudal societies, empirical abstractions of industrial societies, and the ideal type of the industrial society. Perhaps Toennies' work would become more relevant here.

This principle of separating continua for nations and vills may well extend to all types of communal organizations, specifically neighborhoods and households.

*Communal Integration.* Virtually all that has been done in this area has been to observe the existence of entities and to impute an integration to them. But *why* do the parts stay together? If there are bonds, as Sorokin, Zimmerman, and Galpin (1930–32) would have us believe, they are not bonds in the usual sense. If we are to follow the reasoning of Durkheim, we will pay closer attention to the division of labor. But Durkheim was never conclusive about integration, and efforts in the study of stratification have not brought us very far.[1] The suggestion has been made in this book that considerations of convenience are one of the forces integrating vills; that is, vills are integrated in part because of the need to consider simultaneously time, space, and energy factors. These considerations appear most frequent in families as their members attempt to live their lives in a given locality. Presumably, the same integrating force applies to communal organizations in general. But the problem is too important to remain on a speculative level.

Two specific problems merit attention. First, since urban sociologists have so often ignored the family, we know little about it as a communal integrator beyond such obvious points as the integration of wives and children into the system. Second, the lack of data on ethnocentrism in some cities indicates a need for more careful study. If cities indeed are less ethnocentric than folk villages, this may be symptomatic of still other differences in integration.

Because of the importance of integration, more work is needed on community conflict. Of most importance here is the work of such men as James Coleman and Oscar Lewis. But the criminologist also has much to contribute in this area, though it is hardly surprising that he has not contributed more. He has been faced not only with a confusion of basic concepts in the field, but with an erroneous identification. If the error of the prison community can be recognized as such, then more attention can be given to the way in which these formal organizations are integrated (or encysted) into the communal organization. This, of course, is only one problem. More basic to integration is deviance, and it is here the criminologist can make his most effective contribution.

---

[1] Barber (1961) offers evidence for an important distinction between familial, stratification, and local community status which lends much support to the conclusion that stratification is only secondarily related to communal integration.

*Inter-communal organization.* It is understandable that investigators attempt to study their own phenomena to the exclusion of all else. But since phenomena derive much of their meaning from the world around them, abstracting can go only so far. The principle of inclusiveness developed in the last two chapters has shown that communal organizations *include* communal organizations in greater and more encompassing organizations. And communal organizations become the means of integrating other types of social organizations, as well as being integrated by them. Communal organizations are not self-sufficient entities.

But the general statement of such a relation is not the same as specifying the nature of the relationships, in detail. The increasing emphasis upon study of the relationship between communal organizations and their more inclusive systems is thus a wholesome shift in the right direction, and the problems encountered are accordingly welcome ones. The immensity of these problems is suggested by the fact that, though there have been numerous studies in this area (cf. Ford and Sutton, 1961; Steward, 1950), little success has been achieved in drawing these studies together and in isolating the strength and deficiencies of the total effort.

One of the problems has been a failure to recognize different levels: the integration of a satellite city to its metropolis may not be the same type of integration as that of a metropolis with other metropolises, of a metropolis with its region, or of a metropolis with its nation. In these very expressions, however, lies another problem, the frequent vagueness about what is integrated with what. At times, there is a tendency to reify, as Ford and Sutton (1961) have noted; that is, some writers speak of the integration of a communal organization with its "society" without identifying what is specifically involved.

The most promising effort to date is Warren's theory of vertical integration (1963, esp. Chap. 5), in which extracommunal relationships would occur not through the vill as a unit but through specific organizations within the vill. These relations are essentially formal and bureaucratic. But Warren's theory, as yet untested, applies only to the industrial situation developed in the Western World, specifically to America and presumably to Europe. Relationships in other cultures, especially in those emphasizing folk villages, remain unexplored.

Of course, insofar as communal organizations have not been clearly conceptualized and identified, the whole problem of their integration could hardly be confronted, let alone solved. Thus, we are at present faced with many limited studies which trace limited connections of communal organizations with each other and with other social organizations, but aside from the work of Warren, we have no general set of perspectives. The effort required to remedy this situation is a large one. If one of the reasons why community has presented so formidable a problem has been that it is so complex and contains so many variables, how much more formidable will be the problem of intercommunal integration?

*Changes in communal organization.* Of necessity, any theory of social organization must have reference to social change, since change is the nature of the human group. Thus, it is not surprising that although the data used in this study were not historical, they have had relevance for theories which were.

The problem of change in communal organization must of necessity wait on solutions to the problems mentioned above. In other words, we cannot discuss changes in systems until we know what the systems are, or at least until we have some base lines from which to measure. Simultaneous solutions to several problems are often possible, but the understanding of change can never be prior to the understanding of being.

Theories of change in communal organization have consistently clustered around folk-urban variation and, yet, when the evidence for the theories is examined closely, it is found to be very thin. Perhaps the strongest evidence in favor of the theories of writers such as Maine, Toennies, Durkheim, Redfield, and Sjoberg is that they all point in the same direction. Basically, these theories indicate several major complexes of forces. Redfield, Becker, and the earlier writers point to the chief urbanizing variables as increasing heterogeneity and division of labor, accompanied by an ever fuller development of contracts. These forces, in turn, lead to a breakdown of isolation and increased accessibility. Sjoberg goes somewhat deeper in pointing to the development of technology as the principal stimulus to these forces, though he recognizes the necessity of political development and a proper cultural base. He also sees a reinforcement to urban development coming from the cities themselves. The more cities there are, the more thoroughly they stimulate the growth of cities.

These theories have been shown to be consistent with the findings of this book, and they thus provide welcome theoretical support. But more work needs to be done before we can be certain which variables precede which. For example, the argument could as easily be made that diffusion spurs technological growth and that therefore increase in accessibility is more important than technological change. It may even be incorrect to consider either of these variables as prior to the others. Until we have careful socioanthropological studies of communities over several generations, we must be cautious. Information for several centuries would be even better.

The data on folk-urban change has essentially consisted of two types: analysis of historical records and studies of contemporary communities. The strategy has been to attempt to combine the incomplete historical records with careful studies of modern systems. This is a valuable combination, but it cannot take the place of long-term observations of specific social systems. (The Middletown studies, which included a half-century span, are more adequate than most, and even they combine the methods noted here.) To argue that the past may still live in the present does not provide a means for identifying what is past and what is present. (See Goldenweiser, 1937, pp. 507–9, for an excellent discussion of this point.)

Furthermore, the analysis in the previous chapters suggests that folk-urban change is only a part of the picture. The theory of communal organization indicates that there are three basic types of communal change: (1) change within one type of communal organization, as from folk village to city; (2) change from type to type of communal organization, as from a neighborhood to a vill; and (3) change from one social organization to another, as from a social movement to a communal organization. (See Arrington, 1958, for a description of this last process among the Mormons.) Almost all of our effort has been devoted to the first type. And it almost invariably assumes a change in one direction —from folk to urban.

The emphasis on folk-urban change is theoretically pertinent and the assumed direction of change is in keeping with what has been observed in modern times, but this does not mean that the theory is sufficient. For example, though folk-urban change is central to the theory of communal organization, what of changes from one type of nation to another? Enough work has been done in this area that it could probably be readily drawn together, but the synthesis remains to be done.[2] Or, again, most of the change we have witnessed has been in fact from folk to urban systems—but cannot the reverse also occur? The type of social organizations that often have developed in the wake of empire collapse suggest such a possibility. (Note, specifically, the developments after the fall of the Incan, Mayan, Aztecan, and Roman empires.)

Of course, there are theories of social change which take this broader perspective. Sorokin's theory (1937–41) of sensate, idealistic, and ideational supersystems is one of the more relevant. But Sorokin's compass is too broad. We have been able to trace vills carefully from specific cases to middle-range theories without, we hope, leaving any gaps. Sorokin, on the other hand, goes beyond explanations of how any particular group functions vis-à-vis other groups and attempts the ultimate in sociocultural knowledge: predicting the changes in the most inclusive types of social groupings the world has known. In spite of the need for the great systems of sociological theory, there is also a need to build other theories (the prior necessity, perhaps). These must be built from data to prediction so that they may be brought back to data again. This has been the major objective in this book's study of communal organizations.

[2] However, see Krader, 1968, and Parson, 1966.

*Appendixes*

# Analysis of the Systems

Each of the following analyses represents the first stage of the syntheses which resulted in Chapters 2, 3, and 8, respectively. The material is based directly on the quotations from the case studies gathered according to the method described in Chapter 1.

# A

# The Folk Villages

VILLAGES IN THE MODEL

Since there will often be occasion to refer to the individual villages in the discussion of the data, it is necessary to give a thumbnail sketch of the peculiar features of each. Each sketch will include the village name, country or location, and population; its geographic setting and economic base or level; its changes and peculiarities; and the authors' purpose and time of study. (A modified summary of these sketches is presented in Chapter 2, Table 1, p. 28.)

*San Ildefonso*, New Mexico, U.S.A., contains 128 persons. The people are subsistence farmers in an arid, somewhat elevated but level terrain bordering the Rocky Mountain chain. They are American Indians racially, and they are largely Tewa in culture with heavy influences from Spanish and American sources. When studied, the village was in the process of splitting in two parts, called the North and South plazas. The split occurred residentially and to some extent politically and religiously. The U.S. government's influence is increasing through the acculturative effects of jobs and schools. The study was undertaken by the late William Whitman as an anthropological survey of human behavior. The basic data were gathered between the years 1936–39.

The *buraku* (or villages) of *Suye Mura*, Japan, have between 58 to 194 inhabitants and are located on a flood plain encircled by maturely dissected mountains. The people primarily cultivate paddy rice and manufacture silk. The study's author, John Embree, refers to the *mura* as the village. In terms of the present study, however, the settlement patterns known as the *buraku*, of which the *mura* is composed, are the social forms which most closely resemble the other villages. Whenever Suye Mura is mentioned, therefore, reference is to its *buraku*, particularly Kawase *buraku*. The national government is increasingly making itself felt by the installation of schools, military conscription, and agricultural associations. These planned changes are resulting in such unintended consequences as a change from a rice to a money economy and an increased use of machines. Embree investigated Suye Mura in order to provide a social study of a peasant village. His field research extended from 1935 to 1936.

*New Peri*, Manus Island, New Guinea, has between 200 and 330 members. The Melanesian Negroes are almost exclusively fishermen, living on the southeast coast of the Great Admiralty (Manus) Island. They have recently undergone a cultural revolution; in association with a native-inspired messianic social movement, they moved their village from pile dwellings over a lagoon to the shore and drastically increased integration with the outside world by adopting in large measure Western forms of family life, government, and education (they had previously adopted Christianity). Margaret Mead studied these people in 1953 (after an earlier study in 1938) in an attempt to document and understand the effect of rapid cultural transformation.

*Romonom*, one of the islands of Truk in the Micronesian region of the Pacific, contains between 230 and 240 inhabitants. The island is of mixed coral and volcanic origin. In this setting the people gather coconuts, grow taro, and engage in fishing. Early in the present century, a factional conflict split the island into two districts. Since then, the rift has largely healed, though some minor effects still remain. During this time, the islanders have been ruled by German, Japanese, and U.S. governments;

as a consequence, they have given up warfare, have become almost completely converted to Christianity, become highly literate, and have considerably modified their technology. The studies by Goodenough and by Gladwin and Sarason were parts of a program of research on the culture of the Truk islands undertaken by Yale anthropologists in 1947 and 1948.

*Chan Kom*, Yucatán, Mexico, has 251 inhabitants situated in the northern portion of a level peninsula which features second-growth bush as its main form of vegetation. Farming of the slash and burn variety (fire agriculture), centered on corn, is the mainstay of the village. The village had only been recently established at the time of study, and except for that event has had a relatively quiet history (establishing a school, building a road to Chichen Itza, and general consolidation and development). The data were collected by Robert Redfield, an anthropologist, and Alfonso Villa Rojas, the village schoolteacher, during 1930 and 1931. The study is an anthropological (ethnographic) survey, part of a larger project comparing different types of communities engaged in the transition from folk to urban societies (Redfield, 1941).

*Hilltown*, New England, U.S.A., has varied in population from 150 persons in 1767 (the time of its founding) to a maximum of 1,825 persons in 1850. Most of the nineteenth century found the village with more than 1,000 people. Its location in the eroded mountains of New England provided an economic base of not much more than subsistence farming supplemented with lumbering, though other industries were present from time to time. Hilltown is unique among the villages in this study in having farms scattered throughout the village area (that is, the township) in addition to having some residences concentrated in one place. A religious schism occurred early in the nineteenth century in which Unitarians won control over the older Congregationalists (later, Methodism was added). Manpower was seriously depleted by the Civil War (the equivalent of 22 per cent of the employed males were killed while fighting in the Union Army). After 1900, the village became increasingly integrated with the neighboring cities until it is now no more than a middleclass suburb. Only information pertaining to the nineteenth century is used in the present analysis. The township has been analyzed by the sociologists Carle Zimmerman,

George Homans, and David L. Hatch in connection with various studies of social change.

*Kaihsienkung* is situated near the lower course of the Yangtze River about 80 miles west of Shanghai, China, and numbers 1,458 persons. The alluvial plain, intersected by numerous streams, provides the basis for rice cultivation, the main crop for this farm village. Sheep raising, introduced ten years prior to the study, also became an important industry. However, a silk factory that was started at the same time was followed by a decline of the silk industry, an industry which had been carried on by the people for more than a thousand years. The village itself was destroyed in the Sino-Japanese War. Hsiao-Tung Fei, a sociologist and anthropologist, chose the village to describe its socioeconomic system. The period of study was 1935.

*Dragalevtsy*, Bulgaria, with a population of 1,669, is less than five miles from Sofia, the nation's capital. The farms, at the base of Mount Vitosha, produce a fairly diversified agriculture: wheat and rye (mixed) form the main crop, but corn, vegetables, and livestock are also important. Before World War II and the subsequent rise of communism, change had been gradual. During a fifty-year period, formal education had been introduced, the political boundaries of the village had been extended, the national government (non-Communist) had exerted increasing control, and the family had shifted from the large extended form to the smaller, nuclear type. Irwin Sanders' intention was to describe peasant life in the Balkans from the sociological point of view. His field work was done from 1934 to 1937.

*Shamirpet*, India, with 2,494 residents, is 25 miles from the twin cities of Hyderabad and Secundrabad. The land is one of fertile fields and barren rocks, permitting the villagers to grow a wide variety of vegetables and grains and some livestock. The caste system is found here as elsewhere in India; it is formed of 16 groups in addition to the Muslims. The power of the Muslims was seriously weakened when the state of Hyderabad came into the Indian Union in 1948. There is some tendency for caste structure to weaken as individualism and migration become more frequent and as isolation breaks down in general. S. C. Dube, an anthropologist, prepared the analysis as a study of village organization and ethos. Dube directed a team of researchers in collecting data during 1951 and 1952.

*Silwa*, Egypt, with almost 3,500 members, is the largest of the folk villages, and one of the most isolated. Its physical setting, at the foot of the Eastern Plateau, divides the villagers' world into the three distinct parts: the hills (the soil of which is used for fertilizer), the village, and the fields. The Nile should also be added to this physical setting. The main crops for practically every farmer are wheat and millet—vegetables and livestock are secondary. A compulsory school had been established 25 years before the study was made, and it had succeeded in raising the literacy level from 5 to 20 per cent. The villagers have begun to imitate city ways, especially in material aspects. Hamed Ammar relied variously on anthropological, sociological, and psychological approaches in attempting to study education in a village community. A native of the village himself, he collected most of his information in the latter part of 1951.

ELEMENTS OF THE MODEL

Insofar as possible, the elements of the village model are introduced in such a manner as to describe that model with maximum efficiency. The order is not the same as Homan's original analysis of the elements in *The Human Group* (1950). Rather, it is geared specifically to describing the village as a distinctive form of human grouping. (Parenthetically, it must be noted that Homans' categories were used simply because they organized most of the data. There was no preconceived attempt to limit components only to his categories, as is shown by the development of the element of space, which is of course absent from Homans' elements.)

1. *Interaction:* Since this is the most fundamental quality of any human group, it is included first. Activity may or may not be social, interaction is always social. On the other hand, interaction can occur without sentiment, with positive sentiment, or with negative sentiment, and it can occur in non-institutionalized or even non-normative forms.

2. *Space:* This element is considered next because it is one of the features which the village shares with locality groups and which conceivably distinguishes these groups from those which do not emphasize space. In the case of folk villages, especially, space becomes important enough to enter into its structure and function. The reader should bear in mind, however, that the

element of space is considered only because of its importance to a particular kind of group. Most groups can be discussed intelligently by taking space as a constant or as something given. That this cannot be done for the folk village only means that the folk village is a special class of human group, *not* that space is an element on the same theoretical level as interaction, activities, sentiment, and norms.

3. *Activities:* Most of the activities considered here are intimately related to space and should be considered in as close a conjunction with space as possible.

4. *Sentiment:* The order of discussion between this and the following element is essentially arbitrary, though the sentiment of solidarity (that is, the component of homogeneity) serves as an introduction to the institutions.

5. *Institutions:* The various clusterings or organizations of norms that we call institutions present problems peculiar to themselves. They are discussed last because the importance of each institution varies considerably, particularly in its ability to distinguish the folk village from other social forms. Some institutions are central to an understanding of the folk village, others are of little value for identifying the folk village as a special type.

A summary list of all the elements and their components is given in Chapter 2, Table 2, pp. 29–30.

### INTERACTION

*Personal contact.* Each of the villages is composed of a group of people who interact on a personal, face-to-face basis. Whether everyone actually interacts with everyone else, is impossible to say. Ideally, we should know the numbers of the villagers who contact each other personally over a given period of time—say a week or even a month, but such information is not available. On the other hand, the investigators did say that in the Japanese *buraku* and in Hilltown "everyone" knew each other "well." This condition is probably approximated in all of the villages, but the conclusion must be arrived at indirectly.

In Kaihsienkung and in Silwa (the largest village), the precise number of families who were strangers was known (ten and four, respectively). One of these families had been in Silwa for 50 years.

In Chan Kom and in Dragalevtsy, evidence is furnished that at least all of the adult members of one of the sexes know each other. The evidence is particularly clear for the Chan Kom men and for the Dragalevtsy women but only suggestive for members of the opposite sex. The claim is not being made that the rest of the villagers do not know each other—only that the investigators fail to give explicit mention of such contact. It is probable, of course that if all of the Dragalevtsy women know each other, then their husbands, fathers, and brothers also know each other, since the latter were almost invariably born in the village. And it would not be unreasonable to suspect similar knowledge in the case of Chan Kom, since the village is only a fraction of the size of Dragalevtsy.

A different type of evidence must be used for the remaining villages used in this study. Whenever anyone deviated from village norms or whenever unusual events occurred, this knowledge became known at least to all adults. The wireless of gossip is so complete that few if any can hope to shield a secret for very long. The case of Romonom is typical: "It is usually possible to get a fairly complete account of a man beating his wife from anyone on the island within an hour of its happening" (Gladwin and Sarason, 1953, p. 149).

In each of the villages, therefore, all of the evidence points in the same direction. One may wonder about Homans' remark that everyone in Hilltown knows everyone else well, but when the same assertion is repeated by Embree for another village, and when evidence leading to a similar conclusion appears for all of the other villages, one must conclude that not only is Homans' statement possibly true, it is even highly probable. Of course, there is at least one category of villagers who may be omitted from this component of personal contact: the very young. There is, accordingly, no reason to attempt to convert the ubiquity of personal contact into an inflexible law. All members will not be equally acquainted with all others. But as a minimum, the conclusion may be reached that effective social contact in folk villages depends on a high degree of personal knowledge.

*Social processes.* Human interaction may be classified as either solidary or antagonistic (Sorokin, 1947). In this book, cooperation is the solidary process which receives heaviest emphasis,

whereas antagonism is represented mainly by conflict. Cooperation is treated under mutual aid primarily because of the degree
of institutionalization. Mutual aid invariably exists as an institution in folk villages, whereas conflict does not. The more
institutionalized forms of conflict occur in competition.

Nevertheless, conflict is found in all villages. It may be discussed in terms of conflict between and within villages. Inter-
village conflict cannot become too violent when a more powerful outside government is determined to keep the peace, as
happens in so many of the villages. Perhaps for this reason,
conflict remains latent in the form of ethnocentrism. Open conflict between villages flares up only occasionally, specific
examples being found in Chan Kom and Shamirpet.

The data are more complete and specific for intra-village
conflict. The intensity varies, from the virtual civil war which
at one time occurred on Romonom, to the strong factions which
are present in many villages today, to quarrels and other forms
of minor disputes. Factions are most frequently mentioned, but
not for three villages (Silwa, Kaihsienkung, and Kawaze
*buraku*). In addition to Romonom, factions were powerful in
San Ildefonso and toward the close of Hilltown's existence as a
folk village. Factions precipitating varying degrees of conflict
are mentioned for Chan Kom, Dragalevtsy, New Peri, and
Shamirpet, but there is no evidence of their permanence.

The important point is that the villages show no consistent
form of institutionalized conflict. The same conclusion may be
tendered for competition, a process conceived of as a type of
conflict in which the parties cooperate as they conflict, that is,
they agree to abide by norms which pertain to the conflict,
which limit it, and which decide its outcome. Games, of course,
immediately come to mind, and games of some sort are played
in all the villages. But only in seven villages is evidence given
which shows the games to be competitive. Even in the remainder,
however, there were some forms of competition. Among the
pueblo women of San Ildefonso, work has tended to become
competitive; the *buraku* of Suye Mura engaged in inter-village
rivalries; and the people of Kaihsienkung (especially the
women) drive hard bargains with certain types of peddlers.

SPACE

*Spatial integration.* No village was strictly homogeneous in the use of its geographic space. In every village, there are parts, but these parts were also united to form a whole; that is, the space was integrated. There are several ways in which this integration was achieved: (1) by common recognition of the villagers that the village is a unit; (2) by common ownership; (3) by political authority over the territory of the village; and (4), a special case, in those villages composed of clearly separate spatial areas, the areas were still recognized as a unit by the villagers.

1. In all cases, the village was regarded by the villagers as a unit. This unit may have been limited to only part of the area used by the villagers, as in Chan Kom. There, the *ejido* was a unit, communally owned. However, the outlying *milpas* (farms), though cultivated by the villagers, belonged technically to the Mexican federal government. Similarly, in Romonom and New Peri, the village was a unit residentially, but the sea belonged to villager and non-villager alike.

The remaining forms, which apply to seven of the villages, are summarized in the Table 9.

*Table 9.* Spatial integration of villages

| Village | Common ownership | Political authority over territory | Distinctly separate parts form a unit |
|---|---|---|---|
| New Peri | X | | |
| Hilltown | | X | |
| Dragalevtsy | X | X | |
| Chan Kom | X | X | X |
| San Ildefonso | | X | X |
| Romonom | | X | X |
| Shamirpet | | | X |

2. In only three villages was any substantial part of the village owned in common, that is, owned by all members of the village, jointly. In New Peri and Chan Kom, the residential area was held in common, and so was the *ejido* in Chan Kom. In Dragalevtsy, only the meadows and pastures were commonly owned.

3. Half of the villages had clearly defined political rights over

their territory. The other half did not, either because they were not recognized by the government of the larger society (as was the case in New Peri), or because the larger society had not defined political boundaries in accordance with boundaries recognized by the villagers. In the *buraku* of Suye Mura, for example, there was no correspondence between the territory of ownership of land (*aza*) and the political boundaries (*buraku*). However, the people were beginning to recognize the unity of the larger grouping, the *mura*; that is, they felt themselves part of the *mura* as well as part of the smaller *buraku*. In the remaining three villages, the government of the larger society recognized groupings of several villages as the smallest political units in spite of the fact that the folk villages in question considered themselves to be separate entities.

In Chan Kom, political rule extended only over the *ejido*—a territory which included some farms as well as the residences. But the farmers customarily grew crops also outside of the *ejido* in land owned by the federal government. Though the people felt that they had some claim to this land, they also recognized the claim of the federal government. (Whether they were satisfied is another matter.)

4. Four villages were divided into distinct parts. In each case, these parts were also integrated, while at the same time maintaining some form of separateness. San Ildefonso was in the process of forming two new villages (though the process was never completed). The residences had become separated into north and south plazas. The north plaza had the legal governor but had only an informal religious head; in the south plaza the situation was reversed. Yet the two plazas were integrated in their dealings with the U.S. government, in many if not all of their religious ceremonies, and in their economic activities. Romonom, on the other hand, had been healing a similar schism for many decades. There was, at the time of the Romonom study, only one governing official or island chief, though the people still spoke of themselves as coming from one or the other of the older factions. Shamirpet had residential areas for some of its castes separated by narrow strips of land. But each caste was represented on the single village governing council. Chan Kom, as noted, was composed of a single central area together with several outlying ones (that is, *milpas* outside the *ejido*).

Thus, one cannot say the village inhabits one contiguous area. In four cases, such is patently not the situation. On the other hand, if the village is not a contiguous area, the separate parts are tied together, at least politically and usually in other ways.

Only in Chan Kom were all four forms of integration described. Most often, the integration was political, but it could be primarily economic (as in New Peri), or it could be simply an awareness of the villagers that they were separate from other villages, inhabiting one and only one territory—this much at least was present among the villagers of Suye Mura, Kaihsien-kung, and Silwa.

With the exception of San Ildefonso, which at the time of its study was in the act of splitting apart, it is even possible that *all* of the villages were recognized as a unit by their inhabitants in respect to *several* components. Thus, the extent of spatial integration may actually be much greater than is described here. But one must rely on information given by investigators who were generally not looking for spatial integration. The method used in this book affords only descriptions of minimal conditions; that is, *at least* this much is present—there may be more, but more evidence was not given.

*Spatial patterning.* There is no rigid spatial form which all villages follow. However, there are general patterns and tendencies.

1. Each of the villages has developed a settled ecology. At least some of the facilities, especially buildings and fields, are given a relatively permanent location. In New Peri the entire settlement was moved from the water to land, but the pattern of buildings had been stabilized before the move and became stabilized after.

2. All villages displayed the ecological process of concentration; that is, either (1) the residences were all grouped in one place and the "fields" (land or sea) were in some other place, or (2), in the case of Hilltown (the only exception to the residential grouping), there was a nucleus of homes, churches, and the school and town hall with farm residences scattered over the remainder of the township. In other words, whether residences were on the farm land or separated from it, there was a clustering of buildings—an increased density—somewhere in the area utilized by the villagers.

3. Ecological centralization was displayed in a tendency for the nucleus to be in the center of the village areas (that is, the village plus the fields or fishing grounds). At times, however, the village was located to one side of the "center." In either case, one may say that this tendency is present in six of the villages—all villages in this class were surrounded by farms or by the sea from which they lived. Only New Peri, San Ildefonso, and Silwa varied from this pattern (no information was provided for Shamirpet). The fishing village of New Peri was located on a peninsula. In both of the remaining villages, all of the fields were definitely on one side of the residential area. A case might be made, however, for Silwa conforming to some extent to the pattern. It is located between the fields and the hills, and the hills are regularly mined for fertilizer. The reason for Silwa's arrangement is found in the dependence on the Nile for irrigation. Thus, Silwa is "centered" with respect to the total area which is regularly used in the course of the villagers' lives: the hills on one side, the fields and the Nile on the other.

4. There was also a tendency for nucleation within the nucleus, though this tendency could be completely obliterated, as in Kaihsienkung and the *buraku* of Suye Mura. Five villages, however, showed strong sub-nucleation (no accurate description was given for Hilltown): Chan Kom, Dragalevtsy, New Peri, and San Ildefonso were built around plazas (there were two plazas in San Ildefonso), and Shamirpet was grouped around the government offices and shops. In Silwa and Romonom this sub-nucleation was either weak or absent. The government buildings of Silwa (including the police station, post office, and school) were located on the north side of the village, but no information was provided concerning the location of the stores and the mosques ("the finest buildings in the village," Ammar, 1954, p. viii). Romonom had its major buildings—meeting houses, churches, schools—scattered throughout the village but none was located at the extreme ends.

It is perhaps worth noting that the plazas of all four villages which had plazas included at least the religious building, such as mosque, church, or temple.

5. There was a well-established area or network of spaces used as a communication system within the nucleus. Each village had a system of paths (in Kaihsienkung, streams were

added) or at least a central road or plaza. In the six villages for which maps of the nucleus were provided, the network is clearly visible, and it is also verbally described for Hilltown, Silwa, and Shamirpet. In San Ildefonso, however, only the plazas for the north and for the south sections are noted. (Subsequent investigation by the present writer did show subsidiary communication spaces in this village, also.)

The communication system attests primarily to the stability of the villages' spatial patterning. It also serves to document the marked importance of routinized movements within the village area and particularly within the nucleus.

No consistency could be found in the use of land for economic purposes. Villages were devoted to fishing, farming, or both, and even the agriculturalists differed in the crops grown. One can generalize no more than to say that all villages were engaged mainly in primary production. Even so, this was not the only type of production (as will be shown when the economic institution is discussed). Nor was there consistency in property relationships. Some villages had absentee landlords, some were communally owned, and some were composed mainly of small landowners. Most fields were separated from the residences, but Hilltown is an exception. Fragmentation of holdings was displayed in some villages and not in others. Property relations, then, fluctuated radically.

In general, the most constant ecological feature of the villages was their use of space rather than their use of the earth as a physical resource. Factors of distance limited all of the villagers and, consequently, the physical pattern was adjusted by arranging facilities in proximity to each other. Definite patterns of stability, concentration, centralization, and communication within the nucleus were observed. There was some tendency for the nucleus to be located near the center of the village and some tendency for sub-nucleation within the nucleus, but exceptions have been noted. Economic use of land showed no consistency, beyond a general commitment to primary production.

*Vague boundaries.* The term "vague" includes uncertainty or lack of boundaries, conflict in boundaries, and instability of boundaries. Most widespread was the tendency for all villagers to be vague about their boundaries in that they were not confined to those boundaries in the course of their activities.

New Peri was located on a peninsula, Romonom on an island, but although these villagers used the sea, the village boundaries were not on the sea. Chan Kom provides a similar case; though its boundaries around the *ejido* were definite, its villagers were not restricted to those boundaries in making their *milpas*. Indeed, they were not clearly restricted from any area. Kaihsienkung was also noted for lacking clear boundaries. San Ildefonso was in the process of modifying its boundaries as the village moved toward division, and the political authorities responsible for Dragalevtsy changed its boundaries to include other villages. Further, in the religious ceremonies of Dragalevtsy, the village territory was increased in direct ratio to the seriousness of the ceremony. The boundaries between the two districts on Romonom became less important with the passage of time. Finally, Chan Kom, Hilltown, and Silwa from time to time shifted the area in which they farmed or lived.

There was also an inconsistency in defining boundaries. As noted, the *buraku* of Suye Mura used different boundaries to designate political and economic areas. In Kaihsienkung, Shamirpet, Silwa, and later in Dragalevtsy, the boundaries as the villagers conceived of them were not the same as the boundaries set by the national government.

Romonom provides an apparent exception. On the one hand, the villagers were as precise in assigning boundaries as in Western society. But, as in the West, for varying kinds of property in the same space, there are varying kinds of boundaries and sometimes no boundaries. For example, there are fishing rights in water areas, but water itself—especially fresh water—is the property of no one. Apparently, the villagers may travel over certain areas but may not fish in them. One's location in a spatial sense therefore is relatively unimportant. What matters is what is done to the property involved in the space in question. In addition, it will be recalled that the boundaries for Romonom have changed in time. It is thus particularly instructive because its boundaries are so precise. But in spite of their emphasis on boundaries, these villagers also reach the effective condition of having vague boundaries for the village as a whole because they have different boundaries for different activities.

Boundaries, then, help clarify the nature of spatial integration and village awareness. The villagers are chiefly aware of the village within the village boundaries and it is the presence of these boundaries which shows their recognition of the integration of their space. The fact that the boundaries are vague signifies that spatial integration is itself either weak or not complete.

There is also another implication, but one which can receive full attention only when prisons and mental hospitals are brought into consideration. Briefly, sharp and completely consistent boundaries are generally unimportant to the villagers. The nature of the folk village is not defined by any rigid restriction of the socially significant territory which the villagers occupy.

ACTIVITIES

*Base of operations.* This component describes in abbreviated form the general pattern of activities performed by the villagers. It received one of its earliest if not its first expressions by Carle Zimmerman. In speaking of an investigation of Minnesota trade centers, he wrote, " This study suggested a duality of function in the local community. The small elementary trade center was a community where the people carried on their routine day-by-day functions of living. . . . In the larger secondary trade centers, the people participated in the outer world and were accommodated to the 'Great Society'" (Zimmerman, 1938, p. 5). The first of this duality of functions Zimmerman called "localism"; the second he called "cosmopolitanism." (See also Merton, 1957, Chap. 10.) It should be particularly noted that Zimmerman mentioned a *duality* of functions—no communities were exclusively localistic or cosmopolitan.

Talcott Parsons provides a succinct description of this duality : " A community is that collectivity the members of which share a common territorial area as their base of operations for daily activities " (Parsons, 1951, p. 91). The concept of base of operations will be used as the more general concept, including both cosmopolitan and localistic movements.

The village is a localistic base of operations most noticeably in the trips to and from the fields or fishing grounds, perhaps not daily but certainly routinely. Even Hilltown, where a substantial proportion of the villagers lived on their farms, was not an exception but, rather, a variation in the pattern. The Hilltowners used their farm homes as a base of operations into various portions of the fields, to be sure, but they also journeyed frequently to the town's center (the nucleus), to the wooded areas, and to the lumber mills; and the center itself was their base of operations. One may wish to distinguish between inward and outward focusing (or internal and external) bases of operations wherever clustered residences are supplanted by or supplemented with isolated farmsteads, but the pattern of a base of operations remains.

The villagers also use their village as a base of operations into the outside world; that is, in a cosmopolitan sense. These operations may occur with marked and short-spaced regularity, as in the case of weekly visits to market in Dragalevtsy, New Peri, and Kaihsienkung. Though most of the investigators alluded only roughly to the frequency of trips to the outside world, all of them noted the occurrence of such trips and the fact of their regularity.

However, not all of this movement is regular. Substantial segments of villagers leave the village for extended periods before they return. This extension of the base of operations beyond the village limits—both in its regular and irregular aspects—becomes important not only in its own right but as a clarification of one of MacIver's views on community. MacIver felt that the basic criterion of community was found in the ability of a person to spend his whole life there. In view of the significance of MacIver's work in the study of community, it is important that his words be examined carefully. "The mark of a community," he says, "is that one's life *may* be found within it" (MacIver, 1937, p. 9). In a later edition, he becomes even more emphatic: "The basic criterion of community, then, is that all of one's social relationships may be found within it" (MacIver and Page, 1949, p. 9). The word "may," however, is not to be ignored. "But civilized communities," he noted, "even very large ones, are much less self-contained. . . . We may live in a village and yet belong to a community as wide as the whole area of our civilization or even wider. No civilized community has walls around it to cut it off from a larger one." (MacIver, 1937, p. 9.)

The basic criterion is given as self-containment, but it is maintained that communities need not be self-sufficient. Therefore, either (1) the basic criterion is misleading, or (2) most communities lack the "basic" criterion, or (3) the basic criterion requires some other interpretation. The problem is one of isolating the conditions under which the criterion may become empirically observable. How can one know when one "may" or could spend his life in an area? The most rigorous test would be that people (at least some people) did in fact spend their lives in the places in question. If MacIver's criterion is interpreted thus at its face value, attempts to identify it in the ten villages used in this study have not been successful. There was never any mention of any adult in any of the villages who had spent his entire life there. And even if one assumes that under-reporting in this respect occurred in one or two of the villages, one is also struck by the fact that such extreme localization never impressed the researchers as being of any importance. The village which comes particularly to mind is Silwa. There, where most marriages are endogamous (that is, occurring within the village) and where women are rather heavily secluded, it seems *probable* that some women lived all of their days in the village. Still, the probability remains no more than an hypothesis (Ammar never confirms it), and the opposing contention ..that *such localism was not important for most of the villagers*— remains more tenable.

The purpose of the data presented in the Table 10 is to show that large blocks of people have left all of the villages for extended periods before they returned and that, in some cases

*Table 10.* Movements to and from the villages

| Activity taking significant segments of population out of village: | San Ildefonso | Shamirpet | Suye Mura | Romonom | Kaihsienkung | Silwa | Dragalevtsy | Hilltown | New Peri | Chan Kom |
|---|---|---|---|---|---|---|---|---|---|---|
| Children attending school | X | | X | X | | | | | | |
| Pilgrimages | | X | | | | X | | | | |
| Exogamous marriages | | X | X | | X | | X | | | |
| Military service | | X | X | | | | X | X | | |
| Economic employment or trade | | | | | X | X | X | X | X | X |
| Out-migration | | | | | | X | X | X | | |
| In-migration | | | | | | | | X | X | |
| Village moved or was founded | | | | | | | | X | X | X |
| Festivals | | | | | | | | | | X |

(but not all) many persons shifted their permanent residence either to or from the village. Most apparent from Table 10 is the extensive overlapping among the various categories. For example, all of the categories, except the last (festivals), are types of migration. A second point concerns the nature of the data. Many of the categories undoubtedly apply to more villages than shown in Table 10. These data represent only the evidence presented in the various reports, not that which could possibly have existed in the villages.

The evidence permits the following conclusions: (1) In the case of new villages—for example, New Peri, Chan Kom, and Hilltown in its early stages—no adult could have spent his whole life there. (2) For all villages, large segments of the population do not spend their whole lives there. This limitation may be caused by attendance at school outside of the village, by exogamy, or by out-migration. One can also say that (3) large numbers leave all of the villages for short trips and (4) in no village is there specific mention of anyone living his entire life there. Thus, MacIver's criterion patently cannot be applied to the territorial area of the village (indeed, it may not have ever been so intended). Substantial segments of the population do leave, either frequently on short trips or on extended trips. These segments, then, do *not* live all their lives in the village.

It is tempting to say that the folk village provides only the essential things, and that people leave for non-essentials, but such reasoning is dangerous because it assumes that social science has reached the point where it can distinguish all those things which are necessary for social life from those which are not. For example, one would expect that religion is necessary to social life, but the explanation for the need is yet no more than speculative. There is a further danger in that the argument does not explain why many villagers frequently leave and why large numbers leave for long periods. On the contrary, such facts make one suspect that a more likely generalization would be that the outside world also provides essentials.

Fortunately, there is no need to depend upon the literal meaning of MacIver's criterion. The concept of the community as a base of operations is a more profitable interpretation. The village is where most of the main activities of the residents take place. One can thus say that the village supplies the needs of its members for their existence simply because the villages continue to exist.

*Low mobility*. Human social mobility may be defined as the change in social interaction from person to person. Thus, if I change my interaction from the people of one group to that of another, or from the people of one class to that of another, or from the people of one place to that of another, I have moved socially. Social mobility may thus be from group to group (horizontal), stratum to stratum (vertical), or place to place (territorial). These types are distinguishable not only analytically but in actual occurrence.

The degree of vertical mobility is very closely associated with social stratification, and since variation in social stratification among folk villages fluctuates over practically the entire range of extremes, one is probably safe in assuming that there is no constant pattern in vertical mobility among the villages. The evidence for horizontal and territorial mobility pertains primarily to the villagers' place of birth: Most villagers are born in the vicinity of their village, and for most villages, the majority are native to the village. Territorial mobility is low in that villagers do not permanently move great distances from their birthplaces. Horizontal mobility is also low, at least to the extent that many people maintain the same village affiliation during the course of their lifetimes. There are at least four degrees of horizontal mobility. The type mentioned first below probably refers to one of the least mobile populations, though it cannot properly be compared with the others because of the difference in evidence.

1. Romonom, Shamirpet, and Hilltown lack precise information. In Romonom, most marriages occur within the community, that is, village endogamy is high, and one important source of in-migration is thus eliminated. Lineages in the village also extend back at least several generations, thus increasing the probability of a high proportion of natives. In Shamirpet, one may infer a high proportion of native-born among the men because of patrilocal residence, a custom strongly supported by the rest of the family structure (patriarchal, patrilineal, extended families) and a heavy emphasis on tradition. Further, there is no mention of any sudden influx of migrants. (The same kind of negative "evidence" is given for Romonom.) However, one-

third or more of the wives are from outside of the village. Finally, in Hilltown it is specifically noted that the great bulk of in-migration during the entire period of the village's growth was from the neighboring towns.

2. Practically all members of Kaihsienkung and Silwa were native-born. Non-natives comprised less than one per cent of Silwa, and Kiahsienkung contained only 2.8 per cent non-native households.

3. More than three-fourths of the households in New Peri and San Ildefonso contained native-born persons. Between one-fifth and one-fourth of the marriages in San Ildefonso were to non-natives and slightly less than one-fifth of the households in New Peri contained immigrants. (For New Peri, however, see point 5, below.)

4. Dragalevtsy and the *buraku* of Suye Mura followed the custom of exogamy, particularly for wives, (see also the discussion of Shamirpet in point 1, above). In Dragalevtsy, 16.9 per cent of the males were immigrants, whereas 45.4 per cent of the females fell in this class. In Suye Mura, 15.8 per cent of the household heads (males) were not natives, whereas the corresponding percentage for the wives was 80 per cent or more. In both cases, however, almost all of the wives were obtained from neighboring villages.

5. When villages were newly formed—in New Peri, Chan Kom, and Hilltown—almost all of the inhabitants came from the immediate vicinity. Those in New Peri simply moved from the lagoon to the shore. The members of Hilltown seldom came from a distance of more than 20 or 30 miles. The Chan Kom villagers were almost all born within a 40-mile radius—one-third, alone, having come from a single village.

For both horizontal and geographic mobility, one must distinguish permanent and temporary types. Horizontal mobility, further, is analyzed *only* on the basis of a change in village membership. The data do not permit consideration of village subgroups, other than the obvious inference that villagers change groups as they move through the life cycle (for example, children's play groups as opposed to the family life of adults).

When the temporary aspects of village mobility are considered, horizontal mobility seems less frequent, territorial mobility more frequent. The villagers seldom change their group membership, but they often move across their village lines (as was shown in the discussion of the base of operations).

Permanent mobility in reference to the village, of course, occurs only once. But its distance is more quantifiable, and it is found to be short. If the villager changes his membership, he (probably more often she) is apt to do so for a village nearby.

*Continuance.* This component is another residue of MacIver's criterion. If it is moot whether the *village* supplies the needs of its members, there is no doubt that the villagers have their needs supplied somehow. The proof is the ability of the villages to continue. The barest *minimum* number of years which the villages have lasted is given in Table 11.

*Table 11.* Continuance of the villages

| Minimum years in existence | Villages |
|---|---|
| 1,000 | Kaihsienkung |
| 350 | Dragalevtsy, Shamirpet |
| 240 | San Ildefonso |
| 140 | Romonom, Hilltown |
| 60 | Suye Mura, Silwa |
| 4 | Chan Kom, New Peri |

Table 11, however, does not provide a complete picture. In the first place, it gives minimal figures. For example, in those villages to which a minimum age of 60 years is assigned, there is no evidence for the founding dates. All that is known is that the villages have existed for several generations. In the second place, the two youngest villages have a much older social history than their physical ages suggest. New Peri was formed almost completely from Old Peri which, again figuring minimally, would place it in the next older category. Chan Kom, on the other hand, was formed mainly from Ebtun, an established village from the same culture, but still one of undetermined age. Chan Kom, further, was still in existence as late as fifteen years after the initial study (Redfield 1950). This would make its "continuance" extend for approximately one generation, if a generation is defined as the age of the parents at the birth of their first child.

Briefly, then, the evidence for all except two of these villages attests to their ability to persist for several generations or more, and both exceptions were several years old when studied.

SENTIMENT

*Ethnocentrism.* All villagers felt that theirs was the most desirable of all villages or that the village was exclusively theirs, to be actively protected from others. Sentiments concerning the village were often explicitly described. According to the village inhabitants, New Peri, Romonom, Chan Kom, Hilltown (Hatch, 1948), Dragalevtsy, and Silwa were each felt to be better than their neighbors, growing in power or prestige, the center of the universe, or simply a village of which one could be proud.

The only evidence for ethnocentrism in five of the villages studied was a tendency toward exclusion. The *buraku* of Suye Mura expressed milder forms of exclusiveness in stylized parties (reminiscent of potlatch), in other ritual activities, and in attempts of the *buraku* to out-perform each other generally. Village ceremonies and property in San Ildefonso and Kaih-sienkung are reserved strictly for the use of the villagers. San Ildefonso probably carries this feeling to greater extremes with a cultural emphasis on secretiveness. Shamirpet is similar; Dube notes a considerable reserve in initial dealings of the villagers with outsiders, describing their behavior as constricted, suspicious, and guarded.

Ethnocentrism is not restricted only to the village. All villages displayed ethnocentrism toward either some smaller or larger group. In six cases—San Ildefonso, Romonom, Chan Kom, Hilltown, Dragalevtsy, and Silwa—there was a hierarchy of ethnocentrism. The people were loyal to some village sub-group, to the village, and to some larger society which included the village. Kinship loyalty supplements village loyalty in Kaihsienkung and Shamirpet. Shamirpet also possesses castes which cut across village lines. There is no information in Kaih-sienkung of loyalty to the larger society.

No subvillage loyalty is mentioned in other folk villages. But though the authors writing of Suye Mura and New Peri do not speak of a universal loyalty to family, such loyalty seems reasonable. Consequently, all of the folk villages possess ethnocentrism which begins in some village subgroup and includes the village, and all villages except Kaihsienkung extend this ethnocentrism to a larger social system.

*Awareness.* This, and the component to follow, homogeneity and solidarity, were troublesome to classify. They are not sentiments so much as they are the bases of sentiments. Awareness means what the term implies—the villagers know that their village exists. In a sense, awareness is related to ethnocentrism: one is surely aware of that toward which his ethnocentrism is directed. But the evidence for awareness simply indicates knowledge or recognition—factors which can give rise to ethnocentrism and other sentiments but which themselves remain affectively neutral.

Thus, each village has a distinctive name given by the inhabitants and used by them to refer to the village as a unit. Each village also has a headman (chief, mayor, etc.), except for Kaihsienkung (which has two) and New Peri (where the struggle with the New Guinea government confused matters as to whether their government, which did exist, had legal authority). There is evidence also that each village acts as a unit.

*Homogeneity and solidarity.* This component is included as a sentiment for roughly the same reason as awareness was included—it makes a certain type of sentiment possible. The sentiment is, of course, that which Durkheim called "mechanical solidarity." It may even be useful to identify this sentiment with consciousness of kind, as is suggested by T. Lynn Smith (1953, p. 36). To do this, it must be demonstrated that the villagers recognize their homogeneity. Certainly, they recognize their identity in that they are aware of the existence of their village and are ethnocentric about it. Regardless of whether they specifically recognize their homogeneity, however, one can talk with some assurance about the degree to which villagers were alike. (Parenthetically, it should be remarked that homogeneity cuts across many of the components, particularly the institutions.)

Absolute homogeneity is a state seldom if ever reached, a condition in which all parts are exactly the same. Practical homogeneity is more common; in it, all parts are approximately similar. Majority homogeneity is most frequently found, and for operational purposes it may be defined as that condition in which 50 per cent or more of the parts are approximately similar in reference to a given trait (50 per cent is used simply because it is a convenient figure).

The opposite of homogeneity, of course, is heterogeneity. There are essentially two types. Random heterogeneity has no apparent order—in contrast to structured heterogeneity, in which there is some order. This division does not exhaust the logical possibilities, but it will do for our needs.

| | |
|---|---|
| Absolute homogeneity | XXXXXXXXXXXXXXX<br>XXXXXXXXXXXXXXX<br>XXXXXXXXXXXXXXX<br>XXXXXXXXXXXXXXX |
| Practical homogeneity | Xo Xo Xo Xo Xo Xo Xo Xo<br>Xo Xo Xo Xo Xo Xo Xo Xo<br>Xo Xo Xo Xo Xo Xo Xo Xo<br>Xo Xo Xo Xo Xo Xo Xo Xo |
| Majority homogeneity | Xo Xo Xo Xo Xo Xo o o o o<br>oX oX oX oX o X o o o o o o<br>Xo Xo Xo Xo Xo Xo o o o o<br>oX oX oX oX oX o o o o o o |
| Heterogeneity (random) | Xo Xo Xo Xo o o o o o o o o<br>oX oX oX oX oX oX oX oX<br>Xo o o o o o o o o o o o o o<br>oX oX oX oX XXXXXXXXX |
| Heterogeneity (structured) | Xo Xo XXX XX o o o o o o o o<br>Xo Xo XXXXXo o o o o o o o<br>Xo Xo XXXXXo o o o o o o o<br>Xo Xo XXXXXo o o o o o o o |

*Fig. 4*—Types of Homogeneity and Heterogeneity

An important point in understanding these concepts is that the organization of parts has as much or more to do with the degree of homogeneity as the number of qualities involved.

In speaking of homogeneity, especially social homogeneity, one is also speaking of an essential ingredient of Durkheim's mechanical solidarity, a unity which results from possessing common traits, objectives, and experiences. The opposite kind of unity is based upon differences, especially those based on the division of labor and a consequent mutual interdependence.

Since one cannot always be certain of the presence of solidarity, even when he has data which show the presence of homogeneity, conditions of homogeneity will be referred to as mechanical homogeneity.

Differences alone do not necessarily signify organic solidarity.

Examples may be found whenever the parts of a whole are differentiated from each other but the differentiation accomplishes the same end in each case, such as having different religions or different games. The name given here to such a condition is mechanical heterogeneity.

*Table 12.* Relation between homogeneity and solidarity

| Type of homogeneity or heterogeneity | Descriptive term | Durkheim's term |
|---|---|---|
| Homogeneity (any type) | Mechanical homogeneity | Mechanical solidarity |
| Heterogeneity (either type) | Mechanical heterogeneity | None |
| Heterogeneity (structured) | Organic heterogeneity | Organic solidarity |

On the other hand, a differentiation which requires the parts of a group to strive toward different ends such that the parts may in this manner contribute to the whole, Durkheim referred to as organic solidarity. The division of labor is the chief form— a farmer and a carpenter are doing different kinds of work, work which will eventuate in different kinds of products. Both, further, will contribute to the existence of the larger society of which they are a part. In order to preclude making unwarranted assumptions concerning feelings about solidarity, this type of differentiation will be called organic heterogeneity.

Table 12 shows why a degree of heterogeneity is not necessarily equivalent to a given type of solidarity. Structured heterogeneity, per se, does not signify organic solidarity. In order to pass from heterogeneity to solidarity, one must have a division of labor that contributes to the entity that is being considered.

None of the villages were completely homogeneous. Majority homogeneity is the chief form. Further, some degree of organic heterogeneity was found in each of the institutions. Nevertheless, there were several areas in which homogeneity prevailed. First, family affiliation was the universal rule. Rarely is there evidence of anyone without some kinship affiliation in the village. Second, agricultural pursuits (including fishing) form the means of livelihood for most villagers in all the villages. And finally, in each village the majority of the residents were either born in the village or in the immediate vicinity.

Three institutions displayed mechanical heterogeneity. In several villages, families could be either nucleated or extended. Polygyny, further, was practiced in only three villages—and was rare in these. Most villages were homogeneous also in religion. There were three exceptions: Romonom had a Catholic and a Protestant church, but the islanders attached little significance to the difference. Hilltown later in its history had three Protestant denominations. Shamirpet had the most extreme religious variation: a Muslim minority in the dominant Hindu system. Finally, most villages had the same type of government, but decided factions were observable in three. Romonom was at one time split in two political districts, though the rift had disappeared at the time the village was studied. San Ildefonso and Hilltown experienced religious schisms which provided the basis for their political factions.

Organic heterogeneity involves more differentiation than does the mechanical type. But this type of heterogeneity, though found in all institutions, was never extensively developed. Families were mainly limited to age, sex, and kinship statuses. The economic division of labor proceeded largely along familial lines. There was additional occupational specialization in all of the villages, but often it was quite rudimentary and never did it involve more than half of the village (that is, over half of each village was engaged in the same type of occupational pursuits in addition, of course, to the familial division of labor). Similarly, all villages had a priest or religious leader, but few additional specialties, and the government was composed of a ruler, sometimes a council, and little else besides the citizenry of the village. Mothers and fathers shared primary responsibility for the socialization of their daughters and their sons, respectively, and all villages had schools and schoolteachers. Stratification was associated with the division of labor in direct proportion to the importance of stratification in the village. Thus, in Chan Kom there were no great differences between the duties or responsibilities of the various families, whereas in Shamirpet such differences were extreme.

The presence of heterogeneity in the institutions is thus quite apparent. But a qualifying feature is more striking—the heterogeneity for the most part is only barely enough of a difference for one even to speak of heterogeneity. There is seldom more than one type of specialist associated with any single institution. Compare, for example, the village priest or minister and his followers (the pattern approximated by most villagers) with the denominational hierarchies, lay officials, members, non-members and even administrative, preaching, and teaching specializations found in more urbanized congregations.

Homogeneity, therefore, though never absolute, is still prevalent in the villagers' family and economic life and in their place of birth. Heterogeneity, on the other hand, is universal, but it is also little more than rudimentary.

UNIVERSAL INSTITUTIONS

By an institution is meant: "*established forms or conditions of procedure* characteristic of group activity" (MacIver and Page, 1949, p. 15; see also Parsons, 1960, p. 197). An institution is also an organization of norms. Both of these definitions are treated as synonymous. Thus, though norms are discussed as they exist in a more organized context—that is, as institutions—we are nevertheless dealing with norms as one of Homans' elements of the human group (1950).

*Family units.* There is much variation around a hard core of consistency. All villages have institutionalized a sanctioned union of man and woman for sexual relations and childrearing. (Polygamy, as will be noted later, is rare.) The family is also a food production, processing, and consuming unit. Further, wherever the married couple live together, authority is always vested in some male, usually the father.

Kinship in the villages studied displays a decided ability to hold people in the locality. This is shown in two ways. First, except in Hilltown, New Peri, and San Ildefonso, families are either extended or with definite tendencies in that direction. The tendencies may either refer to parents staying with children or the children living in separate dwellings near the parents. Thus, persons related by marriage, birth, or adoption have a propensity to live near each other. One might assume that the exogamy would destroy this relation, but on the contrary, in all four villages where exogamy was practiced to a significant extent, patrilocal settlement (living with or near the father) was the rule (see Table 13). Second, localism is reinforced by customs requiring one of the spouses to settle in the village of some parent, usually the father. The relation of extended families to patri- (or matri-) localism holds for seven of ten villages. Further, it should be noted that the analysis stresses the extremes of the extent to which kinship localizes its members. The tendency toward localism is present in all the villages.

Probably the most common feature which folk villagers share, aside from their village membership, is that they are affiliated with some family within the village. Practically all adults are married (or have been) in the villages of Suye Mura, Chan Kom, Dragalevtsy, Shamirpet, and Silwa. It is probable that some

*Table 13.* Variations in selected familial traits

|  | Nucleated | Extended | Exogamy | Patri-archal | Patri-lineal | Patri-local | Polygyny |
|---|---|---|---|---|---|---|---|
| New Peri | X |  |  | X |  |  |  |
| San Ildefonso | X |  |  | X | X |  |  |
| Hilltown | X |  |  | X | X |  |  |
| Chan Kom | X | X |  | X |  | X* | X |
| Romonom | X | X |  | X* | X* | X* | X |
| Dragalevtsy | X | X | X | X | X | X |  |
| Kaihsienkung |  | X | X | X | X | X |  |
| Suye Mura |  | X | X | X | X | X |  |
| Shamirpet |  | X | X | X | X | X | X |
| Silwa |  | X |  | X | X | X† | X |

\* Matriarchal, matrilineal, and matrilocal.
† Matrilocalism immediately following marriage, followed by patrilocalism.
An X denotes the presence of the trait; its absence, that the trait is either absent or only weakly developed.

Romonom men are not married, and 43 men of Kaihsienkung who are 25 years of age and over are still single (the total population there is almost 1,500). In both of these villages, however, all women are married and, further, the importance of the lineage or extended family is as strong or stronger in these villages than it is in any others in the study.

Information is lacking for Hilltown, New Peri, and San Ildefonso, but there are no accounts of any substantial number of unmarried among those who would be eligible. Further, especially in Hilltown's early days, the family was so important that it is difficult to comprehend how anyone could function adequately in the village without some kinship connection: "the family was the only agency for teaching of farming and housekeeping; reading and writing, and was the indispensable interpreter of religion" (Hatch, 1948, p. 94). There is every reason to believe that the other villages are similarly affected.

Wherever the evidence is clear, then, practically all villagers are affiliated with some family system within the village. Even in the minority of villages for which no data are provided, not only is there no contradictory information, but the central importance of the family in precisely these villages makes their agreement with the rule highly probable. Thus, everyone may not be related to everyone else, but they are almost always related to some villagers.

Usually, descent follows authority; that is, a system of tracing kinship will be structured in a manner which agrees with the system of assigning family rulers. Thus, patrilineal families (where descent is traced through the father's line) are always patriarchal (under the father's authority). But the reverse does not hold: Chan Kom is decidedly patriarchal but traces descent through both sides of the family (bilaterally) with only tendencies towards patrilinearity. Romonom agrees with the principle, although there the system is matrilineal and the maternal side of the family has some authority over the children (specifically, in the role of the mother's brother). Therefore, although some male always has authority, either male or female lineage can be emphasized. (Complete information does not exist for New Peri.)

There are several variations worthy of note. The sanctioning of sex relations in the marital union does not necessarily exclude the possibility of other partners. In New Peri and Romonom, extramarital unions were at least marked (though whether they were practiced by the majority is an open question). Nevertheless, such unions were not approved, at least not by the other spouse. Even in Romonom, where both premarital and extramarital sexual customs were most lenient, adultery was recognized both as grounds for divorce and as a subject for gossip.

Polygyny was found in three and perhaps in four villages (no polyandry was encountered). In all cases it was rare. Shamirpet probably had more plural marriages than any other village: seven Hindu and three Muslim homes were polygynous out of more than 500 households. Multiple marriages were also listed in Chan Kom (which had but one) and Romonom (where the custom continued only among a few). The practice was permitted in Silwa but no reference was given to any specific family.

All in all, once the stable core of consistency is isolated, the extent of variation is impressive. Families may or may not be extended, they may practice exogamy or they may not, males may be emphasized in the lineage and/or in localism or they may not, and monogamy is not the only santioned marital union. The existence of the family as a social, economic, and biological unit seems the most important thing, followed by a tendency to retain kinfolk within the village.

*Primary economics.* There is probably almost as much similarity and more variation among the economic institutions as there is in those of the family. All villages, with the exception of New Peri, grew some form of crop. New Peri was primarily a fishing village, and fishing was also of importance in Romonom and Kaihsienkung. When fishing and agriculture are combined under the heading of primary production industries, all the folk villages are seen to rely more heavily on primary production than on all other industries combined. No village, however, was exclusively productive. Distributive industries (primarily trading and commerce) and service industries (government work, repair services, personal services, etc.) were found in all villages, but variation was marked. For example, everyone in New Peri probably did some trading but no specialist was mentioned. There was one schoolteacher. On the other hand, approximately one-fourth of the villagers in Shamirpet relied primarily on distributive and service industries.

The level of living was low. None of the villages had any marked surpluses. Luxury goods are few, even in Romonom, where obtaining food requires hardly more effort than climbing a coconut palm. Where levels of living are low, where cash money is scarce, and where most persons perform the same kind of labor, one would expect the custom of mutual aid. This expectation is verified in all villages.

Forms of property relationships are quite varied. Communal, familial, lineage, and individual forms of possession are found, both in their pure states and mixed substantially with other types of property. In Chan Kom, the village as a whole or the federal government owned the land. Real property in Romonom generally belonged to the lineage or some part of it. In Silwa, the farmer, himself, was the land owner. Individual ownership was supplemented by absentee landlords in Kaihsienkung and by communal meadows, pastures, and forests in Dragalevtsy. Though information even on real property—let alone all property—is far from systematic, the diversity is nevertheless impressive. Individual possession of land is most frequent, but it is not universal (Chan Kom lacked it), at times it is overshadowed by other forms, and it seldom exists alone.

One additional variation deserves mention. Never did more than two villages rely primarily on the same form of subsistence (fish, corn, rice, wheat, etc.—see Table 1, Chapter 2, p. 28). This variation is important in that it emphasizes the differing ecological conditions under which the folk village has developed.

The pervasiveness of the economic institution must be stressed. Economic considerations figure prominently in most of the elements of village life. The villagers perhaps spend as much or more time in making their living than they do in any other institutionalized activity. The family may provide the only exception, and in many ways it functions as an economic unit. Even the villagers' religion is heavily concerned with agricultural things, the remaining institutions similarly. Of course, insofar as economic concerns penetrate other elements of village life, to that extent these other elements find their way into economics. The relation is undoubtedly reciprocal, but it is nowhere more in evidence than in the economic institutions.

*Religion.* Generalizations concerning religion in the villages are more dependent on the peculiar cultural, local, and historical conditions. In other words, religion does not seem to be intrinsic to village social organization and appears more adapted to the folk village than vice versa.

Each village contained one of the world religions: Christianity (most frequent, found in six villages), Buddhism (Kaihsienkung and the *buraku* of Suye Mura), and Islam (Silwa and Shamirpet). But Shamirpet, though it includes an Islamic or Muslim sect, is predominantly Hindu, and Hinduism does not have as wide a distribution as the other religions. Shamirpet also highlights the fact that the world religion is not necessarily the exclusive one.

Each of these major religions (including here Hinduism) was rather drastically modified to suit local or cultural needs, including association with a system of magic. Though both magic and religion involve supernatural power or beings, there are numerous distinctions (see Davis, 1949). One of the simplest criteria hinges on the factor of control. Magic is pseudo-scientific in the sense that if the right charm is recited under the correct conditions, then the spirits must obey and the desired event will come to pass. If the charm is not successful, it means that one of the participants did something wrong or that some-one else had a more potent magic which overpowered the "original" charm. The magic itself was not wrong—the people involved had somehow erred. This type of belief is contrasted with the religious approach in which one can only ask or peti-tion the god(s) to do what he wants—he cannot control the supernatural. Or, further, one does not even ask—he can only show respect, veneration, awe, or worship.

This distinction can be made for each of the villages. As mentioned, no information existed for Hilltown, but anyone familiar with even contemporary American customs of "bad" and "good" luck would find it hard to doubt the existence of magic there, also. In addition, Hilltowners were Congregation-alists (Puritans) initially and to some extent throughout their history, a denomination which waged an active war against magic (witches) and thereby acknowledged its existence. All villagers therefore supplemented theology with magic, thereby gaining a feeling of some control over the outcome.

Other modifications of the world religions in the ten villages can be roughly described by means of three patterns. In the most common, the world and native religions are integrated. Often, there is a fair amount of give and take. In San Ildefonso and Chan Kom, Roman Catholicism is superimposed on the native religion, but the native religion continues to flourish. Similar changes occur for Buddhism in Kaihsienkung and Shintoism in Suye Mura. New Peri, however, goes a step further. The residents had become Catholic converts, but in reintegrat-ing their culture along Western lines, Catholicism was re-interpreted to fit their newly conceived view of the universe. The new belief is neither Catholicism nor the old religion but an amalgam of both with an addition of features which came purely from the recent history of the village. In Shamirpet, although Islam has remained a minority religion, the local variety of

Hinduism has mingled with regional religious forms of worship.

The second pattern, represented only by Hilltown, pertains to a world religion which, instead of being supplemented by another, has been drastically modified by local cultural and historical forces. Hilltown was originally Congregational but early in the nineteenth century, the villagers joined others in New England in acknowledging the newly developed Unitarianism. Within a relatively short time, the Unitarians became so powerful that they dominated the local government. Finally, Methodism was added. In this development, a typically American (U.S.) pattern is witnessed—a multiplication of denominations within the Protestant tradition. Hilltown, then, differs from the first pattern in creating new forms from old instead of fusing the old with the new.

The third and final pattern is one in which a world religion has largely overshadowed the old. Three villages are represented. In both Muslim Silwa and Eastern-Orthodox-Catholic Dragalevtsy, the villagers no longer clearly recognize the distinction between the old and the new beliefs, the fusion has become so thorough. Romonom has become Christian, but Christian with certain hints of the first two patterns. Both Catholic and "Protestant" churches (denomination unknown) are represented on the island, and the native beliefs have to a large extent fallen into disuse. The islanders, however, see little difference between the two churches and even shuttle back and forth as they feel the need of change.

Thus, although all villages have representatives of the world religions, these religions are never accepted in pure form. They are supplemented with magic and modified according to the villagers' cultural demands. But if the world religion does not remain unmodified, it nevertheless retains enough of its characteristics to be recognizable. Further, it represents an influence and a contact which the villager has with the outside world. (Hinduism must be included here.) Religion is never the sole contact with the larger society, but it is a contact and one which the villagers are reported to consider among the more important. Never, therefore, does religion remain purely localistic.

*Government.* Each folk village has a well-defined system of government. Most authority is held by a chief, mayor, or headman (occasionally, headmen) or his council. Invariably, the headman combines in his office the roles of judge and executive. Legislative functions vary, but usually there is little to legislate. Rule by custom holds sway, at least for most villages.

The structure of authority is institutionalized in that it persists in the forms noted above and is accepted by the people. Some members may not approve of the person in authority, but the structure, itself, remains unchallenged. This condition is most evident on Romonom where the people have an hereditary system of chieftainship. Even under American supervised elections, the hereditary chieftain was "elected" regardless of whether the people thought him the most fit for the office. Similarly, Hilltowners overthrew the old rule of the Congregationalists, but they did so within the structure of township government. And in San Ildefonso, though the south plaza (faction) did not approve of the governor of the north plaza, they also realized that there was nothing they could do about it as long as he held the symbolic "cane of office." He was their legal ruler, and all knew it.

These variations amount to little more than that all villages had a governing system, that there was neither anarchy nor complete democracy. Beyond such a statement, one could always find villages which were clear exceptions.

The rule of tradition was heavy in most of the villages. However, New Peri was in the process of abandoning its traditional ways in favor of Western models. And the Hilltowners were able to unseat the traditional Congregational rule in favor of the Unitarians. A distinction should be made here between structure and content—that is, that part of a pattern of norms which remains unchanged over a span of time (the structure) must be distinguished from relatively minor variations (the content) which take place without modifying the larger pattern. The Hilltowners retained their structure of township government throughout the latter eighteenth and through the nineteenth century. But in unseating the Congregationalists, they radically changed the content, not only by making new beliefs more important than the old, but also by destroying the earlier homogeneity. Similarly, in San Ildefonso, though the village was splitting, no new form of government was instituted. Tradition ruled supreme even in the process of schism. The emerging split amounted only to the formation of a new village (a formation incidentally which was never completed).

Usually there was no more than one chief official, but there were two in Kaihsienkung, and from one to three in the *buraku* of Suye Mura. Often the village head was elected and often unanimously, but the position was hereditary in Silwa and for all practical purposes in Romonom, and in Dragalevtsy it was appointed by the state government. Finally, though often the headman ruled with the help of a formal council, such councils were absent in Dragalevtsy (where they had once existed), in Romonom, and (though the investigator does not make this entirely clear) apparently in Kaihsienkung.

It should be noted, however, that though formal councils may be absent, there is never a case of a ruler who was entirely unresponsive to the people. In fact, except in Dragalevtsy, the headman generally ruled through active consultation with the general population. Dragalevtsy is, in this case, clearly atypical. First, the village council had been disbanded by the outside society. Second, the village mayor, though appointed, mingled closely with the people and was sensitive to their needs. When he attempted to dictate to them, they responded by a quiet withdrawal of efficiency—even to the point of non-attendance at assigned meetings. The Communists altered this situation to some extent, but not completely.

Government, then, is uniform among villages only in the sense of there being a division of labor between ruler and ruled and in giving the ruler rather general powers. However, the division of labor is not sharp. The villagers tend to govern themselves. Some outside society can drastically alter this condition—by, say, destroying the village (as in Kaihsienkung) or by appointing the headman—but these changes represent extraneous forces. Other than these patterns, governments varied markedly and even qualitatively in their structure.

## INSTITUTIONS OF PROCESS

The organizations of norms that are here called institutions of process are not always regarded by sociologists as institutions. Whether they are distributed on a worldwide basis, as is argued for the universal institutions, is not at issue here, since in all of the folk villages studied each of these practices proceeds according to a set of recognized rules. Thus, they are institutions. They also conform to the general concept of processes as types of interaction or social change. Thus, mutual aid is a type of co-operation, stratification is measured by the process of vertical mobility, socialization is regarded as a process in its own right, and recreation may be viewed as an aesthetic process—a type of social behavior engaged in at least partly because it gives pleasure.

Care must be taken to distinguish processes which are found in the villages but which follow no rules, such as conflict, from those to be considered here, which always appear in some insti-tutionalized form.

*Mutual aid.* This institution is an organization of norms re-quiring village members to contribute aid among themselves. No one builds up specific credits or debits. The aid is never paid for directly with cash, though cash loans are sometimes in-volved. Whenever there arise specific cash payments, even in the form of interest, mutual aid in its pure sense is no longer en-countered.

Of course, there are cases in which villagers may keep a care-ful mental record of who gives what, when, and how. But this practice, when found, is probably predicated on the feeling that such accounts will prove of value *if* the occasion to reciprocate should arise; *should* the need arise, aid is often rendered without hope of specific return. Persons who do not always cooperate will not necessarily be denied, but their reluctance will be known, nonetheless.

Thus, mutual aid is diffuse in its goals but specific in its source. It is particularly in the *source* of aid that mutual aid is an institution—a villager expects help from his fellow villagers. On the other hand, mutual aid remains diffuse in its conditional quality. The emphasis is on help when needed, not on what one can buy, for few villagers can buy very much. Mutual aid may, in fact, be described as non-contractual cooperation.

Mutual aid is a practice common within nuclear families. But in all the folk villages, it extended *beyond* the nuclear families to larger kin-groups and non-kin village members. Greater pre-cision on this point is not possible due to lack of information. In Table 14, for example, some folk villages have mutual aid on a neighborhood basis, some on a village-level basis, and some on both. However, one cannot ascertain whether any village truly lacked aid on a neighbor- or village-level basis. Even with this sketchy information, however, mutual aid can be seen to be an institutionalized activity common to the folk village as a whole or some significant segment of it.

*Table 14.* Variations in the description of extent of mutual aid

|  | *Among neighbors* | *In village as a whole* |
|---|---|---|
| Suye Mura |  | X |
| New Peri |  | X |
| Shamirpet |  | X |
| Romonom |  | X |
| San Ildefonso | X | X |
| Dragalevtsy | X | X |
| Chan Kom | X | X |
| Hilltown | X |  |
| Kaihsienkung | X |  |
| Silwa | X |  |

Mutual aid, of course, is primarily an economic institution in all the villages. It functions to insure that one can continue to make a living in spite of uncertainties. But quite often, and perhaps always, it is more than that. The principles of mutual aid extend to religion in San Ildefonso, to the aid of children and wives in New Peri, to public works in Romonom and Chan Kom, to marriage arrangements in Chan Kom, and to recreation in Hilltown. Also, specifically, in Suye Mura, Hilltown, Kaihsienkung, and Dragalevtsy, times of helping one's neighbors are times for recreation as well. One makes a game of help, as it were; if not during work, then after it. Whether this extra-economic mutual aid exists also in Shamirpet and Silwa is unknown. But for at least eight of the ten folk villages studied, mutual aid is more than an economic institution.

There is marked variation in the importance of mutual aid in the villages. Chan Kom, on the one hand, probably institutionalized this pattern to the greatest degree. All adult males were supposed to contribute labor for the village. No one was paid, but no one was exempt. On the other hand, mutual aid in Romonom, though well developed, existed largely within lineages. Mutual aid for the village as a whole, that is, inter-lineage cooperation, was perhaps accentuated more by the

U.S. authorities than by the villagers. As Gladwin and Sarason noted, this cooperation "is rather vaguely felt to be good for the island and in any event is accepted as inevitable" (1953, p. 138).

Though Chan Kom and Romonom are probably the two extremes in commitment to mutual aid, comparisons are difficult to make. In the first place, mutual aid is understandably difficult to quantify. And second, variations between the villages are probably too small to reveal any great differences.

Mutual aid has been contrasted with contractual relationships. An assessment of the importance of this contrast cannot properly be attempted without a standard of comparison. That standard is supplied by the cities.

*Stratification.* Since there is some variation in the literature, a few words concerning the meaning of stratification are necessary. First, status, or the differential evaluation of people, must be distinguished from stratification, or the tendency for statuses to form layers (see Mayer, 1955). One way in which layers are formed occurs when statuses are linked to the family. The status of one member (usually the father) thereby becomes the status of all. This may be called "reflected status." The children, in receiving the status of the parent (they have no other status), thereby become vehicles in the future transmission of the system of stratification.

In at least two cases, and possibly in three, the villagers (or the investigator who is describing them) proclaim their equality, but one can observe status differences in their behavior, differences which are also attached to their families. Since one of the investigators, Redfield, denies the existence of classes under this situation, it is necessary that we examine the evidence in greater detail. Redfield presents his case as follows:

The words written about the village in 1931 on this point might stand to describe the situation in 1948: "There are no social classes. . . . Differences in status are not conferred by birth; some families are more powerful than others because the individuals separately enjoy status and because they cooperate with one another; but social superiority is not conferred by one surname rather than another. Nor are any prerogatives transmitted by inheritance or succession." It is true that the differences between one individual or family and another with regard to either wealth or acquaintance with the city are somewhat greater now than they were in 1931, but now as then, "there are no terms to describe such differences in sophistication within the community and no differences in costume or occupation that might symbolize such differences in status." A man may be described as "rich" or as "having property," but we heard no reference, with respect to the villagers, to "the rich" or "the poor"....

... At any rate, there is no tendency to exclusiveness on the part of the relatively rich or the relatively cultivated. ... Several of the marriages of recent years took place between a daughter or a son of one of the three or four most influential and wealthy families and a son or daughter of a family newly come to Chan Kom or of a family with little property, and most of these marriages were admired and fully solemnized [1950, pp. 76–78].

In other words: (1) There are status differences between families; (2) these differences have increased through the years; (3) the villagers do not refer directly to these statuses; and (4) status differences are no apparent bar to interaction—even to marriage. Thus, Redfield's terms and the terms used here are not quite the same. There are strata in Chan Kom, but the strata are not too important to the people. Some persons would even use the term "class." Redfield does not. But it seems to take more effort to explain away the existence of strata than to admit them. (Redfield came closer to describing strata in Chan Kom in a later book, *The Folk Culture of Yucatán*, 1941, p. 81.)

Hsiao-Tung Fei in his account of Kaihsienkung gives the impression that strata are somewhat more important: ". . . the unequal distribution of wealth in the village is not expressed in a marked variation in the level of daily livelihood. Only a few persons have special and valuable clothes and there are no essential differences in housing and food" (1939, p. 120). But in speaking of one of the village headmen he notes: "Those who are known in the community to be rich will respond to a justifiable appeal for help in order to show generosity and to avoid public criticism. For example, Chou has gained much prestige by subscribing to more than ten [financial aid] societies" (p. 269). And again: "It is true that a child of a poor family has less chance of attaining the position since headmanship has no direct economic reward and requires rather long and expensive preparation (to attain the necessary standard of literacy), but wealth alone does not give power or prestige" (p. 108). To be sure, wealth, alone is not enough, but it is needed, it makes a difference in status, and this difference is attached to families. Again, we would say there were classes.

The situation in Silwa is intermediate between Chan Kom and Kaihsienkung. Ammar writes, "Furthermore the feeling of equalitarianism is so striking in this community that any schematic class-division is very difficult to apply . . ." (1954, p. 39). He notes the extensive similarity in the lives of these farmers, and adds, "Yet all does not mean that they are entirely identical, and the differences are usually in quantity and not in kind. The headman of the village—'Omda'—may have more clothes than others, but his clothes are the same type of clothes tailored in the same style; he may have a larger house than his neighbor but both are built in the same style with the same kind of furniture . . ." (p. 40). The author remarks elsewhere that the office of "Omda" has been in one family for the last fifty years and today is considered hereditary. Thus, although the precise number of strata in Silwa is not known, there are at least two— the family of the Omda and that of other villagers.

It is significant that in Chan Kom and Silwa the villagers firmly proclaim their equality while behaving otherwise. Such a situation has been portrayed with particular force for American society by West (1945) in *Plainsville, U.S.A.* San Ildefonso follows the same pattern: ". . . all men are considered of equal worth except when acting in some official capacity, and even the Governor, once he ceases to hold office, is no better than anyone else" (Whitman, 1947, pp. 25–26). But, as in the other three villages, the evidence does not stop there. "In conclusion, there appears to be a correlation in the North Plaza between wealth and authority, while in the South Plaza, the more conventional of the two, this is less striking" (Whitman, 1947, p. 90). Even more important for our purposes are the following remarks: "Property is inherited within the family. The more important items are, by convention, land and houses" (Whitman, 1947, p. 91).

This lack of recognition—or avowal—of stratified differences should be taken as a datum, itself. It means that the people are either unaware of the significance of the distinctions they make, or that they do not attach great importance to them, or that the differences are subordinated to other things. In any of these cases, the lack of the use of such distinctions clearly weakens whatever degree of structure the strata may have. But the evidence that non-recognition destroys the strata is lacking.

The villages previously discussed display the lowest degrees of stratification. The ranking of the ruling lineages on Romonom was reported to have been "mild." In New Peri, the hereditary distinctions had been somewhat (though not completely) disturbed during the course of its social upheaval. All six of these villages, then, have strata, and the strata are institutionalized; that is, as a minimum, some people are treated with more deference than others. Much of the weakness in stratification can perhaps be attributed to the fact that, in all ten villages, differences between the people cannot be great in view of the fairly uniformly low level of living. Though there are distinctions in status, even the most powerful, prestigeful, and/or wealthiest are not too far from their poorer neighbors either in physical or social distance.

The remaining folk villages reveal more distinct systems of stratification. Dragalevtsy has at least three classes—the intelligentsia (mayor, priest, teachers), the artisans, and the peasants. Hilltown also recognized three classes (though class lines were not precise): a small upper class, large middle class, and a lower class made up partly of hired men and partly of French-Canadians and Nova Scotians who had come to work in the forests. The class groupings of the Suye Mura *buraku* are a mixture of the old *samurai*, farmer, artisan, and merchant classes (the feudal lord has apparently disappeared) together with new groupings based on wealth, "old" native families, and the prestigeful occupations of village officials and school teachers. In these villages, strata are important but not overbearing.

Shamirpet, with its caste structure, is another extreme. Fifteen castes (or subcastes) are grouped into seven prestige layers, each separated by limitations in social interaction. Intermarriage is prohibited between any of the fifteen castes. There is also a Brahmin caste of uncertain status. The Muslims are outside of the caste structure. These imperfections in the system, even in an area notorious for the extremes of its strata distinctions, form an interesting commentary on the failure of people to group themselves according to theoretically neat schemes.

Social layers, then, are present in all the villages. Usually, the structuring is not pronounced, but the variation is extreme. The villagers may not recognize the strata at all. Accordingly, there is undoubtedly something associated with the organization of a folk village which prompts stratification, but in view of the variation, one cannot say that the folk village, per se, is the final determinant in the formation of strata, or vice versa. (See Barber, 1961.)

*Socialization.* The process of socialization is achieved in all villages by the use of school, familial and other facilities. All the villages had schools, but there were important variations. First, none of the systems were indigenous to the village except that of Hilltown and, possibly, New Peri. Hilltown both built its own schools and chose the schoolmasters. The tradition of having schools, however, certainly did not originate in Hilltown. In New Peri, both the school and teacher were products of the village, but the school was conceived as a way of incorporating Western society into the "New Way" of their life. Thus, the school was modeled along Western lines and was, accordingly, as much an import as in the other villages. Generally speaking, then, except in Hilltown, the school is not a thing of the village, and even in Hilltown, significant outside influences may be noted.

Further, the importance of the school in village life differs markedly. Illiteracy in Shamirpet was more than 95 per cent; it probably approached this figure in Chan Kom and was only somewhat lower in Silwa. According to Fei, the school was not regarded by the Kaihsienkung villagers as useful in everyday life. New Peri is intermediate between the above four villages (where literate education was *in* but hardly *of* the village) and the remaining five (which were literate for all practical purposes). The school in New Peri was considered an instrument for realizing the New Way. The hope of the people was in their children, and these they sent to school. The school, together with the schoolmaster, was largely of their own making. Their interest in education is therefore marked.

In both San Ildefonso and Romonom, the school was the creation of outside forces. But the people in the pueblo felt that they had to protect their children from the government school in order that the children might learn pueblo culture. (All were probably literate, however, and thus the force of the U.S. government was quite strong—the government school was one of the main sources of social change.) In Romonom, on the other hand, the school received more toleration.

For the remaining villagers—those in Suye Mura, Hilltown, and Dragalevtsy—schooling was an important part of their lives, not only in maintaining literacy but also in providing an accepted channel of communication between the village and the outside society.

Of course, in all of the villages there were activities which the children had to learn. But the methods of teaching the young were so closely interwoven with the rest of the villagers' life that many of the researchers employed the word "informal" in describing socialization patterns outside of the school. The word "informal," however, obscures some important considerations. Most important, probably, is the fact that primary responsibility for imparting the tradition of the village to its new "recruits" rested with the family. Since male dominance prevailed, it was not uncommon to find the father filling the role of chief disciplinarian. But the close biological and social attachment of child to mother resulted in her becoming probably more influential in the child's early life. It is misleading to claim that socialization is informal *and to that extent unstructured* merely because its functions are delegated to another institution. Socialization *is* structured, though it may lack a *special* structure, one that it possesses exclusively. The structure of socialization is always partly to be found in the family. But the last statement must be supplemented—nowhere is there evidence that the family performs this task alone.

Evidence is clear in seven of the villages that anyone may assist the parents in the socialization process. For example, in both the smallest and the largest villages (San Ildefonso and Silwa), non-familial villagers administer beatings to wayward children without consulting the parents. Therefore, in all except Suye Mura, Hilltown, and Kaihsienkung, socialization is truly a village affair, though the family is probably dominant; and the only reason for excepting these three villages is that evidence is not provided. But where one either knows or is aware of practically everyone else, where everyone is remarkably alike, and where even the government is sensitive to the things desired by the village as a whole, it would be virtually impossible for any village family to confine the socialization process to itself.

As would be expected where there exists a division of labor between the sexes, the task of teaching the boys their life's work is reserved for the fathers; the girls, for the mothers. Evidence is clear for this type of structuring in all villages except Suye Mura, New Peri, and Hilltown.

Thus, the structure of socialization (apart from the school) is as follows: The family plays the most important part, followed by other villagers, presumably anyone else (even children). Within the family, a further division of educational labor corresponds to the economic division. This structure is definitely present in most of the villages and probably in all.

Not only is there structuring of teaching roles, but there is structuring relative to what will be taught. Boys are to be taught men's work; girls, women's work. It is also possible that there is further patterning. In San Ildefonso, Suye Mura, Romonom, and Kaihsienkung, there are relatively well-defined expectations as to what is to be learned and at what time. Children are not regarded as simply ignorant adults. The villagers recognize developmental stages, stages when children cannot learn, stages when they can learn more, and stages when they can learn only special tasks. It is not clear to what extent these expectations prevail in the other villages.

There seems to be no other institutionalized method of teaching, but one must be careful in such an appraisal. Institutionalization is most visible in its sanctions, and these are apparently most often visible during times of deviance. But, since there are practically no deviants in these villages, one seldom learns how the villagers would react to other teaching methods. For example, Mead gives much attention to the learning of life roles by imitation and participation. She stresses the great amount of time which parents devote to teaching the children, patiently repeating a word as many as fifty or sixty times. What would happen if someone tried another method, such as telling the child to keep still or to go somewhere else? No one does, and sanctions accordingly remain invisible.

In Dragalevtsy, on the other hand, there was a reaction to deviance. When confronted with "newfangled" ideas of child rearing from the village doctor, one woman commented, "Are children gods or kings that older people should tremble over them?" (Sanders, 1949, p. 114). This remark, when linked with the pattern of expected child-submissiveness in this village, is obviously invoking a negative sanction. From other remarks by Sanders, a similar reaction from other women in the village appears probable. For example, regardless of their age, children were expected to show respect for the father; social distance was marked. Socialization in Dragalevtsy is authoritarian.

On the island of Romonom, institutionalized sanctions to childrearing are apparently absent in the village as a whole. Beatings are administered, but the cause for beatings as well as severity varies widely in different families. Similarly, though children are given much freedom, there is a point beyond which they may not stray. "This point again varies widely as determined by different parents, from an attempt to keep the children home practically all the time to almost complete unconcern over their whereabouts" (Gladwin and Sarason, 1953, p. 87). In the face of such variation, there are understandably no records of negative sanctions, and one is probably safe in concluding that there is an absence of norms governing methods of teaching.

Two generalizations concerning non-school socialization are possible. First, there is no common method of socialization. New Peri is "progressive," Dragalevtsy is authoritarian, and no method is discernible for Romonom. Second, socialization outside of the school is institutionalized to some degree in all of the villages. There are well-recognized educational goals, and different degrees of responsibility are assigned different persons in the socialization process.

*Recreation.* As was true also of stratification, the villagers occasionally minimized the importance of recreation. The residents of Silwa believe that games, singing, and related things are only for children and the very old. Yet, like the other institutions, recreation asserts itself in all villages, even in Silwa.

The activities which make up recreation include feasts and festivals, games (including gambling), music and songs, dances, and stories (including poems and plays). In its institutionalized forms, recreation may be at least partly defined as a patterned and pleasure-giving behavior performed in a group or in groups. One is tempted to say that recreation is performed for its own sake. But the same activity which is so performed may also be performed as a part of another institution. In fact, all forms of recreation mentioned above have been integrated with the religious institution in some of the villages, though they have also existed separately.

Feasts and festivals are the most universal type, including parties, banquets, and celebrations. All villages used food in their recreation, whether in the rather elaborate banquets of Suye Mura and the food contests on Romonom or as rewards for the players of certain games in San Ildefonso. Most commonly, such food-use appeared in festivals or celebrations, particularly in weddings and religious ceremonies.

Games were invariably played among adults and often among children. The particular type varied—gambling, cards, or athletic sports were found in all villages, though the precise nature of the games was not specified for Kaihsienkung. It is interesting that in Silwa, where recreation for adults was frowned upon, there were nevertheless at least two forms of adult games, one secular and one religious.

Music and songs constitute the third theme, though no mention is made of either musical instruments or songs for Hilltown; however, the close association of music with Christianity affords no doubt that the Hilltowners were no exception. Similarly, evidence is not provided for music in Kaihsienkung at the time of its study (though its presence was not denied), but there had been operas performed in the village in the past, attesting to a musical tradition. Finally, in Silwa, singing was permitted only for children, adolescents, and the aged, but when ceremonies demanded music (as, for example, at weddings), adolescent boys provided it. It should also be noted that musical instruments, other than the drum, were not always described (they were not noted in San Ildefonso), but where instruments were not mentioned, singing was.

One may conclude, therefore, that celebrating, playing, and singing are found as patterned, group-performed activities in all of the villages. Silwa forms the most interesting case—it constitutes no exception, though one gathers that it would like to: "the children's world which, being considered transitory, uneconomic, and even frivolous, is in most cases despised by the sober adults. To describe a grown-up's action as 'childish play' is to condemn it, and such a phrase is highly offensive and might lead to bitter altercation, even blows" (Ammar, 1954, p. 154).

Silwa's attitudes and the consequent reality form an interesting commentary on the power of recreation to persist even when it is ostensibly given a negative value.

In mentioning Silwa, one should also mention Suye Mura, where all five recreational types discussed above are found, and in addition the villagers have their own peculiar recreational form of the geisha. Suye Mura had more forms of recreation than any of the villages, though this difference in quantity may have been only a reflection of the researcher's interest.

No other recreational form was clearly universal and, curiously enough, that includes children's games. Redfield claims: "Until the school in very recent years introduced ball games and other games involving 'teams,' there were, in Chan Kom, no competitive games, not even races, jackstones, or marbles" (Redfield and Villa Rojas, 1934, p. 191). True, one does not necessarily have to compete in order to have institutionalized play, but Redfield does not mention any form of group play for children. If Chan Kom were the only exception, one might wonder. But there was no account given of such play for the children of Kaihsienkung; it was only mentioned that collecting grass to feed the sheep was congenial to them "because it permits a free run in the wild with their companions without any interference from the elders" (Fei, 1939, p. 37).

If it can be said that children's recreation is not necessarily institutionalized, then the sociological importance of recreation is emphasized. Since adult play is patterned, play is not merely functional for childhood irresponsibility. In its group form, it probably fulfills an important social role.

Dances are another form of recreation which were not universally mentioned—that is, no data are given for Hilltown, Shamirpet, Silwa, and Kaihsienkung. Stories, poems, and plays were encountered only occasionally, though here a different type of problem was raised. When is a tale a story and when is it a religious myth? Might there at times be no distinction? Since there were no completely satisfactory answers to these questions, no conclusions can be offered.

Commercialized recreation is available in most villages, if not all (information was absent for San Ildefonso, New Peri, and Romonom), but two points must be made: (1) Such recreation is generally of no consequence. Movies, for example, are noted as rare in Suye Mura and Silwa, and they were hardly mentioned for Chan Kom. (2) Commercialization is often no better than partial, even where it is present. The most pertinent examples are the tea shops in Kaihsienkung and the taverns in Dragalevtsy. These were commercial in that refreshments were purchased, but the refreshment was only a setting for the gossip (or "discussion") which was the major focus of attention and which, of course, was not paid for. Most villagers, then, are in contact with commercial recreation, and in some the influence is noticeably increasing (as in Suye Mura), but such activities are at best secondary and occasional.

Non-institutionalized recreation was, of course, present in all of the folk villages. Where social interaction is as intimate as it is in these villages, then gossip can hardly be ruled out (it has been called the twin sister of neighborhood) and neither can visiting. When sex is included in this category, then the importance of non-normative play bulks large—perhaps largest—in the villagers' lives.

An interesting question is posed by the above materials. Why is recreation so decisively institutionalized even where the people look down upon it and even where (in all villages) so much exists in unpatterned form? One can probably explain the existence of play in terms of the high-energy diets of humans and their extensively developed nervous systems, but such biological factors only explain play in the sense that man shares it with other mammals (see Kroeber, 1948). They do not explain its social and patterned nature. Villagers like to play, and they do so in groups and according to traditional forms. Recreation may be a more serious part of human society than is suggested by its inherent levity.

# B

# The Cities

The choice of the five cities was governed largely by the same criteria used for the folk villages: Relatively complete case studies were required, each from a different culture. The abundance of U.S. studies and the paucity of those from other cultures presented a mixed problem. Middletown was selected as one of the U.S. representatives because of its position in the literature and because of the intensity of the investigation which it received. New Orleans was added because of the practical consideration that I knew it better than any other: it was the city in which I was reared and on which I have done two sociological studies. It thus fulfilled the scientific desideratum of being primary data. It also presented a much greater diversity of cultural background than did Middletown and it was, as well, the most metropolitan city in the sample.

The choice of non-Western cities was more limited, merely because so few case studies were obtainable.

THE CITIES

Each of the cities is briefly introduced in the following pages. The description generally follows the outline employed in the sketches of the villages. (A summary of the descriptions is given in Chapter 3, Table 3, p. 42.)

The urbanized area of *New Orleans*, Louisiana, included 660,000 people at the time (1950) when data were gathered used in this study. Located not far from the mouth of the continent's largest river, the Mississippi, the city is a major port. Other industries have been added to this commercial base. Numerous cultures have met and mixed in the city since its founding as a French colony in 1718. In addition to French, Spanish, and "American" peoples, there are Germans, Irish, Italians, and others. Negroes are from both "American" and French cultures. They constitute slightly less than a third of the city's population and have extensively influenced it, first as slaves, later as relatively unprivileged free men, and recently as a group insisting upon more equitable treatment. The city was initially studied in order to discover whether its largest Negro area was a community and later (using the data for the same time period—1950) as an analysis of the sociological and demographic differentials between its Negro and white inhabitants (Hillery, 1951, 1952, 1954 and 1957). Use has also been made of Gilmore's (1944) perceptive study of the city's human ecology and Fichter's intensive analysis of one of its Catholic parishes (1951).

In 1934, the population of *Merida* was estimated at 97,000 persons. The city is located in the northwestern portion of the relatively flat and dry Yucatán Peninsula and in the area of commercial *henequen* (sisal fiber) production. Merida is a hub of trade and finance, serving as the center of communication from its hinterland to the world. There is not much machine industry on the peninsula, but Merida has most of what is there. Change has been relatively uneventful. After the Spanish invasion and founding in 1542, the most significant development was a gradual shift from a status structure of conqueror and conquered to one based on an upper-class, European-oriented culture and a lower-class culture derived from Mayan and peasant elements. Achievement of independence, the revolution of 1915, and accompanying economic expansion broke the city from its isolation and greatly increased contacts with the outside world. Today, Merida "stands out among the communities of Yucatan as the place where the old culture has suffered the greatest amount of disorganization and where new ways of life, borrowed from other urban societies or developed under the stimulus of its own urban conditions, are most in evidence" (Redfield, 1941, p. 35). Redfield employed the data gathered by Hansen (1934) in making a comparative study of four communities chosen to represent points along a line of contrast from the city of Merida to the Mayan hinterland. Although historical connections are given substantial attention, the basic time of observation is 1934.

*Middletown* is easily the youngest of the cities to be studied, the first permanent settlement in its county occurring in 1820. By 1935, it had grown to an estimated 47,000 persons. The criteria by which it was chosen by the Lynds are informative: a temperate climate, a rate of growth sufficiently rapid to reflect social change, an industrial culture, but one not dominated by a single factory, substantial local artistic life "to balance its industrial activity," absence of any outstanding peculiarities which would make it atypical of American communities, and finally, it should be chosen from America's Middle West. The city was also selected for its small Negro and foreign-born population. Apart from rapid growth (Middletown increased more than seven-fold in fifty years), the most significant change was experienced during the Great Depression. The city was studied twice by Robert and Helen Lynd (1929, 1937). Both investigations were prompted by an interest in social change. The present analysis relies more heavily on the second study.

At the time of its study (1947–48), the city of Ch'u numbered 31,000 and its county contained 150,000 persons. Located in the Yangtze plain, the town relies most heavily on agricultural products and on the labor of artisans. The city dates at least as early as the T'ang dynasty (618–906 A.D.). Approximately one hundred years ago, the Taiping rebellion inflicted devastation to an extent that was not matched even by the Japanese invasion or the recent civil war. By the 1870's the population of the county was estimated at one-third of its pre-rebellion size, though many of the *émigrés* subsequently returned. Ch'u is the most racially homogeneous of the cities studied, practically the entire population being Mongoloid. Homogeneity, however, is apparently confined to this single trait. Morton Fried (1953) studied Ch'u and its county in an attempt to provide an analysis of extrafamilial associations in a large "community." Field work was carried out during 1947 and 1948.

The precise number of persons residing in *Timbuctoo* was impossible to determine because of the large transient segment, but Miner estimated 6,000 inhabitants in the minimum permanent population of 1940. The location of Timbuctoo reasonably near the Niger River and on the edge of the Sahara provides probably one of the more ideal breaks in transportation available in the area. The satellite village of Kabara located on the high water channel serves as its port, whereas the city itself is the terminus for caravans. As with Ch'u, the age of this African city is unknown. It was a seasonal camp of the nomadic Tuareg in the first written accounts around 1,000 A.D. During most of its history, the city has been under the dominance of some foreign power, and its historical periods are periods of occupation: the Mandingo domination (fourteenth century), the Moroccan conquest (late sixteenth and early seventeenth centuries) and numerous periods of shorter duration wherein the city was subjugated by other peoples, mostly Tuaregs. Only during the fifteenth and part of the sixteenth centuries were the native Songhoi able to exert their own control. The recent half-century of French occupation has brought about some limited change. Ethnic composition reflects this history of dominance: the city is composed primarily of Tuareg slaves (Bela), Arabs, and Songhoi. Horace Miner (1953) chose Timbuctoo in order to provide more light on folk-urban theory and particularly to supply a need for non-American urban studies. His field work was conducted during 1940.

INTERACTION

*Primary and secondary contact.* The stranger is inescapably an integral part of each city. In Merida, even as far back as 1860, the *barrios* (neighborhoods) were isolated from each other to such an extent that incoming families had to expect to be treated as outsiders. Barrios were more open and strangers more acceptable when Redfield wrote in 1934. Impersonality extended even to religion: an individual attending mass is among strangers with whom contacts are casual and secondary. Similarly, there is in Middletown's culture little of the suspicion of the stranger as a potentially dangerous person. A Middletown citizen remarked in 1925: "People know money, and they don't know you" (Lynd and Lynd, 1937, p. 62).

The importance of the stranger in Ch'u is extensive and pervasive. The typical store clerk, for example, has the companionship·of his wife for only a brief fraction of the year. In the majority of cases, clerks spend most of their time with individuals to whom they are either distantly related or not related at all. More important, informality of contact is institutionalized in the sentiment of *kan-ch'ing*. This sentiment is an alternative to friendship, recognizing exploitation and even ameliorating it. *Kan-ch'ing* presumes a much more specific common interest, possessing much less warmth and more formality of contact than does friendship. It is the property of all classes. This extreme degree of institutionalizing a sentiment between persons who are not members of a primary group causes Fried to ask: "Is *kan-ch'ing* merely one specific attempt in a particular culture to reconcile the personal contacts of a kin-organized society with the impersonal relationships which are demanded in all cultures which operate through a civil organization?" (Fried, 1953, p. 227). Persons who develop *kan-ch'ing* between each other will, of course, not remain strangers. Yet, the sentiment can be initiated with strangers, and therein lies its significance in the present context.

The stranger is probably most important in Timbuctoo, the smallest of the five cities studied. This importance is seen in several ways. First, there are the seasonal nomads who supply milk and meat. Second, there are the transient traders who are part of this social system to such an extent that the city is almost always functionally larger than its permanent population (6,000). Third, each of the three major ethnic groups—Tuareg slaves (Bela), Arabs, and Songhoi—dominates one or more quarters of the city. Within these quarters an individual may be known fairly well, but outside, the situation differs. His family identity will largely be unknown and in many cases he must speak a language other than his native tongue. Songhoi, the native Sudan language, is the lingua franca in these occasions. In such cases, external symbols of status become very important and an emphasis is placed on dress. "Even friends may be so unfamiliar with one's actual economic condition that a show of opulence can give increased status" (Miner, 1953, p. 25).

The situation in New Orleans fits easily within the extremes of the other four cities. Obviously, half a million inhabitants could hardly be intimate, and strangers can and do enter the city and remain unknown as strangers, even while interacting. This condition is, of course, facilitated by the city's variegated ethnic composition. The position of New Orleans as a major seaport means, further, that persons who are obviously not native are observed frequently.

Indeed, most of the residents of New Orleans were probably born elsewhere. Inference for this statement depends primarily on data obtained from a random sample of 96 households in the city's largest Negro section (Hillery, 1952). Respondents were composed of 72 persons (75 per cent) who were born outside the city. The incidence of migration is thus high, and other evidence shows that migration rates are twice as high or more in the white as in the Negro population. (It is instructive to examine this sample also in respect to the number of people who were members of the same formal groups. With minor exceptions no *two* persons could be found, *both* of whom belonged to the same two or more organizations. The roles of the people are thus extremely segmented, though they are all of the same ethnic group and are all residing in the same area of the city.)

When one attempts to become more specific concerning the role of the stranger, evidence becomes weaker. Unambiguous data are present only for New Orleans. In that city, one tends to draw "friends" from distances greater than adjacent homes. The urbanite does not always know his neighbors—they only live nearby, or, to use Bessie McClenehan's term (1929), the nearby residents often become nigh-dwellers rather than neighbors. In the role of the nigh-dweller, the acceptance of the stranger becomes institutionalized. The sample data (mentioned above) readily establish the existence of the nigh-dweller: Of those persons listed as close personal friends, 69 per cent lived more than two blocks away. On the other hand, 12 per cent of the respondents knew none of the persons who resided directly across the street, 25 per cent knew some of the residents, and 56 per cent knew all of them (6 per cent had no persons dwelling across the street from their home). Such data confirm the writer's observations in many other portions of the city.

Strictly comparable information does not exist for the other cities. The Lynds speak of a decline in neighboring in their first study of Middletown, and though the proportions differ, the spread of friends over the city is equally evident: more than two-thirds of the best friends of the mothers of both working-class and business-class wives who were interviewed lived within six blocks of them, whereas approximately half of the best friends of the present generation of working-class wives and less than one-fifth of the best friends of business-class women interviewed lived within six blocks of these women. No other evidence was found concerning nigh-dwellers for the three other cities.

Mass communication, in the broadest sense of the term, is more in evidence. In each of the cities there is some means for moving large quantities of men or materials. The caravan is the chief mechanism for Timbuctoo, and in all probability it is the inefficiency of this device that is responsible for Timbuctoo's relatively small size. Ch'u and Merida rely heavily on railroads. To rail transportation, Middletown adds automobiles. Though motorable roads are found in all of the cities, automobiles are mentioned with frequency only in the American cities. (Merida had approximately two automobiles per 1,000 inhabitants.) New Orleans, of course, is a major seaport.

The emphasis on social communication in the city is thus one of quantity. What *kinds* of people come to the city (in terms of who knows them) becomes generally of little consequence. These observations do not mean that the city is composed of strangers. Primary groups abound, as will be noted below, particularly (of course) in the form of the family. But there are at least three levels of urban social interaction: (1) the primary groups, (2) the secondary groups which probably link most of the primary ones, and finally, (3) sheer anonymity even (and at times especially) in interaction, which functions in such a way that natives and foreigners are treated alike. It is on this final level that the stranger can and does function.

*Social processes.* Most of the social processes are discussed in other sections of this appendix, especially in connection with heterogeneity and contract. This is because the sociologically more significant aspects of social processes are their institutionalization. This section considers the processes which are relatively uninstitutionalized, and in the case of cities, these are the antagonistic ones.

As in the folk village, no consistent form of conflict could be identified within the cities. The closest approximation would be that of ethnic conflict. Certainly, this type occurred in New Orleans, Middletown, and to some extent in Timbuctoo. And Merida "represents the result of four centuries of interaction: a single society, with social classes, racially indistinct" (Redfield, 1941, p. 59). Even class conflict, where it does exist, is sporadic and proceeds according to no set form.

Thus, although conflict does occur within all of the cities, the city is not a system in which one faction is eternally at war with another. Perhaps the nearest that cities come to displaying a common form of conflict is found in the consistent reports of deviant behavior among urbanities. However, the deviant does not necessarily conflict with the larger society, and he is never totally deviant. But deviance is of special importance in understanding urban life and is so widespread that it can only be understood after other components have been examined (see below).

SPACE

*Spatial integration.* The most striking aspect of urban spatial integration is its economic form, though the city is never integrated only in this way. Timbuctoo shows the economic pattern as clearly as any of the cities. Its markets are the focus of impersonal contact between the various ethnic groups. Indeed, it was this importance that caused the Moroccans to shift one of the major markets from the center of the city to its outskirts—nearer the fort where the pasha's troops could apply force whenever needed. The markets are similarly integrative in Ch'u, and as in Timbuctoo, there are two markets; one is located approximately in the center of the city, the other at the East Gate, part within and part outside of the city walls. This location on both sides of the walls means that the integrative powers of the market area are not confined solely to those persons residing within arbitrary boundaries.

The importance of the retail business district in Middletown can be inferred from its position: roughly in the center of the city, in the area most accessible to most people. True, the manufacturing industries produce products valued at approximately two and one-half times the sales of the business district, and the factories employ about four times as many workers. But the factories are dispersed throughout the city and do not act as a focal point for trade.

Merida, though larger, probably lacks the manufacturing importance of Middletown, but the dominance of its center is, if anything, more important. This is the place where one works, buys, or seeks diversion. The barrio squares also constitute secondary business districts, but according to both Hansen and Redfield, these are subsidiary. It is probably important to observe that the integrative powers of the center have grown with the city. The separation between the barrios and the center was more marked in earlier years, particularly when the Spanish and Yucatecans constituted separate ethnic groups.

The picture is the same for New Orleans—numerous secondary and even sub-secondary shopping centers scattered throughout the city and the adjacent parishes. But the major shopping and business district, "Canal Street," continues to dominate the commercial life of the city, whether in banking or retailing. The business district, however, is not in the center of the city— and apparently never was—due to the commercial importance of the Mississippi River.

One is forcefully reminded of Weber's terse phrase, "the 'city' is the market place" (Weber, 1958, p. 67). Although the statement is an overemphasis, as is any ideal type, it is instructive to compare the integrative powers of the market and of government. Political boundaries by no means include all of the city's residents. Each of the five cities has a suburban fringe of varying proportions. Though the fringe may be excluded politically, it is never excluded economically, and therein lies the importance of the retail markets.

There is another spatially integrative force: class or status structure serves, at least in part, to place the various areas of the city in some sort of relation with each other. First the evidence: the Bela and Arab slaves of Timbuctoo live on the outskirts of the city, and residential land values increase as one goes to the center. Middletown has its upper- and middle-class residential areas as well as a part of the city located "across the tracks." Middletown is characteristically American in giving different areas of the city high residential value and other areas high commercial value. At one time, however, before modern transportation had made its influence apparent, it was socially more desirable to "live in"; that is, closer to the center of town. Merida is similar to Timbuctoo in having the upper-class residential area located toward the center of the town—social status shows a tendency to decrease as one moves out of the city.

New Orleans is a mixture of these tendencies. A product of different sociocultural influences, the American metropolis contains one of its choicest upper-class areas near the center of the city, no more than a few minutes' walk from the main business district (this is the French Quarter, although not that part normally seen by tourists). And, as one goes from area to area within the city, he meets pockets of older residential areas which refuse to comply with "normal" ecological forces—strips of residential areas located along St. Charles, Esplanade, and Carrollton Avenues are cases in point. (See Firey, 1947, for paralleled developments in Boston.) Generally, however, the better residential areas are farther away from the central business district in Gentilly and Metairie. New Orleans, then, like Merida and Timbuctoo, shows remnants of an earlier time in having higher residential land values located closer to the city's center. But like Middletown, both residential and commercial values tend for the most part to be separated.

Fried only gives part of the necessary information concerning Ch'u. He does note a tendency for commercial values to concentrate near the center of the town and near the city wall, explainable primarily by the greater foci of human traffic at these points. In addition, one of the lower status groups is clustered on both sides of the city wall (described more completely in connection with ecological processes, below). Thus, regardless of where the upper-class areas may be, they are not exclusively in the center of town—these are commercial areas. Similarly, they cannot be clustered near the city's walls—these are the areas of commerce and the residence of certain lower-status groups. And, finally, no matter where other status groups may be, parts of the city can be delineated as areas inhabited by lower-status persons.

The relation between this patterning and spatial integration is to be found in Durkheim's concept of organic solidarity. The city is composed of differences, and these differences are reflected spatially. But the differences do not merely stem from a chaotic congeries—there is a system: this system, at least for these five cities, is partly found in the various status levels into which the city is divided. Stratification integrates these areas, particularly in the interdependence it sets up among them, as when domestics work for the rich. Stratification thus puts the differences and heterogeneity in some order. And though the force, itself, is not a spatial one, it has spatial consequences.

The territory of the five cities, then, is in each instance integrated economically by some commercial (retail) center, generally located toward the center of the city, but not invariably so. The cities are all also partially integrated politically. And all of the cities are integrated to some degree through the organization of the spatial distribution of their status groups. Thus, although economic forces are the chief spatial integrators, they are not the sole ones.

*Ecological processes.* None of the theories of urban spatial patterns ("ecological" theories) can be defended by reference to the five cities. Certain classical ecological processes show up clearly, however. Most noticeable is the specialization among various areas according to ethnic, status, or economic functions—that is, the ecological process of segregation. Ethnic segregation occurs in all of the cities except Ch'u. New Orleans segregates Negroes and whites (though not completely), and its history is dotted by the invasion and succession of various waves of immigrant groups in numerous parts of the city. Merida had an initial pattern of Spanish and Indian segregation which, however, tended to disintegrate with time and accompanying racial hybridization. In recent years, only a colony of Syrians was large enough to form a visible area. Middletown segregated Negroes and whites, and Timbuctoo segregated Arabs, Tuareg slaves, and Songhoi ethnic groups.

Status formed another basis of segregation, generally allying itself with ethnicity (where ethnicity was present). There appears to have been, *at one time or other*, a clear pattern in which *distance from the center of the city was inversely correlated with status*; that is, the closer to the center of the city, the higher the status. The correlation is not perfect but it nevertheless showed itself at some time in the history of each city. New Orleans displayed the pattern in its earliest years, as did Merida and Middletown. The city of New Orleans, proper (now roughly the "French

Quarter"), was reserved for the French. Other immigrant groups settled in less desirable lands outside the city. Merida reserved the center of the city for the Conquistadores, and Middletown's preference to live "close in" was evident in the period antedating the automobile.

The correlation between status and distance from the center is still evident in Timbuctoo. The data for Ch'u, however, are incomplete, but there is a decided tendency for seasonal agricultural laborers to settle in huts of mud and straw located in sections on both sides of the city wall. Nevertheless, the correlation is still present, since these laborers were undoubtedly the lowest of Ch'u's social strata.

A third pattern of segregation was found in the economic institutions. Again, however, the process appears only at certain times in the city's history. All cities had centralized market places or business districts. Most of the cities had one major shopping area. Timbuctoo and Ch'u had more. Beyond this, the degree of economic segregation depended on the complexity of economic specialization. New Orleans, Merida, and Middletown had industrial areas (though only recently). In Ch'u and Timbuctoo, however, segregation was not so evident. There was an attraction of the center and even a tendency for specific commodities to cluster at certain locales within the market. But there could be little further segregation since major industries other than market institutions were relatively lacking.

In each of the five cities, a centralization process helped integrate the segregated areas. The correlation of status and distance from the center of the city is one such integrative force, though not always is it displayed. In the three larger cities—New Orleans, Merida, and Middletown—automobiles had reversed this correlation, with the centralization of retail (or market) functions exerting an ever increasing force. Miner assures us that the force was always present in Timbuctoo, and economic centralization was clearly noted in Ch'u by Fried. In the earlier history of the largest cities, however, political and religious institutions apparently assumed the centralizing function. Jackson Square of New Orleans was the location of the Roman Catholic cathedral and the government buildings, as was the central square of Merida. (One should note, however, that Jackson Square was located with reference to the geographically dominant Mississippi River rather than to the city's geographic center.) In both cases, the marketplace was nearby but clearly secondary. Thus, various institutions exert different impacts in the centralization process. Exactly what the centralizing institution will be is a culturally relative phenomenon, though the centralizing process, per se, is common to many cultures.

An additional process appears in all of the cities, though its significance is not readily apparent. In each city, many if not most of the segregated areas, whether economic, ethnic, or class, are named. There are occasional exceptions—in New Orleans, for example, the largest area of Negro settlement in 1950, located approximately in the city's geographic center, was unnamed. The importance of the names is another matter, for in none of these cities is one impressed with strong social cohesiveness within most of the areas. Even where ethnic segregation is present, the homogeneity is seldom absolute. Often there is some loyalty to a named area, but equally or more often the names appear to serve only as identifying symbols.

The opposing process of decentralization is not as evident. A movement to the suburbs, especially of the upper classes (in which are placed the nouveau riche, for purposes of this discussion) was found in each of the three largest cities. It is noteworthy that families living within two *li* (a *li* is about one-third of a mile) of the city walls of Ch'u are also counted among the city's residents. The question arises, has this always been the custom? Did walls demarcate the city in earlier times or have they always merely enclosed a place to which some of the city's residents could retire in time of trouble? In any case, there is a decentralization process of another sort in Ch'u. The city wall seems as much an attractive force as the center, and there are clear tendencies for markets and people to cluster at least at some of the city's gates, located at the four cardinal compass points. These areas may not be suburbs but they are decentralized.

Timbuctoo provides the only questionable case. Miner notes the "presence of peripheral suburbs of straw huts," but there is no evidence that the people moved from the center of the city or any other part. Nomads also settle on the city's edge, but this is more the process of concentration than decentralization. That decentralization occurs within the city was noted earlier, but the reason was a peculiar one—the desire of the Moroccan pasha to shift the market's location in order to bring the populace under more efficient control.

Each of the cities had an elaborate network of communicating paths or streets. The network is important, in spite of its obvious nature, for without it, the city could not function. But not to be missed is its extensive and elaborate nature, penetrating each city in the fullest sense of the word, such that all inhabited parts are not only near the network but most often adjacent to it. It is the visible facet of the cities' social interaction.

The impact of geography on the cities' spatial patterning may vary from extreme to inconspicuous. The Mississippi River twists New Orleans into such tortuous shapes that (in part) a special study of its ecological pattern was prompted (Gilmore, 1944). Ch'u is also oriented toward a river. Middletown and Timbuctoo, however, are both built on flat land, and the city in each case has been allowed to spread almost as it would. The river through Middletown has exerted only a slight influence in that some industry is located upon it. All of the older cities, incidentally, depend in part on water transportation, whether the body of water is adjacent or (as in the case with Merida and Timbuctoo) some miles away. Both Timbuctoo and Merida have satellite ports.

*Vague boundaries.* As was true of the folk villages, the term "vague boundaries" is meant to convey two ideas. First, some area belongs to the city, and this area is demarcated by some kind of boundary. But, second, the boundary is either fluctuating, changing, or in conflict with other boundaries. Each of these terms is used in a specific way. A fluctuating boundary shifts with the activities of the inhabitants; a changing boundary is consciously moved. Conflicting boundaries occur when boundaries are not congruent.

New Orleans shows all three tendencies. Technically, the city is coterminous with the Parish (county) of Orleans, but much of the city's population has spilled over into the adjacent parishes. Except in political matters, the residents pay little attention to the boundaries. Suburban living is not a handicap to city employment, and vice versa.

Boundary fluctuation has occurred in at least two senses. Political boundaries, of course, grew as the city grew, though such change virtually stopped when the population reached the parish boundaries. Suburban areas however, are still growing.

Conflict in boundaries occurs also in the sense that political boundaries of the "city" include vast tracts of land which contain few inhabitants. Most of New Orleans is, as far as territory is concerned, a marshland. Thus, if one attempts to delineate the territory of the city, he will obtain entirely different perspectives, depending on whether he employs residential or political boundaries.

Redfield offers few comments on Merida's boundaries, but he does describe a fluctuation in the residential occupancy of the city's edge. This was the portion of Merida in which suburbs were growing—and failing. Whatever may have been the stability of political boundaries, the actual area in which Merida's inhabitants reside is and has been in a state of flux.

Middletown has also experienced the conflict of suburban with political boundaries described in New Orleans, just as it displayed tracts of land which were politically within the city but residentially uninhabited.

The wall surrounding Ch'u would appear to be an obvious and definite boundary. The wall is obvious, but the precision of that which it bounds is another matter. On both sides of the wall is a major shopping area and the dwellings of the seasonal agricultural laborers and, further, all inhabitants within two *li* of the wall are counted as city residents. Boundary fluctuation also occurred in the past, although the present city "limits" have not altered for fifty years. The conflict in boundaries, however, still appears. The seasonal workers are permitted to build their huts outside the city walls—but not within. Yet, all who are within two *li* are city residents. For some purposes, then, one set of boundaries suffices, whereas for other purposes another set is used. In addition, it was seen that the seasonal workers blurred even the boundaries assigned specifically to them in that they infiltrated within the city walls. Finally, in spite of the above distinctions, the city is also regarded as an integral part of the county of which it is the seat. Thus, another set of political boundaries is used for still additional purposes.

Timbuctoo may be delineated by means of its buildings, including two forts, two mosques, and a shifting periphery of straw huts. Miner does not speak of political boundaries. The periphery is composed of slaves, recently emancipated slaves, serfs, low-class Arabs, and "mobile bush folk who know and care so little about the city that they are willing to live here" (Miner, 1953, p. 44). In addition, there are the nomads who seasonally camp around the city with their herds and flocks, supplying milk and meat to the population.

Three major questions remain: whether political boundaries are always present; if present, the degree of their importance; and, whatever their importance, the extent to which the boundaries are transgressed. This much, can be said: Political boundaries are not of major importance to the inhabitants of the city, particularly in relation to the place of residence and the place of interaction. More generally, one can point to a definite pattern in which the residential areas on the outskirts of each of the five cities fluctuate noticeably in territorial extent. City boundaries, in brief, are vague in that they are fluctuating, changing, or in conflict with other boundaries—and all three of these conditions have been found in a single city.

ACTIVITIES

*Base of operations.* As with the folk village, the city is a base of operations both in the sense of localistic and cosmopolitan movements. In its cosmopolitan functions, however, each of the five cities outstrips the folk village. The city is a base for journeyings to places thousands of miles away, and in some cases, literally to any part of the globe. Of course, what is "far" and what is "near" is subject to cultural (especially technological) interpretations, but Table 15 helps to describe the progressively more distant and repeated contacts which the members of the five cities make with the world at large.

According to these criteria, Ch'u and Timbuctoo are more isolated, followed by Middletown and Merida, with New Orleans easily the most cosmopolitan. Ch'u is the most isolated when one considers that it is on a rail line while Timbuctoo is not. In other words, Ch'u has more access to communication but uses it less. The only distant ventures Fried noted took place during the recent civil war, though there were probably earlier ones as well. This type of cosmopolitanism, of course, comes only at infrequent intervals. And although the distances are not given, it must be remembered that distance is culturally relative. That which is considered distant in Ch'u may be of no real

consequence in Timbuctoo. The remarkable fact, notwith-
standing this relativity, is the extent of cosmopolitanism in each
of the five cities.

But distance is not the only feature of cosmopolitanism. All of
the cities have institutionalized activities related to their contact with the "Great Outside." Most often, this institutionalization is represented by a rail terminus (Timbuctoo had none) or

*Table 15.* Cosmopolitan features of city life, by approximate distances of
contacts

| City | *More than 1,000 miles* | *1,000 to 100 miles* | *Less than 100 miles* |
|---|---|---|---|
| New Orleans | Numerous sea, air, and rail connections linking the U.S. and Latin America | Transportation center for the lower Mississippi Valley | Close contact with southern Louisiana and the Gulf Coast |
| Merida | Two airlines operating | Capital of Yucatán; rail hub for hinterland | Port of Progresso serves as the shipping point of Merida |
| Middletown | Upper-class children go east to school | Private and commercial planes average over 500 miles per day | Estimated 10,000 leave for other towns and resorts "every fine Sunday" |
| Ch'u | Travel to other places during the war | Close contacts with Shanghai; some brides not from the immediate vicinity | Closely connected with Nanking; trading and familial ties with people residing nearby |
| Timbuctoo | Occasional trips to Mecca; more frequently to Morocco and Algeria | Principal commerce from Taodeni mines in central Sahara | Town of Kabara serves as river port of Timbuctoo; trading in the "bush" |

an airfield (the three largest cities), or even a port. Further, not
only were there usually *places* where the cosmopolite could
expect to terminate (or begin) his journey, there were also
places where he could expect to stay. Obviously, this applies to
hotels, and they are specifically mentioned in Ch'u and Merida.
New Orleans has scores of them and, though the chroniclers of

Middletown are silent on this score, one cannot doubt the presence of hotels there also. Timbuctoo provides the discrepancy, again. Travelers "lodge with residents of the city with whom they may or may not have been previously acquainted. Strangers can apply to the city chief for lodging and he will direct them to one of these hostels" (Miner, 1953, p. 63). Most of the traveling traders stay with persons known through trade connections or those recommended by friends.

The institution which Timbuctoo illustrates so clearly is found in its "system of accommodation for strangers" (Miner, 1953, p. 63). For most cities, the system is commercially based. In Timbuctoo, the base is also commercial, but not in the usual sense: "The owners of the lodgings often fulfill a directly commercial function, acting as middlemen in the sale of transients' goods" (Miner, 1953, p. 63). The principal difference from other cities is that lodgings in Timbuctoo are not purely contractual, although they do contribute to contract formation.

As indicated, the city is also a base for the cosmopolite. Each of the cities had populations which were not members of the city, per se. The three largest cities had one or more colleges or universities, and thus they had student populations at least part of which would not be native to the city. In addition, most of the cities had categories of people who could be called permanent transients. Traveling salesmen are, of course, a part of American culture, which would include both Middletown and New Orleans. Timbuctoo and Ch'u have other categories. Seasonal agricultural laborers, though not city members, occupy a significant segment of the life of Ch'u. Timbuctoo, of course, depends on caravans, and is thus in constant contact with nomads, specifically the Arabic Berabich and the Tuareg. Each of these peoples come to and stay in the city for considerable periods but are not permanent residents.

Ch'u has a more borderline case of "permanent transients"—store clerks. Some come from places as far removed as Shanghai, others from much closer locations, but none known to Fried established new and separate residences in Ch'u. "The typical clerk in a store in Ch'u enjoys the companionship of his wife for only a brief fraction of the year" (Fried, 1953, pp. 43–44).

The homes of the residents are bases of operations for traveling to the business districts and there are also other localistic contacts. Visiting patterns among friends have already been noted in New Orleans and Middletown, and the existence of friendships was noted in the other cities as well. It would appear unreasonable to confine friendships only to immediate neighbors. The city in this sense is composed of an interlocking mesh of bases of operations, both within the space it occupies and from this space to the outside world.

How many persons live their life within the city? Basically, the question is not answerable with the data at hand, though there are some indications. More certitude can be given negative evidence; that is, it is possible to indicate which segments could *not* have lived their life within the city, and these are considered first.

As the city enacts its cosmopolitan functions it necessarily sends members from it, at least temporarily. Also the five cities have permanent transients. And finally, the stranger is an integral part of the city, particularly in relation to one of its most central elements, that of interaction.

In addition, another segment of the population could not have lived their lives there, simply because they were born elsewhere. This category is discussed in the section on mobility, below, but it may be noted that those citizens who were born elsewhere constitute noticeable proportions of all the cities, from probably a majority in New Orleans to perhaps a minority in the cities of Ch'u or Middletown.

It would be useful to know the extent to which these four segments supplement each other and to what extent the same persons are involved. Whether a person is a transient or a citizen, he may use the city as a base of operations, can have been born elsewhere, and can be a stranger in certain situations. It would seem logical to suppose that most people in a city sooner or later fall into at least one of these categories. It is known for one city (New Orleans) that *most* people have spent at least part of their lives elsewhere, but, with this exception, the data do no more than indicate that large and varying proportions are contained in each category.

There is no direct evidence on the converse condition—persons who have lived their lives within the city boundaries. There are, however, some allusions to this condition. Fried mentions that "brothers will remain together, in all likelihood, for their lifetimes" (1953, p. 64). How many would leave the city in its cosmopolitan functions is another matter. In Middletown, the Lynds give one brief mention of a "lifelong resident" (1937, p. 466). But, as in the case of Ch'u, we are provided with no clue as to whether such a resident ever left the city for any reason.

No evidence of any life-long residents is available for the other three cities—not to mention evidence of anyone who has *never* left the system. Even in New Orleans, the writer has not encountered anyone who has never left its bounds, nor has he ever spoken with anyone who knew such a person. Of course, in a city of more than half a million persons it is only logical to assume that some of its members have never passed beyond its corporate limits. The same reasoning applies to the other cities. Still, the more important fact remains: the city cannot be described as simply a collection of life-long residents. The student of community is faced with the problem that MacIver's criterion (that is, that all of one's social relationships may be found within the community) fails to explain the behavior of many and even, at times, most city members.

Of more interest is a statement by the Lynds: "Those unsatisfied souls who remain in Middletown tend often to carry on difficult lives of outward conformity and unhappy underlying rebellion" (1937, p. 64). The implications of this observation are central to a corollary of MacIver's criterion, that the community may satisfy all of its residents' needs. The Lynds provide us with the observation that, for some of its members, the city is clearly a frustrating instead of a satisfying condition.[1]

The point to be made is not that MacIver's criterion is untrue. Rather, that it has been stated in an untestable manner, for when one says one "could" spend his entire life in a place and does not specify the conditions of that possibility, then whatever is eventually tested will differ from the original criterion to the extent that conditions are specified. More to the point are Zimmerman's and Parsons' concepts of localism, cosmopolitanism, and base of operations. These do all that MacIver's criterion can do, and they do it in a manner that can be observed.

*Mobility.* Two of the three types of social mobility are to be considered in this section: horizontal and territorial. The move-

[1] One should note in this connection that MacIver considers the city to be a community (see MacIver and Page, 1949, index).

ment from stratum to stratum (vertical mobility) is treated in the section on stratification.

Transportation has been seen to be a significant and even an essential part of the cities' existence; territorial mobility was discussed in relation to the cosmopolitan's base of operations. Migration is a third and probably more important aspect of territorial mobility. From 1949 to 1950, approximately 33,500 persons moved into the Standard Metropolitan Area of New Orleans, or 5.2 per cent of all persons one year old and over. For the fiscal year of 1949, the net movements in and out of the city, itself, was 13.4 Negroes per 1,000 population and 45.9 for the whites. Of the three processes that change population sizes—migration, birth, and death—migration was highest in the white population and was higher than the death rate among Negroes. (For Negroes, as previously mentioned, the sample interviewed by the writer showed 75 per cent born outside the city, and, as noted, during the same year the migration rates for whites were higher than those for Negroes.)

Studies of three widely separated areas in Merida (one middle-class and two lower-class) revealed 26 per cent born in the hinterland. An additional 2 per cent of the city's residents were foreign-born and an undetermined number came from elsewhere in Mexico. In 1950, 58.9 persons had moved into Middletown from another county for each 1,000 persons who had lived there in 1949. Note that this rate is higher than that for either Negroes or whites in New Orleans. Remaining data for Middletown are of a different order, and none are presented for 1935 comparable to the two larger cities. Roughly half of the boys and a third of the girls residing in Middletown when they graduated in 1916–19 had not returned to the city to live in 1925. Further, Middletown's working class was heavily re-cruited from first- and second-generation farm stock. Finally, the major part of Middletown's very rapid growth (seven-fold in fifty years) was by migration.

Evidence in Ch'u is more sketchy. The volume of migration was known to have greatly increased during the Taiping rebel-lion a century earlier. For recent times, only two observations were offered. First, a large number of individuals or family groups were detached from extended families in other provinces. Second, membership in the merchant guilds was composed of many persons whose native place was not the county in which Ch'u was located. In addition, seasonal agricultural laborers reside partly in the city, and those are considered non-native by the citizens of Ch'u.

Migration data for those who reside in Timbuctoo is also incomplete. It is reported only that the Arab Berabich and the Tuareg nobles and serfs are nomadic, and that the Tuareg slaves (Bela) live in the city, many of whom are possibly migrants.

Territorial mobility is also related to horizontal mobility in that movement to the city means establishing new group ties. The realignment is also relatively permanent, even in Timbuctoo. The Tuareg slaves may not sever their ties with their masters (though sometimes they do), but their urban residence forces them to establish new urban ties.

A change of residence usually involves some change in neighbors and thus it involves horizontal as well as geographic movement. In New Orleans, the percentage of persons who moved from house to house within the city (1949–50) was almost three times as great as the percentage that moved to the city (12.3 vs. 4.2 per cent). The evidence for Merida is more indirect but could indicate as high a degree of movement. The social and spatial mobility within the city was great enough to practically destroy the old barrio communities of which the city was once composed. Statistics are more extensive in Middletown. The workers form a pool of quickly interchangeable semiskilled "human machine parts." Among the business class, moving is often a "natural and highly approved" accompaniment of rising income and opportunity. Residential mobility was also high. For example, 10.2 per cent of the owners had moved within less than three years, as contrasted with 76.2 per cent of the renters (slightly more than half of the residential units were rented). And, as in New Orleans, persons moving from house to house (1949–50) constituted a much larger percentage in Middletown than those moving to the city (11.4 as contrasted with 5.9 per cent).

Fried does not dwell on residential mobility, but he does speak of a great degree of horizontal mobility among both the lower and middle classes. Seasonal agricultural laborers provide a labor pool for both rural and urban employers. Even among the more completely urban workers, there is a good deal of individual mobility, a person not only changing status (vertical mobility) but changing jobs within the same status level. Finally, at least one of the middle-class families that Fried investigated intensively had "considerable mobility of family members." Although Fried does not provide sufficient quantitative data, he nevertheless leaves an impression of extensive fluidity in Ch'u's population.

Job mobility is relatively low in Timbuctoo, controlled largely by the guilds. French interference has led, however, to the breakdown of control over the selection of novices to certain crafts, and this situation may change even further, leading to the possibility of greater movement. More important is the influence of Timbuctoo's significant transient population. This element, alone, is a force leading to a high volume of horizontal mobility. The prevalence of divorce among the Arabs, for example, is attributable in part to the practice of transients marrying local women and leaving them on departing the city. On a wider level, contact between the various quarters seems extensive and frequent. Various tricks which a man plays on strangers, enemies, or those from other ethnic groups are the subject of proud descriptions to his intimates. Robbery was once part of the accepted pattern of life, and shrewd exploits are expected outside of the family and ethnic group. Therefore, the degree of horizontal mobility also seems high in Timbuctoo. There are indications, however, that horizontal mobility in this African city is lowest among the five cities studied, chiefly in the marked importance of heredity in ascribing group membership.

The cities are, accordingly, places of a high degree of mobility, both territorial and horizontal. Although the five cities vary in the extent of their mobility, particularly in the horizontal variety, there can be no doubt that their members do not as a rule remain in one place or retain contacts with only one group.

*Continuance.* The age of the cities can be ascertained with more accuracy than the age of the folk villages (see Table 16), probably because of a greater emphasis on record-keeping, poor as these records may sometimes be. (For example there is no founding date for Ch'u or Timbuctoo, the oldest two cities; the earliest recorded date is given.) Therefore, no great importance should be attached to the apparent difference: over five centuries for the cities as compared with more than two centuries in the villages. The more important point, as in the case of the folk village, is that these systems have been in existence generally for much longer periods than have their members. Whatever needs are *not* satisfied, enough *are* satisfied to maintain the system for extended periods of time. (This, of course, is one valid aspect of MacIver's criterion.)

*Table 16.* Minimum age of the five cities

|  | Earliest Date (A.D.) | Date of study | Minimum age in centuries at time of study |
|---|---|---|---|
| Ch'u | 618–906 | 1947–48 | 10.4 |
| Timbuctoo | 1000 | 1940 | 9.4 |
| Merida | 1542 | 1934 | 3.9 |
| New Orleans | 1718 | 1950 | 2.3 |
| Middletown | 1820 | 1924 | 1.0 |

Methodologically, another point to emphasize is the younger age of the cities in the U.S., especially since New Orleans is one of the nation's oldest. An age bias is consequently inherent in the data for U.S. cities. To the extent that American sociologists have relied on Anglo-American cities for their generalizations, to that extent they have been using historically atypical cases. Further, modern cities are atypical in that they dominate rural areas. In earlier periods, the dominance was reversed, if only numerically (see Price and Hillery, 1959, pp. 4–9). In the wider view of history, then, Timbuctoo and Ch'u are more typical.

SENTIMENT

*Ethnocentrism.* Data from the three largest cities show that the residents of each believe that theirs is the best city. In New Orleans, this sentiment is expressed in many ways, especially newspaper descriptions of sport events and the promotional activities of the Chamber of Commerce and similar organizations. From conversations with people in all of the city's major status levels, it can be attested that this ethnocentrism is widespread and deepseated. To many residents of New Orleans, it is unquestionably the "best" city—with no exceptions. Other cities may be obviously bigger, richer, or whatever, but even when faced with such evidence, the New Orleanian has been heard to state, "I like New Orleans better."

In Merida fifty years before its study, the strongest loyalties were to the respective barrios rather than to the city as a whole. When Hansen studied the barrio inhabitants in 1934, however, they considered themselves primarily city people—even the humblest feeling superior to persons born outside of the city.

In speaking of "The Middletown Spirit," ethnocentric remarks are frequently encountered. People "should be loyal, placing *their* family, *their* community, *their* state, and *their* nation first" (Lynd and Lynd, 1937, p. 407). And, again: "Middletown people should shop in Middletown. 'Buy where you earn your money'" (p. 410). There is an intense localism in Middletown; citizens feel it is "the finest place in the world," (p. 378), a view also promoted by the press, Chamber of Commerce, and other groups. Of course, there will always be room for improvement, and these very organizations will be in the vanguard of debate on such measures, but the sentiment is clearly that of making what is best "better." Parenthetically, one should note that these are majority views; there is a minor discord to be noted below.

Definite evidence—either positive or negative—does not exist for Timbuctoo or Ch'u. Urbanites there are ethnocentric about various things, as will be indicated, but the investigators do not comment concerning the peoples' sentiments about their city. However, conclusive contradictions are also absent. For three of the cities, then, ethnocentrism is definitely present; in two others, the evidence is not complete.

Although one cannot be certain whether the city, per se, is involved, a hierarchy of ethnocentrism is found in all of the cities. The citizens of Middletown and New Orleans were enjoined to be loyal to their family, community, state, and nation. The hierarchy in Merida begins with the family, proceeds to the barrio, then the city, and finally to Yucatán. In Timbuctoo, loyalty to one's kin supersedes loyalty to one's ethnic group; there was some loyalty to the quarter; and at least lip-service was paid to loyalty to the followers of Mohammed. This latter sentiment was "the one value shared by all natives" (Miner, 1953, p. 75). Similarly, extra-kin relations in Ch'u complement preexisting ties of conjugal or affinal kinship.

An interesting quality is found in some of the data used to infer ethnocentrism in New Orleans and Middletown. It is to the decided advantage of such groups as the press and the Chamber of Commerce that ethnocentrism be promoted, and thus the "loyalty" seems somehow less genuine. A distinction is necessary between values that are ultimate and ends in themselves (such as sentiments associated with religion and family) and ends which are instrumental (such as economic or educational ends). It sometimes happens that ultimate ends become instrumental, such as the values of someone who goes to church merely to meet people. Conversely, instrumental ends can become ultimate, as in the case of a scholar or a miser. The "use" which the Chamber of Commerce and the press make of ethnocentrism seems to transmute ultimate to instrumental values.

One should not conclude that all urbanites treat ethnocentrism as an instrumental value, but, perhaps ethnocentrism has always had an instrumental quality. Admittedly, this quality was not visible in the folk village, but it is probable that the vested interest in the folk village is more readily identified with the social system as a whole. In other words, one is ethnocentric about the folk village "because" it is to his best interest to do so, but in the absence of any competing interests, this "reason" is never apparent—not even to the folk villagers.

Additional comments are needed about competing and deviant loyalties. There were several Negro respondents in the New Orleans sample who did not want their children to grow up in that city. Occasionally, a Middletowner would break through the official view (the Lynds describe it as a "front"), as did the well-to-do wife who exclaimed in private conversation, "This is just a twenty-five-cent town" (Lynd and Lynd, 1937, p. 434). The Lynds also mention political apathy as a dominant trait. In nineteenth-century Merida, gang fights took place between barrios. Fried notes a complete and well-developed realm of non-familial contacts in Ch'u, independent of kin connections, which may on occasion compete with kin ties for the individual's loyalty. In Timbuctoo, though data on loyalty to the city are not furnished, one is expected to be loyal to his family, ethnic group, and quarter. And yet, numerous cases are cited where sons financially cheat their fathers and where thieves steal even from members of their own groups.

These disloyal members are always described as in the minority, or (in Timbuctoo) at least as recognized deviants. But the presence of such deviants reveals that loyalty in these cities, even when it exists, is never complete. The cases of Merida and Timbuctoo are even more informative. At one time, the barrios of Merida clearly took precedence over the city in terms of the people's loyalty. Evidence points strongly in the same direction for Timbuctoo: it is one's family *and* ethnic group *and* quarter which is of importance there, and there are *several* distinct ethnic groups and quarters in the city. When a Bela is acting toward an Arab or a Songhoi (and each has his "vice versa"), the only morals appear to be those of expediency.

Urban ethnocentrism may therefore actually be quite weak, appearing only as long as other loyalties do not conflict. The evidence we have is merely suggestive, but it would seem possible that should economic interests, for example, conflict with city interests, then economic interests would come first. Seldom, however, do such interests conflict. More often, the sentiments concerning the city adjust to the other sentiments, and it is only in rare cases, as in Merida in the earlier century or Timbuctoo of today, that one can view sentiments which have not become integrated.

*Awareness.* The quality of being aware of the city as a whole is included with sentiments primarily because it is a precondition of sentiment. Awareness is also, however, a precondition of interaction, in the sociological sense of the term, and this component could as well have been placed in the earlier discussion. Although one can note its quality as a precondition—as that which is necessary for—the existence of sentiment and interaction, the quality of awareness is distinct from both. To know of a group, to interact with its members, and to have a sentiment concerning it are three different things. This difference will become especially apparent in the examination of evidence for awareness in cities where there is no clear evidence for ethnocentrism.

Another important feature in the concept of awareness is found in its distinguishing qualities. Awareness is necessary to the existence of any social system in its functioning as a collectivity in Parson's sense (1960, p. 171), for it is awareness that helps set the collectivity apart from others in the minds of its members. This quality becomes particularly important because the city's vastness and heterogeneity might seem to mitigate against awareness of it by its inhabitants. That size and heterogeneity do distort this awareness will become evident—but they do not prevent it.

There is no doubt that the inhabitants of the three largest cities are aware of their city. Ethnocentrism was readily apparent and each of the cities has a name and a central government. There are additional considerations, but more comments should be given to the two remaining cities, since they present unusual problems.

Fried was somewhat vague about awareness in Ch'u. He has these comments: "In the original characters . . . the Ch'u character has no meaning other than to designate this local area. The *hsien* character . . . stands for 'county,' and, when combined with a place name, may mean either a county or a county seat. Thus, Ch'u Hsien means either the whole county . . . or the seat of government of that county, an ancient walled town" (1953, p. 6). Thus, "Ch'u Hsien" has a double meaning, and one aspect of this duality is an awareness of the walled city of Ch'u. Further, whatever the name used, it is clear from Fried's remarks that the inhabitants distinguish between the county and the county seat. The town, further, has a wall. It also has laws, including those which govern who shall and shall not be admitted to the city without passes (that is, the seasonal agricultural laborers). And, finally, Fried consistently refers to Ch'u as a collectivity separate from the county as a whole, though he also notes that it is closely integrated with the county —certainly these are not incompatible states.

Timbuctoo provides another case, and one which opens up important nuances. Miner states rather clearly that awareness is well-developed: "The greater part of the culture which is common to all the people of Timbuctoo consists of this religious core, the common knowledge of the physical aspects of Timbuctoo, the mutual recognition of commercial custom, and the recent general recognition of French dominance" (1953, p. 74). So far, all seems clear. But when one considers the fact that the *French* are dominant, and that the French are not originally from Timbuctoo, the question arises, just what is it that the people of Timbuctoo are aware of? In addition, Timbuctoo is composed of three major ethnic groups and additional minor ones, and solidarity and ethnocentrism do not ordinarily extend beyond the ethnic group. Thus, most of the inhabitants of Timbuctoo will be "aware" of that part of Timbuctoo they come in contact with and, for the various ethnic groups, these parts will not tend to be common parts.

The same observation may be made for most of the cities. That the people have an awareness of the city cannot be denied. This awareness is heavily conditioned by the fact that people tend to live in certain parts of the city to the exclusion of others, and their movements from their bases of operations over the city are not likely to give each resident a common viewpoint. (Recall the analysis of spatial patterning in this instance.)

The case of Timbuctoo, in particular, is instructive on another point. Ethnocentrism concerning the city was in doubt, but Miner gives clear evidence for the component of awareness. The significance of this statement lies in the ability to distinguish between the two components: one being a positive sentiment; the other being an act of recognition.

*Heterogeneity and organic solidarity.* The same conceptual distinctions are used for this component that were employed for *homogeneity* in the folk village. The reasoning, briefly, is that Durkheim's mechanical solidarity can be measured by mechanical homogeneity (wherein all traits are alike) and mechanical heterogeneity (in which traits may differ, but they do not add to the functions of each other; for example, different religions or grocery stores). Organic solidarity, on the other hand, is measured by organic heterogeneity, that is, by a division of labor.

None of the cities were "absolutely" or even "practically" homogeneous in respect to any trait (see Fig. 4, p. 226). In three cases, cities were homogeneous for a majority of inhabitants relative to a single item, but never was such an item universal. Thus, Timbuctoo was almost completely Muslim, but no other city had such religious homogeneity. Ch'u was composed almost solely of Mongoloids, racially, and Middletown was also racially "pure"—over 90 per cent Caucasoid. New Orleans had a minority of Negroes, but the Caucasoid majority was composed of French, "American," and other ethnic groups. Slightly more than half of the permanent population of Timbuctoo was

Songhoi (approximately 58 per cent), but this "dominance" would not apply when transients appeared in sizable numbers. And Merida had undetermined mixtures of Europeans and Mayans.

Such homogeneity is probably not significant. But there is one aspect of urban homogeneity which is highly significant and which has been virtually ignored in the literature: most city residents—even most adults—are members of some family or marital union. With this exception (and it is an important one), the city is to be described as a system based on heterogeneity rather than homogeneity.

Organic heterogeneity was most highly developed in the economic sphere. Timbuctoo probably had the smallest number of specialists: more than 34. From here, the number mounted rapidly until the population of New Orleans was reached. This city is divided into 11 major occupational categories representing 469 types of specializations and 13 major industrial groups pertaining to 148 more detailed categories. (For greater detail, see the section on economic institutions in this appendix, below.) Nor were the cities occupationally homogeneous in that they did not contain farmers, for all of the cities had some population devoted to farming. True, the proportions were invariably small, but this was true of most occupations. Wherever there are statistics, seldom did an occupation or industry claim as much as one-half of the employed population. (Middletown was the single exception: more than half of its employed male population was engaged in manufacturing industries.)

Organic heterogeneity was also conspicuous in governmental and religious institutions. Each of the cities had a division of labor between administrative, enforcement, or judicial aspects of government. In other words, the functions of coordinating various political decisions, of enforcing political and economic norms, and of judging economic and political disputes were usually carried out by different groups. Although legislative functions were separate in the three largest cities, no such separation was clearly mentioned for Ch'u. Timbuctoo was an "occupied" city and had been for much of its history; as such, its legislation came from either the administrative or police bodies (usually both).

Religious hierarchies were relatively elaborate in all of the cities, whether the people were Muslim, Buddhist, Taoist, Roman Catholic, or any of the innumerable Protestant denominations (especially in New Orleans and Middletown). There was also a division of labor between the practitioners of magic and religion. Of course, in all of the cities there were people who practiced both, but more important, each city had "specialists" in both areas, whether the Songhoi smith (magician) and *marabout* (student of the Koranic word) in Timbuctoo or the palmist and minister in New Orleans and Middletown. New Orleans, of course, has voodoo practitioners.

A similar division of labor is found in the family—clearly for four cities, and probably for all. From the institutional point of view, the "labor" of sexual relations was divided between the family and the institution of prostitution. (Prostitution is not mentioned in Merida, but it is probably safe to assume its existence in that city.) Of course, in many cases, prostitution is more approximately considered an instance of mechanical heterogeneity, since both husbands and single men can avail themselves of it. But insofar as the practice is a sexual outlet for unmarried men, organic heterogeneity is attained.

Since each of the cities has a well-developed system of stratification, organic heterogeneity is present in this institution also. Similarly, a division of labor is found in school and familistic socialization.

Only in institutionalized recreation was there lack of evidence concerning organic heterogeneity. A division of labor occurs in all cities for feasts and music but is not always apparent in games. In New Orleans and Middletown, where team sports have been developed to a high degree, the division of labor in recreation is both extensive and elaborate. But no such picture is given for the smallest cities, Timbuctoo and Ch'u, specifically for team games. Team games there were, but of the type in which everyone engages in a common activity.

The more important point is that organic solidarity was clearly developed in all of the institutions discussed here (mutual aid requires separate treatment—see the section on contract, below). Little comment is required about mechanical heterogeneity. With a well-developed organic heterogeneity, extensive mechanical heterogeneity is not surprising (though not theoretically necessary). Thus, briefly, several types of families are found in all the cities as well as numerous duplications in the economic sphere, several types of religions (though Timbuctoo had but one), varied practitioners of the magical arts, and numerous forms of recreation. Only in government, stratification, and socialization is mechanical heterogeneity (in an institutionalized sense) not readily apparent.

The conclusion that is most dominant is that the difference in heterogeneity between folk villages and cities is not sharp. Folk villages possessed some organic heterogeneity, though rudimentary. Conversely, homogeneity was found in all of the cities. In fact, homogeneity is probably as rudimentary in cities as heterogeneity is in the folk village. The pervasive nature of both conditions is crucial, for since they are found throughout both systems, it suggests that the continua uniting folk villages and cities is at the same time real and significant.

UNIVERSAL INSTITUTIONS

The heterogeneity of the cities makes discussion of several institutions difficult. In many cases, variations within the city occur both for ethnic and for status groups—and sometimes the two are merged. All of the cities have upper and lower classes—most have middle classes as well—and some of the variation follows these class lines. Other cities add ethnic groups as well. New Orleans has white and Negro segments (with Negroes assuming a caste-like lower status), Merida has European, mixed, and Mayan elements (Mayans forming the bottom layer), and Timbuctoo has Songhoi, Arab, and Bela (the latter being slaves of the Tuaregs).

These status and ethnic distinctions will not always be made, but they will be used often enough to require the reader to take cognizance of them now. (Of course, the folk village also has status distinctions, but life styles are not as drastically affected by them.) The same definition of an institution applies here as for the folk village: An institution is an organization of norms (including other institutions).

*Families and individuals.* Since the family is one of the most important components in the model of the folk village, a detailed consideration of families in the cities is of particular significance. The family in the folk village is a sexual, socializing, and economic unit, having male rulers and spatially retentive qualities for its members. In the cities, all of these aspects are modified drastically and some practically disappear, but the family remains.

Although the family is institutionalized in all of the cities, the most apparent feature of its structure in four of the cities is instability. (Ch'u is a special case.) The basic measure of stability used is the proportion of divorce—and the rate in Timbuctoo must be astronomical. Of the three major ethnic groups, the Songhoi usually marry at least twice and Arabs perhaps more often. "The younger Arabs have a distinctive attitude toward divorce. Both sexes place some positive value on the rupture of marriage. After some years of marriage, a man's friends may begin to tease him about keeping one woman so long" (Miner, 1953, p. 197). These two groups constitute five-sixths of Timbuctoo's population. The rate among the remaining sixth, the Bela, is not known, but the Bela did have the highest rate of prostitution of any ethnic group, so one would conclude that most residents of Timbuctoo do not expect to live out their lives in an unchanged marital union.

The rates of divorce in Middletown and Timbuctoo cannot be directly compared, but apparently Timbuctoo has the higher rate. In Middletown between 1925 and 1935, the rate varied between 36 and 50 divorces per 100 marriages, or from 3.1 to 5.4 per 1,000 of the total population. The data, however, do not end there. Many high-school students increasingly felt that marriage need not be final since divorce is no longer a disgrace. Furthermore, the incidence of male desertions was increasing. Finally, "the very heavy majority of Middletown's divorces come from the group of people on whom financial cost might be expected to operate most heavily as a deterrent to divorce," that is, the working class (Lynd and Lynd, 1937, p. 155). In other words, the high divorce rate in Middletown is significantly established in the mass culture.

The information for Merida is not completely comparable with that for Timbuctoo and Middletown. In 1934, the *number* of divorced persons per 1,000 population for the *municipio* (county) of Merida was 6.9; for the city it was 7.4; and for the entire state of Yucatán it was 5.2. This cannot be compared with Middletown's figures, where the total persons divorced at any given time is unknown (as contrasted with the number who become divorced during one year). Thus, Merida's rate is probably the lowest of the three cities discussed—only a slight tendency for Middletown's current divorces to accumulate would push its number of divorces proportionally higher than that of Merida.

And yet, the rate for the Yucatán city was certainly higher than that for the entire state—and the state was much more rural. Whatever may be Merida's absolute position, relative to its culture it has a high divorce rate and, in terms of the criterion adopted here, a high degree of family instability.

The rate of divorce in New Orleans is strikingly higher than that in Merida: 17.0 per thousand for males and 25.9 per thousand for females (21.6 for the total population). The ratio in New Orleans is thus three times higher than that in Merida. The relative position of New Orleans is also higher: the rate of divorced persons in the entire state of Louisiana was 11.6.

The data suggest that Timbuctoo had the highest incidence of divorce, Merida the lowest, with New Orleans and Middletown ranged between.

No comment was furnished on the frequency of divorce in Ch'u, but evidence is provided on the absence of divorce and the stability of the nuclear family. Concerning relationships within the nuclear family, Fried comments, "The variations themselves range from the tightest mutual dependency of related individuals to practical repudiation of responsibility" (1953, p. 67). This range of variation, technically speaking, takes the population *just short* of the act of divorce, and if Fried's statement is taken at face value, then no divorce occurs in Ch'u.

There is also positive evidence. For those with small or no surpluses, the nuclear family is the productive and distributive unit, the social organ caring for young and old, and the primary recreational unit. Though "no family in Ch'u is economically, politically, or religiously a unit unto itself, in each of these areas the first focus is within the nuclear family" (Fried 1953, p. 97). Under such conditions, divorce would be a quite serious matter, for it would tend to disrupt this fundamental and basic unit. If the family is as brittle as it appears in the other four cities, one would expect to find some sort of compensating mechanism to permit change in the sanctioned sexual unit. Only two are mentioned, however: secondary wives (or concubinage) and prostitution. Concubinage was not often practiced, though several cases are cited. Similarly, there were few prostitutes, and the city of Nanking was a source only for those with sufficient wealth to go there.

Among the five cities, therefore, the family varies from an extremely volatile to an extremely stable unit. Probably the only generalization applicable to all of the cities is that most of the inhabitants will be part of a familial and marital system during their lifetime.

The presence of single persons in the population is an important counterpart to an examination of family structure. If Redfield has correctly interpreted Henry Maine—that society has changed from a system of families to an aggregation of individuals (Redfield, 1941, p. 210)—then the number of persons without family ties is important. There is practically no information on the number of persons without kinship connections in the cities, but there is data on the number of adults who do not marry. Among persons 15 years old and over, 26.6 per cent of the Middletown males and 19.0 per cent of the females were single in 1930. The corresponding percentages for New Orleans (the 1950 population 14 years of age and over) were 25.3 per cent for males and 20.4 per cent for females. In these two Anglo-American cities, then, approximately one-fourth of the males and one-fifth of the females are to be found living in the single state.

Timbuctoo has an important transient population and, accordingly, at times has a high proportion of unattached males. In a particularly informative sentence, Miner remarks, "Unmarried Arab men, transients in the city, and all the single men too old or unattractive to find willing sweethearts, frequent prostitutes" (1953, p. 179). Each category refers to the single state.

Many persons in Ch'u "remain unmarried and know no relatives" (Fried, 1953, p. 66). These are mainly beggars and itinerant workers, on the one hand, and, on the other, store clerks, apprentices, and government workers who spend long periods away from their family. Thus we meet another device which permits changes to be made in the nuclear family, specifically in that individuals are permitted to separate themselves from the family unit. The separation may occur either prior to or subsequent to marriage. In spite of the infrequency of divorce, and realizing that separations are not always voluntary, temporary suspensions of marital contacts occur—and even the lack of formation of marital ties in the first place.

Accordingly, in all the cities there were persons who were either unmarried, divorced, deserted, or who were separated from their families. And in four of the cities, the marital bond displayed evidence of instability, from absolute to a relatively high frequency. These five cities, in other words, were systems of individuals with *and* without families.

The position of the family in the cities differs in other ways from that in the folk villages. First, the socialization function can be rather drastically curtailed. Fourty-four per cent of Middletown's families in 1930 had no children under 21 years of age living in the home. Such data are only suggestive—they do not tell how many children these families had at one time, but it is unlikely that the two figures would be equal. The sample data for New Orleans give a similar picture: of 96 households, 49 were childless at the time of the study (that is, 51 per cent). Thus, approximately half of the families or households in these two cities were not fulfilling a socialization role. The socialization activities were more completely performed by the families in the other cities, but the point remains that one cannot claim that the family fulfills the task of socialization in the city.

A second difference between the family in the city and the folk village is that the family is less of an economic unit. It is probably still a consumption unit in practically all cases, but wherever the division of labor involves a separation of residence and occupation, production thereby tends to separate from the family. Taking only the smallest cities, note such occupations as troubadours and donkey drivers in Timbuctoo, or porters, wheelbarrow men, and pole carriers in Ch'u. The removal of a significant element of production from at least some families is enough to show that the family in the cities has in certain cases lost its economic unity. And one specific role is lost: since few of the city dwellers are farmers, the family cannot be a food-producing unit as it is in the village.

The high degree of mobility of urban residents would preclude the family having any universal retentive powers. In other words, the family—and even the nuclear family—lacks the power to retain its members within the city (or within the population from which the migrant came originally).

The family in the folk village was dominated by males— even if descent was matrilineal. This generalization does not apply to the city. One instance was found of a widespread female rule of households (the term "matriarchal" cannot be used since many of these women were not mothers). In the sample of the Negro population in New Orleans, 56 households (58 per cent) were found in which a woman was recognized as the head. The pervasiveness of this pattern is important: it is found among women with children and women without them; and it is found among women who live with their husbands (19 households) as well as among women who live apart from their spouses. Even if the pattern is a cultural peculiarity, which it no doubt is, it renders the generalization of male dominance inapplicable to the city. Further, if a folk village were patrilineal, it would also be patriarchal, and this rule cannot be applied to the cities.

Both nuclear and extended families are found in all of the cities, the difference being in emphasis. In Timbuctoo, Ch'u, and Merida, different segments of the population will favor nuclear families, others will favor extended types. In the Anglo-American cities, nuclear types are favored, but different classes will at times develop extended families, whether through choice (upper classes) and/or necessity (lower classes). In all, the variation is the most striking feature. Even with respect to polygyny, variation occurs in the degree to which it is relatively favored (Timbuctoo and Ch'u), whether it has a quasi-institutionalized flavor (Merida), or whether it is flatly illegal (Middletown and New Orleans) but nonetheless possible.

In summary, there are two themes. The first is the lack of any qualitative separation between the folk village and the city. There are differences, but they are of degree. The second theme emphasizes change instead of disorganization. The reaction here is specifically to Redfield's pioneering efforts in his *Folk Culture of Yucatán* (1941), wherein he applied the term "disorganization" to the city family. Perhaps the term is still applicable in many ways, but it should not lead us to overlook the fact that something else has also happened: The city has transmuted the family rather than disorganized it. The family's social role is more limited in the city. It is a smaller system—in functions as well as often in members. It is also in many cases more readily changed and more mobile. The family, in short, has been divested of what may be regarded as many non-essentials. In this process, some disorganization has occurred—perhaps even extensive disorganization—relative to the folk village. But to call the transition "disorganization" and to leave it at that is to ignore some of the positive aspects of the family's position in the city. For the family does not assume a mere passive role of disintegration in the city. It still provides various services, but it provides them in a pattern which is markedly more flexible than that in the folk village.

*Secondary economics.* The discussion of economic institutions revolves around three major emphases: a division of labour between each of the cities and other cities; a division of labor between the citizens *within* these cities; and the degree of individuality which the city residents have developed.

Max Weber has proposed a useful economic classification of cities: A two-fold division is made between producer and consumer cities, with consumer cities separated into those of the rentier and merchant or trade types. (In rentier types, the level of economic activity is determined by independently wealthy or pensioned citizens [Weber, 1958, pp. 68–70].) Two additions to this classification are used. Trade cities are dichotomized into those based on local and foreign trade, with foreign trade referring to anything not connected with the immediate hinterland. Producing cities, in turn, are divided between factory and hand production. Rentier and trade types of consumer cities are also referred to as internal and external consumer types, respectively.

Each of the cities in this study has populations engaged in most of these activities, but there is a marked dominance of certain types in each city, as shown in Table 17. Most cities appear under two types in the upper portion of the table. As Weber has noted, "actual cities nearly always represent mixed types" (1958, p. 70). Table 17 shows first the logical relationships among the theoretical types, then the relationships between the various cities, with the types rearranged below. The rearrangement shows that the pattern of specialization does *not* depend on size. There is a relationship, to be sure, but Timbuctoo occupies the reverse position that it would occupy if population size were the sole consideration. With the exception of Timbuctoo, the other cities fall into place generally in relation to their number of inhabitants (note that New Orleans and Merida could be interchanged). At least one specialization does not appear among the five cities—there are no "rentier" or "service" cities (such as St. Petersburg, Fla., would be). Also, the entries in Table 17 are given only for the dominant specializations. The generalization bears repeating that such specialization has been developed to some extent in each city—though Timbuctoo is an exception in that it has no factories.

*Table 17.* Dominant economic activities in the five cities

| | New Orleans | Merida | Middle-town | Ch'u | Timbuctoo |
|---|---|---|---|---|---|
| *Consumer:* | | | | | |
| Internal (rentier or service industries) | | | | | |
| External (merchant, trade, or distributive industries) | | | | | |
| Local | | | X | X | |
| Foreign | X | X | | | X |
| *Producer:* | | | | | |
| Small (hand industries) | | | | X | |
| Large (factory industries) | X | X | X | | |

| | Tim-buctoo | New Orleans | Merida | Middle-town | Ch'u |
|---|---|---|---|---|---|
| Consumer, foreign | X | X | X | | |
| Producer, large | | X | X | X | |
| Consumer, local | | | | X | X |
| Producer, small | | | | | X |

Timbuctoo is the most extremely specialized of the five cities; it is a commercial city and not much of anything else. Of course, it has hand industries, trade with the people in the bush, and doubtless inherited wealth producing rentier types. But the life blood of the city is centered on commerce, a commerce based upon a hinterland reaching a thousand miles to the north and the west and half of that distance to other points. The population has grown and declined in direct ratio to the frequency of trade contacts. The height of the yearly commercial activity centers on the departure and arrival of the great winter caravan of approximately 5,000 camels. Practically all of the men and many of the women are engaged in trade. Timbuctoo also functions as a river port by means of its satellite village of Kabara. The exchange of "foreign" goods so overshadows everything else that no other major or dominant specializations are visible.

New Orleans and Merida both belong to the same scale type, since both emphasize commerce and manufacturing. In New Orleans, the distributive industries (transportation, communication, and other public utilities; wholesale and retail trade; and finance, insurance and real estate) clearly dominate in number of persons employed. Though other investigators describe this city as "low" in manufacturing (Harris, 1943; Duncan and Reiss, 1956, p. 393), their classifications are relative to the United States, a country with one of the most extensive manufacturing developments in the world. In New Orleans, the single industrial category of manufacturing is second only to that of trade in number of employed.

Merida supports itself chiefly by commerce and manufacturing. "All lines of communication, both with the hinterland and with the outside world, converge upon it. It is the hub of trade and finance" (Redfield, 1941, p. 19). Most of the manufacturing in Yucatán is concentrated in Merida: "railway shops, several cordage mills, an electric-power plant, a brewery, and many smaller shops and factories for making decorticating machines, furniture, cigarettes, soap, vegetable oil, soda water, matches, and tiles" (Redfield, 1941, pp. 19–20). As is true of any large city, its hinterland, alone, cannot support it. The city is dependent on other parts of Mexico and on the world beyond as well as on the Yucatán peninsula.

Middletown, of course, was originally studied because it represented an "industrial" (that is, manufacturing) culture. But since, like New Orleans, Middletown is in the United States, it is not surprising that Duncan and Reiss (1956) classify Muncie (Middletown's actual name) as medium in manufacturing. This classification also shows Middletown specializing as a maintenance trade center, that is, as a local, external consumer city.

The county of Ch'u is primarily engaged in agricultural production, to which may be added the labor of artisans who work from raw materials. "The bulk of the town population, however, relies on the exploitation of both categories of workers for its wealth" (Fried, 1953, p. 24). The result is an extensive market service to the county and an intricate development of hand industries. Ch'u does have commercial ties with the outside world, but no mention is made of factories.

Timbuctoo represents the most urbanized type in that its commerce is specialized in foreign trade, whereas Ch'u depends on its own hinterland for its commercial activity. Ch'u's manufacturing activities are on a scale smaller than that of any of the cities, except Timbuctoo. But Timbuctoo is too specialized to have developed any manufactures significantly. Lack of manufacturing in Timbuctoo may thus be regarded as a consequence of its extreme specialization and thus, according to this measure, its extreme urbanization.

The division of labor within the cities is readily described for four of the cities and clearly inferred for the remaining one. These data are presented in Table 18. For New Orleans and Middletown, the industrial classification of the 1950 census is used (1930 data for Middletown are not comparable). The terms for Timbuctoo and Ch'u are those employed by their investigators.

Although all recorded job and occupational descriptions are used for Timbuctoo and Ch'u in Table 18, only relatively broad classes are given for New Orleans and Middletown. The reason, of course, is that the division of labor is vastly more extensive there than shown in the table. New Orleans has persons in each of the 148 detailed industrial classes, ranging from two persons in synthetic fibers to 12,829 males in water transportation. The industrial classification for Middletown in 1950 includes only 77 items, and of these one is vacant (knitting mills). The largest category contains 3,039 males employed in motor vehicles and motor-vehicle equipment.

In Timbuctoo and Ch'u, the specific industrial and occupational terms probably represent the minimum specialization. But these specifications differ in an important way from those in the two Anglo-American cities. Quite often, functions that are more specialized in the larger cities are combined in the smaller cities. Thus, smiths in Timbuctoo are also magicians

*Table 18.* Industrial composition of four of the cities

| Industrial classification for New Orleans and Middletown | Timbuctoo | Ch'u |
|---|---|---|
| Agriculture | Farmers | Truck farmers |
| Forestry and fisheries | .... | .... |
| Mining | .... | .... |
| Construction | Masons | Painters, masons, carpenters |
| Manufacturing | | |
|   Furniture and lumber and wood products | .... | Lumber yards |
|   Primary metal industries | .... | .... |
|   Fabricated metal industries | Smiths | Blacksmiths, tinsmiths |
|   Machinery, except electrical | .... | .... |
|   Electrical machinery equipment and supplies | .... | .... |
|   Motor vehicles and equipment | .... | .... |
|   Transportation equipment, except motor vehicle | Donkey breeders, camel breeders | .... |
|   Other durable goods | .... | Pottery shops |
|   Food and kindred products | Butchers, bakers | Slaughter house and butcher shops, candy makers and bakers, beancurd makers, rice polishers, noodles and processed wheat products makers |
|   Textile mill products | .... | Cloth shops, cotton ginners |
|   Apparel and other fabricated textile products | Tailors | Tailors |
|   Printing, publishing, and allied industries | .... | .... |
|   Chemicals and allied products | Charm-makers | Herb stores, incense and candle makers |
|   Other non-durable goods | Slippermakers, sandalmakers, tanners, basket weavers | Cigarette makers, charcoal jobbers, fuel grass jobbers, leather tanners, basket makers |

*Table 18 (cont.)*

| Industrial classification for New Orleans and Middletown | Timbuctoo | Ch'u |
|---|---|---|
| Not specified manufacturing industries | .... | Firecracker makers |
| Railroad and railway express service | .... | .... |
| Trucking service and warehousing | Shippers | Transport firms, import good stores |
| Other transportation | Donkey drivers, caravaneers | Pole carriers, rickshaw men, porters and coffin carriers, wheel-barrow men |
| Telecommunications | .... | .... |
| Utilities and sanitary services | Water carriers | Water sellers |
| Wholesale trade | Wholesalers | Livestock commission merchants, grain ex-changes |
| Food and dairy products | Milk vendors, (vendors of various foods) | "Groceries," eating oils stores, fruit stores, salt stores, tea stores |
| Eating and drinking places | .... | Restaurants |
| Other retail trade | Market retailers, shopkeepers, cloth vendors, wood vendors, tobacco vendors | Peddlers, "other" (i.e., jewelry, sign shop, gold exchange, etc.) |
| Finance, insurance and real estate | Money lenders, landlords | Speculators, userers, landlords |
| Business services | .... | .... |
| Repair services | .... | .... |
| Private households | .... | .... |
| Hotels and lodging places | .... | Hotels and bath houses |
| Other personal services | .... | .... |
| Entertainment and recreation services | Troubadours | .... |
| Medical and other health services | Barbers, healers | Barbers |
| Educational services, government and private | Teachers | Teachers |
| Other professional services | Marabouts | Priests, abbots |
| Public administration | Cadis, emirs | Various public officials |

and are therefore professionals as well as workers in fabricated metal industries. Bakers, to take another example, manufacture their product as well as sell it, and thus they belong under manufacturing and under food and dairy products. The difference is in the degree of specialization: Although all of the cities have an intensive division of labor, the process has gone farther in some than in others.

The inference may safely be made that Merida lies somewhere between the extremes represented by New Orleans and Timbuctoo: (1) industries of commerce and manufacturing are dominant in Merida, whereas in Timbuctoo, only commerce is dominant. Thus, Merida would have more specialties; (2) factory industries characterize Merida's economy rather than the handicraft of Timbuctoo (and Ch'u, for that matter), and thus one could expect to find even greater specialization; (3) Merida had a population more than 15 times that of Timbuctoo, and although there is not a 1-to-1 correlation between population size and occupational specialization, there is some relationship. The increase in the absolute number of specialties is only too apparent. Accordingly, the conclusion is that Merida is at least more specialized than Timbuctoo.

The incomplete nature of the city family as an economic unit has been discussed earlier. The question remains, what is it that fills the gap? In a more immediate sense, economic activity shifts from the family to other organizations. These organizations are of course controlled by individuals, but they are individuals in the sense that their social relationships have been changed—from individual membership in a family to membership in some non-familial organization.

These comments may oversimplify one point—the city must not be viewed as having abandoned the family, even economically. A shift in emphasis occurs such that the family ceases to be practically the only means by which the social system operates to that in which an important emphasis is placed on individuals apart from their family positions—and even at times in total disregard of family positions. Most individuals in all of the cities have family connections, and in many cases the family is and can be an economic unit. But all families are not such units.

In contrasting individuality in Timbuctoo with the "folk community," where the line between religious, family behavior, and economic activities is exceedingly difficult to draw, Miner observes: "In Timbuctoo it is often easy to make such a distinction. A market economy requires specialized and individualized activity. In these activities, the market rewards secular and impersonal behavior. This fact, plus the inherent conflict between different traits of cultures in contact, results in interrelations of a non-folk type" (1953, p. 274). Miner goes on to note that even the obvious need of a community-wide organization is obscured by lack of understanding which arises from heterogeneity and the apparent rewards attainable by disregarding tradition.

The description for Ch'u is more definite. It has been noted that although many individuals have no family attachments in Ch'u, the nuclear family, itself, is rather strong and stable. However, the essentials of wealth production and the consumption of food are carried on by the large household rather than by the nuclear family. Thus, there are qualitatively three types of situations: nuclear families, households, and unattached individuals. These situations parallel three distinct types of financial organization occurring in Ch'u: nuclear family enterprises, extended family stores, and partnerships. The last are "individualistic" organizations, and they comprise over 25 per cent of all shops, mainly the largest ones. In addition, there is another level, one which rises above the households, families, and individuals. In the economic sphere, this organization was found in the merchant guilds, to which all who wanted to do business in Ch'u had to belong.

To this discussion of individuality should be added the sentiment of *kan-ch'ing* (described in the section on interaction), a sentiment essentially integrating kin and secondary contacts. It is thus particularly relevant here.

Redfield's discussion of Merida is even more suggestive of the pervasiveness of individuality. Secular and pecuniary considerations "do not fully prevail" within the family—one does not drive a hard bargain with a kinsman. And yet the family is a scene of pecuniary and bargaining activities. Indeed, on the whole, "the attitudes in Merida are such as to approve of many sorts of business dealing within the extended family and even within the parental family, with the understanding that such dealings are more friendly, personal, and informal than are such dealings with persons who are not relatives" (Redfield, 1941, p. 160). In other words, to some extent the family has become the locus of individualistic (that is, non-familial) activity—and preferably so. More interesting, it is not always possible to keep "friendly, personal, and informal" sentiments in such transactions. The people of the lower class recognize a conflict in that business dealings tend to lead to quarrels or because business dealings must be guided by self-interest, a viewpoint difficult to maintain in transactions with relatives.

The Lynds give one specific utterance which attains a succinct relevance: "The city's economic and associated institutions operate by long tradition on the theory of each man for himself..." (1937, p. 34). The individuality of economic endeavor can be described even more precisely for both New Orleans and Middletown, at least in 1950. Table 19 shows that unpaid family workers are almost non-existent, private wage and salary workers most numerous. But "individualism" has invaded the

Table 19. Class of worker for New Orleans and Middletown, 1950 (per cent)

|  | New Orleans: non-white | New Orleans: white | Middletown |
|---|---|---|---|
| Males |  |  |  |
| Total employed | 100.0 | 100.0 | 100.0 |
| Private wage and salary workers | 86.3 | 72.8 | 84.2 |
| Government workers | 7.4 | 13.6 | 6.0 |
| Self-employed workers | 6.2 | 13.5 | 9.7 |
| Unpaid family workers | 0.1 | 0.1 | 0.1 |
| Females |  |  |  |
| Total employed | 100.0 | 100.0 | 100.0 |
| Private wage and salary workers | 87.5 | 77.7 | 79.8 |
| Government workers | 8.1 | 15.2 | 13.8 |
| Self-employed workers | 4.0 | 5.8 | 5.8 |
| Unpaid family workers | 0.4 | 1.3 | 0.4 |

family even further in that in at least some instances, persons in the class of private wage and salary workers are actually related to each other. The case of one such New Orleans family illustrates this point. The business was founded by the father, and each of the three sons were given shares and key administrative positions. After the death of the father, one son bought out the shares of the others, demoted them, and assumed control —illustrating the principle that even in family businesses, hired relatives may fall into monetary rather than familial classifications: The *economic* relations become non-familial.

Money is central to the economy of each of the cities. Timbuctoo once used a system of exchange based on cowrie shells, but the shells were true money, as shown by their fluctuation in value relative to the stock of gold hoards during times of famine. And in Merida at one time, price-haggling was the custom (as it perhaps still is in Ch'u). The haggle has been superseded by the fixed price—but the price is there. And, of course, a money economy is thoroughly ingrained into the cultures of New Orleans and Middletown.

Money is a peculiarly economic medium, but it has important non-economic implications. As Fried points out in speaking of Ch'u, "The use of money clears the way for immediate interpersonal relationships on a massive scale without benefit of prior meeting, introduction, or kinship" (1953, p. 124). In other words, money becomes a highly abstract and simple form of contract.

*Religion.* Religion exists in each of the cities and in one way or another influences most of the inhabitants. (The intensity of this influence is another matter and will be reserved for a functional analysis.) Timbuctoo is almost purely Muslim. "The belief in Allah and his prophet Mohammed is the greatest unifying force in Timbuctoo. It is the one value shared by all natives" (Miner, 1953, p. 75). Such a degree of religious homogeneity is found in none of the other cities. Ch'u contains Confucianism and ancestor worship (perhaps "ancestor reverence" is a better term), Buddhists, Taoists, religious societies, and two small bodies of Catholics and Protestants. Merida is predominantly Roman Catholic, but there has been enough anti-Catholic sentiment that the cathedral was once sacked by a mob. The city also has Protestants (since 1879), Spiritualists, Theosophists, and Naturists. According to the 1936 Census of Religious Bodies, Middletown (Muncie) had 50 churches in 29 denominations. The Methodist Episcopal Church was the largest, containing 22.8 per cent of the total reported members 13 years old and over. For the same age group, New Orleans reported 33 denominations with 284 churches; Roman Catholics, as might be expected, formed the largest share: 69.5 per cent. Interestingly, Negro Baptists constituted the next largest group (9.8 per cent).

By no means, therefore, can one say that cities are religiously heterogeneous. Timbuctoo is clearly homogeneous, as are Merida and New Orleans from the point of view of the majority. Only Ch'u and Middletown are probably heterogeneous in religious composition.

This heterogeneity is mechanical, but most of the religions in all of the cities have a division of labor. The religious hierarchy is the obvious example. This hierarchy extends to both the natural and supernatural world, as in the Roman Catholic religion. The Muslim hierarchy in Timbuctoo is one of prestige. In the supernatural sphere, it descends from Allah to Mohammed, to the saints, and finally to the ancestors. There are also living saints, sanctified by public opinion. Marabouts appear next in the hierarchy, followed by their students and these probably followed by the faithful. Non-believers form the bottom or "outcaste" layer, but the number of these are negligible. A division of labor for religious functions, however, is more clearly developed between the marabout and the cadi. The marabout is learned in the Koran, writes magical Koranic charms, prognosticates the future, and works supernatural cures. The cadi, on the other hand, is simply a judge of Koranic law.

Information for hierarchies is limited to the secular aspects of religion in Ch'u. Both Buddhists and Taoists have a hierarchy of at least a temple head (or abbot), priests, and followers. The Buddhists and Taoists have monks. There were also Catholics and Protestants, as noted. In Middletown, hierarchies were also developed by various Protestant denominations.

All cities in the study have religious societies, such as the Catholics' Knights of Columbus, the Methodists' Wesleyan societies, the various Muslim religious orders, or the religious societies in Ch'u. These organizations permit those with the greatest religious interests to come together and, thus, set the more devout somewhat apart. The organic nature of this differentiation is in the division of society into those of manifestly nominal as opposed to intense devotion.

Magical practices are also found in all of the cities. The distinction is the same as that used for the folk village: magicians control the spirits, whereas the (religious) gods control the people. Magic is extensive in Timbuctoo, involving an elaborate complex of genies, fetishes, grigris, vampires, fortune tellers, etc. Merida has black magic and witches, with apparently a sharper division of labor than Timbuctoo: marabouts work in magic as well as religion, whereas Catholic priests oppose magical practices. Of course, the marabouts were apparently limited to Koranic magic, as opposed to the non-Koranic magic of the sorcerers, and to this extent a "division of labor" did appear, symbiotic though it may be.

Magical practices were also extensive in Ch'u. The distinction between practitioners of magic and religion, however, does not appear well developed—the Taoist monks were known to be a source of both.

Belief in magic is generally disfavored in urban Anglo-American culture. People are apt to disguise such beliefs by talking of "luck," both good and bad, and an elaborate set of rituals and charms have grown up in connection with such "luck." Accordingly, it may be safely assumed that both New Orleans and Middletown have magical beliefs. In addition, in Middletown, as in New Orleans: "Patent-medicine advertisements still pepper the pages, as well as advertisements of doctors not recognized by the medical profession, . . . and advertisements of 'Madame Claire, Palmist'" (Lynd and Lynd, 1937, p. 375). New Orleans—at least as late as 1950—still contained persons who believed in the potency of various voodoo practices, such as scrubbing steps with brick dust to remove the evil effects of gris-gris (the pronunciation and meaning is the same as that found in Timbuctoo). One white man and several Negroes are known to adhere to these beliefs. Of course, procuring information of this sort—given the unfavorable cultural definition—is extremely difficult. Advertisements in Negro periodicals would lead one to conclude, however, that the faithful (or even those who would rather not "take a chance") are at least numerous enough to be commercially noticeable.

How important is religion to these urban cultures? The intensity of beliefs varies widely from city to city. The apex probably is found in Timbuctoo, whereas religious observances in Ch'u are described as relatively minor events. Merida includes the few Catholics who identify closely with the church, a great number of partial or nominal Catholics, and a large minority of frankly dissident or disbelieving cultists and others. There is equal variation in New Orleans—from faithful church attendance in the Negro sample (averaging approximately a visit a week), to nominal attendance, to frank atheism (though this is rare). Middletown appears more ambivalent. Manifest loyalty to Christian beliefs is demanded (at least for Christians), "but when this world of religious values cuts athwart Middletown's labor problem, or the city's devotion to such more immediate symbols as those identified with 'patriotism,' people's reactions are almost unvaryingly determined by their loyalty to those more immediate things rather than to the religious symbols" (Lynd and Lynd, 1937, p. 310).

It is often stated that one of the functions of religion is support of the mores. The data for the five cities in this study cast serious doubt on such a conclusion. How can the mores be supported by such frankly half-hearted or shallow belief? Timbuctoo may seem to be an exception, but as is true of all five cities, one may also ask about it, *which* mores are supported? Certainly religion in Timbuctoo does not prevent the inhabitants from different quarters from considering each other fair game in any market transaction, even for "unethical" practices. And yet, all are of the same religion.

Having offered this criticism, perhaps another interpretation should also be offered. Four of the cities have ingrained in their culture a belief in life after death. Ch'u is slightly different in that it reveres ancestors rather than believes in an afterlife. But a quotation is helpful: "The younger gentry had little or no use for the Taoist temple and its few priests. . . . The most important day of the year, as far as the Taoist priest was concerned, was the holiday . . . on which day the evil spirits of disease are driven away. . . . Hardly anyone, even the most outspoken of the young landlords, refuses to give something in return [for the magic prints] to the Taoist monk for fear of angering him, which might lead to disaster" (Fried, 1953, pp. 201–2). If the belief in life after death is interpreted as a *fear* of death, and the fear of the Taoist monks as an indication of basic insecurity (perhaps associated with death), then religion becomes an element in bolstering the morale of a people, or in sustaining their esprit de corps. Of course, insecurity need not be confined to a fear of death, but it seems a common thread. (In this connection, see Malinowski 1955, pp. 50–53.)

*Government and power.* The division of labor in government has already been described (see the section on heterogeneity). The theme here is government power. The distinctions of Bierstedt (1950) are used: *power* is latent force, *force* is manifest power, and *authority* is institutionalized power. Force may also be described as the application of sanctions or the reduction of alternatives. In all of the cities, force was the basis of power, although it was not always readily visible. Sanctions could be applied by all of the city governments, and the ultimate threat was the reduction of alternatives to the point where an individual had no alternatives but to do the will of the police or soldiers (or die).

There was also authority in all cases—a city government of some sort was recognized by the people as the seat of power. But whether authority was more important than power (that is, power "in the raw") was another matter, and this condition varied in each city.

The French, as the conquerors of Timbuctoo, wielded more power than authority. Authority was vested in the emir (chief) and the chiefs of the city quarters, in the cadi (judges), and in the patrilineal family. This authority was bolstered, at least *in part*, by Koranic law, for even this system was generally not operative except under outside control. Over this hierarchy ruled the French, who reserved for themselves the administration of all major corporal punishment—that is, the application of force.

Authority in Ch'u was more important. The Nationalist government stood at the top of a hierarchy which filtered down through the provinces, *hsien* (county) governments, and terminated finally in the *pao* or group of households. Except in the case of deviants, such as bandits, the legitimate nature of the government was recognized and used. Power seldom became manifest in force because of this institutionalization.

The mixture of Middletown's power and authority is different than in either of the two smaller cities. On the one hand, there is the duly elected government constituting the authority. These political institutions, however, have "fallen into disrepute because of the meager calibre of men" who run for office (Lynd and Lynd, 1937, p. 89). On the other hand, there are economic interests who do not want to rule directly, but who do not want too much interference with their affairs. They do not want authority, but since they are efficiently organized, they gain power. The most powerful of such interests is a family designated by the Lynds as the "X's." This family does not dictate, but it nevertheless controls. Since its power is not institutionalized—is not legitimate—the family (and its economic interests in general) possess power rather than authority.

Information is meager concerning government of Merida, but it appears to resemble that of Ch'u. That is, the national government assumes the greatest authority through a centralization of political controls.

The government of New Orleans typically is a political "machine" of the variety well described by Lincoln Steffens (1931). Such organizations generally operate as a link between the political and economic forces of the city. Since the machine as such has no authority, much of its power remains invisible (and thus particularly latent). The New Orleans machine has at least been partly visible in that its manifestly political arm has been named. Earlier it was known as the Choctaw Club; now it is called "The Old Regulars" (see Heberle, Hillery, and Lovrich, 1953). Since 1946, however, a non-machine candidate has held the mayor's office.

In only two cities, then (Ch'u and Merida), were the forces in power also those of authority. Of the remaining three cities, two displayed a government with less power than that held by others in the city (that is, the native rulers of Timbuctoo in contrast to the French, and the political officials of Middletown in contrast to the "X" family and other economic interests). New Orleans shifted between these two situations.

Regardless of the dominance of power or authority, in none of the cities—not even in Timbuctoo—was total power in use. In other words, there was no evidence that the total life of the inhabitants was controlled or even that such control was attempted. Even in Timbuctoo, where occurred the most extensive use of power, the French permitted native rulers and judges to function.

INSTITUTIONS OF PROCESS

*Contract.* Although contract is the form of cooperation more typically found in the cities, mutual aid appears to some extent.

Following Smith (1953, pp. 523–26), we may refer to both mutual aid and contract as types of cooperation. (In this sense, of course, they more properly belong under the element of inter-action. But we are here focusing interest on institutions.) Mutual aid is essentially non-contractual. It refers to norms setting forth the expectation that the members of the system should contribute aid to each other (not always in economic matters) without calculation of specific remuneration (Hillery, 1959, p. 238, n. 7). Contract, on the other hand, operates through a formally constituted organization, by means of definitely specific rules.

Timbuctoo most closely approached a system of mutual aid in the *koterey*, a fraternal society to which every adult native belongs. But there are three important qualifications. First, there is no city-wide organization. At the most, these societies are integrated only on an ethnic basis, and even then not always. Second, membership is in terms of individuals rather than families. Third and most serious, among the Songhoi, the city's largest ethnic group, one can and does belong to more than one *koterey*, and in these cases cooperation is "purely on a money basis. The *koterey* are becoming increasingly like mutual insur-ance companies" (Miner, 1953, p. 174). It is this specification which keeps the *koterey* from being completely an institution of mutual aid, in the sense that the means to cooperation are specific instead of diffuse.

None of the remaining four cities have mutual aid even to the limited extent of Timbuctoo, though it can and does occur, of course. For example, during the depression of the 1930's, many Middletown landlords were willing to let the rent lapse (in part because of a desire to have their properties occupied by trusted tenants instead of standing idle). And in New Orleans, specific-ally among the lower classes, neighbors have been known to take in victims stranded by floods. But circumstances prompting such help are rare. Further, since one never knows that this help can be expected, it can hardly be looked upon as institutional-ized, as normative, in the sociological sense.

Most of the behavior of city residents, then, is not covered by mutual aid; the most important type of cooperation is the con-tract. The basis of the contract is primarily to be found in its specialization. Whereas the obligations and rights of mutual aid are diffuse, those of contracts are specific. Parsons elaborates this quality when he describes four of the essential fields which must be adequately defined if the contractual system is to be stable: the *content* of the contract must be defined, the *means* of securing the assent of the other party to the contract must be delineated, limitations must be placed on the degree of *risk*, and *societal interest* must be specified (1960, p. 145).

The industrial specialization noted in the section on economics is basically a manifestation of contract. The content of the contract, that which a person must (and must not) do is specified, as are the legitimate means of gaining such specializations (contracts) and the degree of risk involved. And once a social system has committed itself to industrialization or commercialization (as all of these systems have), then fulfillment of contracts definitely becomes of societal interest, particularly in the sphere of government.

But specialization is not confined to economics. Organic heterogeneity has been repeatedly noted in the other institutions and must be noted again. The most general feature common to this heterogeneity is that of contractual obligations and rights. Even the family, basically a non-contractual institution, was found to be subject to its influence.

And then there is money. In itself, money is a written contract between the citizen and his government. Thus, though it is an economic means, money has a non-economic basis. Further, and more important in the present context, money can be used for ends that are not strictly economic in the sense of making one's living. Such institutionalized activities as commercial recreation, religious contributions, educational tuition, taxes, and even commercialized sex illustrate the point.

Contractual behavior is not found everywhere in the city— note the family and recreation (where all is not commercialized) —but it clearly permeates most of the city. In fact, were there no contracts, none of the five cities described in this book would function.

*A note on urban deviant behavior.* There is a qualitative increase in the extent to which deviance is *reported* in the cities. The purpose of this note is not to treat deviance as an element, however, since even criminals (except, possibly, psychotics) conform to a vastly greater degree than they deviate—in clothes, speech, use of money, etc. The importance of deviance is not to be found in the act of deviance but in that which it represents.

In Merton's theory of anomie, he proposes five types of individual adaptation, summarized in Table 20 (Merton, 1957,

*Table 20.* Individual Adaptation

| Modes of adaptation | Culture goals | Institutionalized means |
|---|---|---|
| I Conformity | + | + |
| II Innovation | + | − |
| III Ritualism | − | + |
| IV Retreatism | − | − |
| V Rebellion | ± | ± |

KEY: + = acceptance
− = rejection
± = rejection of prevailing values and substitution of new values

p. 140). As has been noted, the most prevalent type of adaptation is conformity. The other types are deviants. Though doubtless all types are found in all of the cities, the only consistent evidence is confined to innovation, such as petty larceny, burglary, banditry, and fraud. These crimes are listed for each of the cities except Merida. Redfield offers no evidence concerning crime in Merida, but he notes that "a modern police system was organized" as early as 1902 (1941, p. 34).

Why should evidence for innovation be second only to that for conformity? Innovation points to the presence of contradictory norms among groups sharing the same types of culture, and of course this is the situation found in each of the cities. The contradiction arises from heterogeneity. Mechanistic heterogeneity seems most responsible; that is, the condition in which different kinds of means (such as religions) are used to attain the same ends. But organic heterogeneity should not be ruled out, particularly when the means of adaptation available to the lower classes are limited while at the same time the culture emphasizes the importance of adopting the common goals, such as pecuniary achievement.

But more important than heterogeneity and money is the contract. There is a chain of links stretching from deviance to the contract, and not the least of these links is the quality of individualism and the separation from complete control which individualism suggests. For it is characteristically the individual with whom a contract is made. Money is the simplest and most flexible type of contract, and the frequency with which deviance is concerned with money thereby becomes important (as in larceny, burglary, fraud, etc.).

Thus, deviance, itself, is not a significant feature of city life. The more significant feature is the contract and the heterogeneity and individualism which breed it. Deviance is important as a type of evidence indicating the nature of certain crucial features in the type of social system under investigation.

*Stratification.* The range of statuses in the cities is extremely wide. Whether stratification is built of personal characteristics, family lineage, achievement, power, authority, or possession (Parsons, 1953), the people in each city differ widely. Timbuctoo contains slaves, serfs, poor tradesmen, rich merchants, and nobles. The recognized classes in Ch'u include officials, landlords, merchants, peasants, tenants, and workers (combining county and city classes), though there was much overlapping. In Middletown and New Orleans, classes are heavily based on occupation and wealth, though family does assume importance (more so in the southern city). New Orleans also has a caste-like system separating Negroes and whites. The classes of Merida are founded primarily on differences of occupation, origin, race, language, and literacy. The upper class tends to be predominately of white ancestry, the lower classes Mayan, but racial mixtures vary throughout the scale. The situation is similar in Timbuctoo, though Caucasoid and Negroid are substituted for white and Indian, the white population again forming the upper layer.

In several cities, there are separate systems of stratification existing side by side. Timbuctoo, has separate systems for each of the three ethnic groups: Arab, Songhoi, and Tuareg. The foreigners in Merida also form a parallel status structure. In New Orleans, the situation is more complicated. Though almost all whites regarded almost all Negroes as their inferiors, the Negroes do not necessarily acquiesce and, in addition, the Negroes have developed their own class structure.

The degree of vertical social mobility varies between the cities, though there is always some movement. Timbuctoo has slavery in both the Tuareg and Arab populations, and though slaves may now attain their freedom, this was not always as possible. Status achieved by economic means had long had some importance, but it was more limited in earlier times by the ascription of roles on the basis of ethnic group, state of servitude, and family position. Mobility, in brief, has always been possible in some instances in Timbuctoo, but it increased under French rule.

Ch'u differs from Timbuctoo in that the overlapping of class lines is more marked and class mobility is recognized. "A man is known not only by what he is but also by what he was and what, in all likelihood, he will be in one year or ten or twenty" (Fried, 1953, p. 18). But though a man may move from peasant to merchant during his lifetime, the move from merchant to landlord is not recognized by the people (even though the merchant may acquire land). This distinction is thus more rigid than those separating other strata. Further, intermarriage between classes is infrequent.

Redfield succinctly describes Merida's changes in class movement: "The old social classes . . . were based chiefly on genealogical connection with originally distinct ethnic groups (although wealth was important in determining the social position of the individual in relation to other members of his own class); the new social classes are based on wealth, education, and occupation" (Redfield, 1941, p. 166). And, since the new classes are based heavily on achieved status, movement between classes is correspondingly more frequent.

With the exception of ethnic differences, class movement is probably as frequent and rapid in New Orleans and Middletown as in any of the other cities—often more so. But in discussing Middletown's industries, the Lynds speak of the increasing appearance of two social ladders rather than one. The working-class ladder is becoming shorter, harder to climb, and leads nowhere in particular. The other is "a long and repaying one but beginning a long jump above the plant floor" (Lynd and Lynd, 1937, p. 72). New Orleans adds the Negro-white caste-like condition wherein movement is practically always one way and in secret (into the white population). Also, though of less frequency today, there are remnants of the old planter aristocracy whose fortunes have declined—proud, clannish, and attributing more status to themselves than others can quite manage to accord.

It is impossible to rank these cities on any consistent scale. Ch'u probably has more mobility than Timbuctoo, and Merida has more than Ch'u, but New Orleans is very similar to both Timbuctoo and Middletown. Further, at different times in the history of the cities, the speed of class movement has varied. The only generalizations remaining are that the distances from the top to the bottom layers is great in all cities, and that all have some degree of vertical social mobility.

*Socialization.* All of the cities have schools that they had established, though the complexity of the school system varied. The simplest organization was that of Timbuctoo. The teacher was a marabout—a man learned in the Koran. He complied to no fixed standards—the more learned he was, the more respected he became. Some of his students were pre-adolescent sons of the wealthier families who were turned over to him for day-long instruction. Others were apparently less fortunate, for Miner remarks that alms could be given to students to assist them in their Koranic studies.

Educational specialization is markedly greater in the other four cities: All have one or more high, middle, or college preparatory schools, and three of the cities contain one or more colleges or universities. (Ch'u, on the other hand, sends its college students to other cities for their education.)

Both Ch'u and Timbuctoo contain a system of apprenticeship for youngsters entering the crafts, and New Orleans—in addition—has numerous programs of on-the-job training. Merida and Middletown probably have corresponding institutions.

The degree of literacy varies, from almost complete in New Orleans and Middletown to a condition where most inhabitants are illiterate, as in Timbuctoo or even Merida. (Fried is not specific for Ch'u, but the level of literacy probably approaches that of Merida.) Median years of schooling completed in 1950 for the adult population were higher for Middletown (9.7 for males and 10.3 for females) than New Orleans (8.1 for males and 8.6 for females). On the other hand, "the great majority" had no education in Timbuctoo. Merida had 73 per cent of its population classified as "literate," but most "ordinary" people read and write little and laboriously.

Institutionalized socialization in the family is poorly developed. The *aims* are fairly well defined in all cities. The families are at least expected to teach the children to speak and to conduct themselves in interpersonal relationships—for example, to have "manners." The educational *structure* is also consistent in part: the mother generally assumes the greater burden in all cities. The role of the father as a teacher is seldom described, but his position appears consistently as the ultimate source of discipline. There does not seem to be any common *method* of socialization in the family, however. Children may be punished or rewarded frequently or seldom, consistently or inconsistently. In New Orleans and Merida, "among all classes corporal punishment is often unregularized and capricious" (Redfield, 1941, p. 193). In addition, some parents of New Orleans, Middletown, and Merida compound the issue by psychological experiments in child-rearing. Methods of child-rearing may be institutionalized in Timbuctoo and Ch'u (the data are not clear), but regardless of the situation in these cities, methods of familial socialization are certainly not institutionalized in all five cities.

*Recreation.* The same universal recreational practices appear in the five cities as appeared in the folk villages: feasts, festivals, games, and music. There were also other forms. Gift-giving and children's games were noted for all cities except Merida, though the absence of these practices in a city as heavily influenced by European culture as is Merida seems unlikely. Dances were mentioned in all cities except Ch'u. Similarly, plays and stories were not mentioned in Timbuctoo and Ch'u—not even motion pictures were described. Timbuctoo, however, does have the interesting occupational specialty of troubadour. Whether these are poets, musicians, or both is not stated. Gambling, finally, was not mentioned in Timbuctoo or Merida.

Specialization has influenced two of the universal forms of recreation, either by producing a division of "labor" directly in the recreation or through some organization which serves it. Industries have grown up to supply prepared foods for feasts in all of the cities. There is the specialty of musician in each city. As mentioned earlier, however, games do not necessarily have specialization—none was observed in Timbuctoo and Ch'u. On the other hand, many games in the largest three cities have elaborate organic heterogeneity, involving not only players but spectators as well (paid admissions, reporters, etc.).

The commercialization of recreation is extensive. By commercialization is meant contractual hiring of persons to perform some given service. Festivals are universally commercialized. For example, musicians in Timbuctoo are paid to play for the wealthy on the birth anniversary of Mohammed, the clerks of Ch'u are given money to visit a bath house at the eighth-month festival, and toys, candies, and food are purchased for various festivals in the larger cities. These examples could be multiplied, but they should also be qualified: festivals are not *necessarily* commercialized. Commercialization has occurred in part only. The same may be said of music, though this form of recreation is probably heavily commercialized in all of the cities. Games, again, do not invariably succumb to this process (they do in all of the cities except Timbuctoo and Ch'u). Gambling is practiced in Ch'u, but this type of game does not necessarily require the hiring of anyone and thus is not necessarily commercialized (at least by definition).

Where motion pictures are present, plays and stories may become automatically commercialized, as happened in the three largest cities. Interestingly, commercialization preceded rather than followed the cinema—the theater is one of the oldest forms of commercial art in European culture.

Miner notes for one of the games of Timbuctoo—an almost ceremonial game of hockey called *alkura*—that it contributes to the social solidarity of the various quarters. When the more neutral term of organic heterogeneity is translated into Durkheim's organic solidarity, the place of recreation as a medium for reinforcing cooperative norms appears as much in the city as in the folk village. The universal specialization and commercialization of recreation in the cities shows merely that the form of cooperation has changed from that of mutual aid to that of contract.

Thus, recreation helps to emphasize the theme that folk villages and cities exist on continua. Accordingly, it is quite understandable that some recreation was commercialized in some of the villages (though not in all of them) and not all of the universal forms of recreation are commercialized in all of the cities.

The mixture shows the nature of one continuum between the folk village and the city. Recreation both reflects and stimulates cooperation, and cooperation is one of the central elements on which both cities and folk villages are built. The form changes as the system changes, but the basic nature of this institutionalized process remains.

# C

# Total Institutions

The data in this appendix necessarily stand in a different relation to the rest of the book than do the preceding appendices, for several reasons. First, we are dealing with a negative case. As will be apparent prisons and mental institutions are not the same order of things as are folk villages and cities. However, prisons and mental institutions have often been treated as communities, and thus they must be considered here. They cannot be dismissed on a priori grounds, for the basic approach of this book is that in the present instance theory must be built from data. And since data are emphasized, then data must be presented here as for more positive considerations (as with the preceding appendices).

But the most important consideration is that these systems represent a conceptual borderline for folk villages and cities. It is because we can say that total institutions are not vills that we can say further that nations, neighborhoods, and families are related to vills rather than to total institutions. From this point we are able to distinguish the entire field of communal from formal or complex organization.

313

THE SYSTEMS STUDIED

The five total institutions studied are outlined generally according to the scheme used for the village and the city. Summaries appear in Chapter 8, Table 6. Insofar as practical, the components are the same as in the vills, under the null hypothesis that the systems have no qualitative differences.

*Belmont Hospital* was established as part of the Neurosis Centre at Belmont Hospital in England. The full population, including the staff, numbers more than 135 persons. Since the average length of stay for inmates is short (two to four months), considerably more persons have been in Belmont than indicated by the population at any one time (8,607 persons had been admitted up to May, 1950). The hospital was only three years old when studied, and the still experimental atmosphere was quite noticeable in the report. The Unit was developed to investigate the chronic unemployment neurotic. Maxwell Jones and his associates (1953) reported their experiences in organizing the Unit from 1947 to 1950.

*Caudill's hospital* is unnamed and unlocated, except for its being in the United States. It was founded approximately thirty years ago as a research and teaching unit attached to a medical school. When studied, the inmates and staff included somewhat more than 70 persons. William Caudill (1958), an anthropologist, conducted the research during 1951–52. His basic goal was essentially descriptive: to obtain objective and detailed information on a psychiatric hospital by a scientifically trained observer.

*Southern Hospital*, originally the State Lunatic Asylum, opened in 1861 with fifteen patients. In 1950, it had 2,960 patients in a total population of 3,570 (424 medical and 186 non-medical employees). The yearly average number of patients, however, was 4,800. The development of Southern is best characterized by unplanned and random growth. The asylum was studied as a social organization by Ivan Belknap (1956) during 1951 and 1952. His work is noteworthy for its completeness.

Clemmer's is the classic treatise on prisons, if not on total institutions. It was intended as a description of the formal and informal organization of a conventional prison. In effect, as Donald Cressey comments in a foreword to Clemmer's book, the prison is treated as a social microcosm of conditions and processes in the broader society. It is the younger of the two prisons studied here. The oldest cellhouse was built in 1878. The inmate population was composed of 2,300 prisoners when studied (1931–34), and had a staff of 200. As happens with many studies of total institutions, Clemmer (1940) chose not to disclose the identity of the system.

The New Jersey State Maximum Security Prison (herinafter designated the *Trenton Prison*) was first built in the last decade of the eighteenth century. Its modern inmate population of 1,200 is smaller than Clemmer's, but the staff is larger (300). Gresham Sykes (1958) studied this prison (apparently in 1954) by means of a variety of techniques, including questionnaires, interviews (with both inmates and guards) and personal observation. Sykes' main emphasis is on the use of power and its influence both on staff and inmates.

A word of caution before proceeding to the analysis: There is a strong temptation to speak of total institutions as they *could* be rather than as they are. Someday the total institution as described here may cease to exist, in spite of the fact that from what we know of Rasphuis (Sellin, 1944), approximations to them have existed for more than three centuries. But vastly more important is the realization that the systems we are about to analyze are what we have now. We are thus describing what exists (as nearly as the resources will permit)—not what might be.

INTERACTION

Interaction revealed itself in three patterns. First, there was a network of system-wide contacts linking most or all of the population in each total institution. Second, interaction tended to cluster, such that there were degrees of isolation, both individual and structural, in each system. And finally, there were informal as well as formal structures in all of the total institutions.

System-wide contacts were intentionally formalized in Belmont in at least two ways. (1) Every weekday morning there was some form of "community" meeting attended by all patients and some of the staff. (2) By means of psychodrama, patients' problems became "known to everyone on the Unit" (Jones *et al.*, 1953, p. 64). In Caudill's hospital, on the other hand, this system of communication operated chiefly through the patients on an informal basis. The patients were in contact with the greatest number of persons and had the greatest access to both doctors and nurses. "This circumstance would help to explain the seemingly mysterious process by which patients often sensed or even knew what was happening in the hospital before this information was available to other role groups" (Caudill, 1958, p. 336). In Southern, certain key personnel assumed central roles in the communication network. In practice, the asylum operated in three subsystems: maintenance, custodial, and technical (medical-psychiatric). Although each subsystem was isolated to some degree, strategically placed attendants, a personnel manager, and the assistant superintendent kept the superintendent informed about important problems.

There were two system-wide means of contact in the prisons. The first was rigidly institutionalized by the staff and was directed chiefly toward custody. The prison officials felt that their first duty was to prevent escapes, and they kept enough contact with the inmates to insure a high degree of success. But there was another network which depended more on the volition of the prisoners. Clemmer saw this informal structure as partly institutionalized in the role of the runner or prisoner-messenger. Persons in this role formed a very effective grapevine which extended widely throughout prison life. Prisoners, for example, found it impossible to keep a disease such as syphilis a secret, because of the hospital visits required. The motives for grudge fights, similarly, would "spread to the entire community of 2,400 persons" (Clemmer, 1940, p. 218). Sykes does not explicitly describe a grapevine, but the interaction network was nonetheless vigorous. Prisoners lived in an "enforced intimacy" in which "each man's behavior is subject both to the constant scrutiny of his fellow captives and the surveillance of the custodians. It is not solitude that plagues the prisoner but life *en masse*" (Sykes, 1958, p. 4).

Yet this system of contacts is not complete in any of the institutions. There are various degrees as well as kinds of isolation. First, "structural isolation" seals off various parts of the institution by means of barriers to communication. The barriers are greatest between staff and inmates in the prisons. Southern

Hospital added an additional barrier between the technical staff and the rest of the population. The hospital was operated in practice by the attendants, and the technical staff interacted with the patients largely through them. Several nurses of Caudill's hospital had not been on the locked ward for years, and several had not been on the open ward. The least degree of structural isolation was at Belmont. The staff-inmate split was purposely minimized by group therapy and by the formal meetings of most of the Unit. Nevertheless, the staff chided the patients for shielding a thief who had been plaguing the Unit and for a "false sense of loyalty or fear of reprisals" (Jones *et al.*, 1953, p. 178). Thus, the inmates themselves erected a barrier, one which was apparently broken in some cases but by no means in all.

There was also "individual isolation." Clemmer found that 960 men (41.9 per cent) had no definite or intimate social relationships. Sykes noted the same process, but gave no percentages. Both writers apply the term "atomized" to the inmate population. Of course, the severe neurotics and psychotics would tend at times to be fairly well isolated in both Southern and Caudill's hospital. Belmont kept such isolation at a minimum by means of two policies: (1) severe character disorders were expelled, and (2) the task of encouraging participation at sessions of group psychotherapy was shifted to the patients themselves. Few were isolated at Belmont. And yet, here and there are accounts of "persons too ill to be responsible" (Jones *et al.*, 1953, p. 42), and of efforts to be sure that "feelings of rejection by the group [were] avoided as far as possible" (p. 86). The phrase "as far as possible" is an admission that not always was the effort successful. And then, there is explicit mention of "desocialized" patients who feel "outside the [therapeutic] community" (pp. 31–32).

The informal structures in these systems may be appropriately designated as cliques for the most part, that is, non-institutionalized primary groups. They were strategically located throughout the total institution, certainly in all of the inmate populations and explicitly in the staff of Belmont, Southern, and Caudill's hospitals. There is no reason to believe that cliques were lacking among the staff of the prisons.

A closer look at the prison situation is instructive. Clemmer categorizes the inmates into primary groups (one-fifth), semi-primary groups (two-fifths), and the "ungrouped" (two-fifths). Sykes creates approximately the same impression by describing two extremes: "collectivistic" prisoners, who offer fellow captives mutual aid, loyalty, affection, respect, and united opposition to staff; and "individualistic" prisoners, engaged in a war of all against all, each seeking only his own advantage. The population of prisoners is a mixture of both extremes, "balanced in an uneasy compromise."

The ultimate effect is that inmate systems are inherently unstable. Indeed, because of contradictions generated by the "grouped" as opposed to the "ungrouped," it is incorrect to speak of an inmate system at all. One may only speak of a number of inmate systems, and then only with the realization that not all inmates operate within systems.

That the inmates of the mental asylums represent varying degrees of isolated or "atomized" individuals is evident. But none should conclude that the "atomization" is complete—no more than is true of prisoners.

SPACE

*Boundaries.* The boundaries of total institutions are "pathologically" sharp, and this fact makes a great deal of difference to all concerned. Thus, this component necessarily differs from the "vague" boundaries of folk villages and cities.

The sharp boundaries surrounding prisons and mental asylums of course are an indication of concern with the problem of custody. At one extreme is Belmont, where no mention is made of locked or disturbed wards, and there probably are none. Those who do not respond to controls of a non-violent nature are discharged; the problem is "solved" by avoiding it. But there are still regulations concerning boundaries. Inmates must secure *permission* to leave the Unit, permission in the form of passes, and these passes are in the hands of the doctors, not the patients. These passes are denied to some patients. Further, those who do not heed the regulations are discharged. In other words, either the inmates submit to the total control of the institution or they cannot belong. Initial submission may be voluntary, but once the inmate enters the system, he surrenders his freedom to come and go.

Still, Belmont is not nearly as concerned with custody as the other total institutions. In addition to the institution of passes, Caudill's hospital has locked wards for more disturbed patients. Thus, there are two sets of boundaries, both sharp. Nor is there conflict between them. Persons are assigned to locked wards depending on their unwillingness to submit to the staff's requirements for custody.

The problem of multiple boundaries increases in Southern, in part because of that hospital's size. It has windows with security screening and, instead of the institution of the pass, there is parole, with the implication of greater supervision. Southern also contains the criminally insane, thus necessitating tighter boundaries than is true even for most inmates in maximum security prisons.

The boundaries around the prisons are obviously sharp. Sykes' description is relevant to both prisons: "A massive wall 20 feet high separates the free community from the prisoners, serving not only as the final barrier to escape but also as a symbol of society's rejection—for this is a fort to keep the enemy within rather than without" (1958, p. 3). The staff sets these boundaries, and thus, although they are concerned with them, they may transgress or move over them at will. In this sense, the boundaries are sharp for both staff and inmates, but the behavior toward these boundaries is qualitatively different.

*Spatial pattern.* There seems to be no pattern in the use of space that is common to all total institutions. Both of the prisons are small (approximately 13 acres) and have high walls, but the similarity ends there. Although both Belmont and Caudill's hospital are probably quite small, Southern is very large—200 acres, though this area includes farm land.

There is no way of knowing whether all of the asylums have walls, since no descriptions are provided, but there is an impression of drabness in all cases (this could be due to the emotional rather than the physical atmosphere). The nearest approach to a pattern is a tendency for wards, cells, offices, and rooms to take the place of homes, courthouses, churches, factories, etc., but even this tendency is not always exhibited.

The lack of pattern suggests that space, per se, is not of central concern. It becomes important only to the extent that it can be used for the specific ends of the total institution. These include custody in prisons and both custody and treatment in asylums.

*Spatial integration.* The main evidence for spatial integration has been given in the two preceding sections. For present needs, four items may be used initially: the sharpness of boundaries, the lack of other patterns, the concern over custody, and the different relations of staff and inmates to both custody and boundaries.

Custody is important in all cases, but variations occur in the extent to which boundaries are crossed. No inmate may pass the boundaries of any of the custodial systems without staff permission, but in the prisons this permission is given very seldom. It is given more often in Southern Hospital, with even more frequency in Caudill's hospital, and with most frequency in Belmont. Thus, a shift in orientation toward the use of space takes place; the space is *used* by the staff for accomplishing varying purposes. Space, itself, is not an independent variable governing or limiting interaction. Since prisons and asylums use space somewhat differently, each should be considered separately.

Custody is the overriding concern of the prison staff, although it is only one method of using space in the control of the prisoners. Space is also a limiting condition, since once custody is violated (for example, in escapes), so is control. Reciprocally, staff tends to increase spatial restrictions as inmates violate prison rules. Solitary confinement is one extreme, extension of the prisoner's commitment is another (that is, loss of "good time," as this extension is referred to in prison argot). Extension of commitment is not only an extension of prison rule but it is also a temporal increase of spatial confinement. Space, in other words, is used as an instrument of control, both with respect to the prison's boundaries and with respect to the space within the prison.

In the asylums, custody is also a problem, but not the chief problem. The concern is not simply to keep the enemy within; there is also the quality of asylum, itself, of sheltering the relatively helpless. In addition, it is easier to treat the mentally disorganized when they are conveniently located than on an "out-patient" basis, and, at times, they can only be treated in confinement.

In other words, custody is not always developed for custody's sake in the asylums. It is used for treatment purposes. Southern

Hospital, in being both a prison and an asylum, combines both methods. The criminally insane are maximum security patients and custody is modified only by the fact that the patient is sometimes incapacitated as well as hostile. Restrictions in use of space vary according to the willingness of the patient to conform to custody. Space is thus used in a fashion similar to its use in prisons. But greater freedom is permitted other patients, including " parole " on the hospital grounds. And when the patient becomes " rational," he will be freed, depending on the staff's interpretation of his conditions. The important point, of course, is that mental disorganization, not custody, is the real problem. When the problem is solved, the need for custody ceases.

In Caudill's hospital, the emphasis swings to treatment, though custody remains (passes and locked wards being examples). This shift in emphasis is revealed in this conversation between two psychiatrists.

*Dr. Reynolds:* This raises the whole question of the use of rooms. Should rooms just be assigned on a priority basis? . . . I feel there should be freedom to move patients around. . . .

*Dr. Scott:* Wait a moment! Look what you said there! Freedom to move them around. Really what you meant to say was freedom to discuss with them about the move. This business of sort of assuming authoritative control over the patients [Caudill, 1958, p. 288].

If a patient is well enough, he is given a pass to town. Some patients even attended parties given by an ex-patient who had rented an apartment in town after her discharge. Again, custody is important for treatment; otherwise, it is expendable.

Belmont represents the extreme in the minimum use of custody. Depending on their condition, inmates are either retained within the Unit or are given passes. Patients requiring maximum security precautions are not allowed to remain. In Belmont, then, there is only the task of custody; it is not a problem.

Spatial integration in the custodial system is thus not something sui generis but is responsive to other causes: custody or treatment. Distance usually presents no problem for social interaction. All are equally near, for practical purposes. The problem, instead, is how to use this space for the specialized ends of the organization in question. Space does not help to integrate the organization. Rather, the organization uses space for various ends, whether these be integrative or divisive.

### ACTIVITIES

*Base of operations*. Total institutions function as bases of operations—with three serious qualifications. Most important, prisons and mental asylums are bases for their inmates only when staff gives permission. Without this permission, there is no base of operations, only confinement. Second, it is no longer sufficient to refer only to cosmopolitan and localistic bases of operations, as was possible when discussing vills. The localistic type must be further divided into internal and external subtypes; that is, those activities which take place within the total institution and those which take place outside of it. Although unnecessary for the other local systems, the nature of the confinement renders this distinction mandatory in the case of custodial systems.

The third qualification hinges on the staff-inmate split. Staff is not subject to the limitations imposed on the inmates. For some staff members, specifically those who dwell on the grounds, the total institution *is* a base of operation, both localistic and cosmopolitan. But not all staff "live in," and for those who do not, other sites become the base. Even among those who live in, it is the staff themselves who control the confinement, and it is they who can "violate" it as needed. Accordingly, the distinction between staff and inmate renders the base of operations a qualitatively different phenomenon in total institutions than in vills.

Since the control exerted by staff varies, one would expect variation in the degree to which different total institutions function as bases of operations. And such is the case. The prisons become almost completely localistic and internal bases of operations. Furthermore, these function only for some of the prisoners, not all. Those in solitary confinement obviously lack any sort of base of operations. Only trusties, if there are any, can use the prisons as external bases of operations for journeying to the town, or, in a more cosmopolitan sense, to other towns. But the exceptional position of trusties serves only to strengthen the contrast with other inmates.

Discharge and parole are qualitatively different things: they are institutions of population maintenance and as such will be discussed under institutions. Briefly, it should be noted that when inmates leave by either of these two means (or by escape), the entire base of operations is changed to some other social system.

Both Southern and Caudill's hospital are internal bases of operations for only some patients: those confined to locked wards obviously cannot participate. But there are open wards in both institutions, and Belmont is run entirely in this manner. Thus, the asylums are quantitively different from the prisons in the greater freedom of movement permitted. But the basic task of custody is still present. *Some* patients are *permitted* to move about at will, others are not, and those in the "permitted" categories can be placed in the prohibited categories, if the staff sees fit.

The same argument applies to all three asylums in the case of external and cosmopolitan operations. Southern gives furloughs and leaves of absence (of shorter duration than furloughs), and Belmont and Caudill's hospital give weekend and daily passes. All of these institutions, however, place conditions on the patient's return. Thus, it matters not whether a visit home is called a cosmopolitan operation or not; the patient operates from his base only at the sufferance of the staff. Otherwise, he has "escaped," which means he is no longer subject to the institutional controls.

The total institution as a base of operations is peculiar in another way. This peculiarity is found in the lack of a population segment found in the vills—children. Paradoxically, this *lack* prompts certain superficial comparisons with vills. (1) There are many similarities between children and inmates (though the obvious distinctions should not be confused), one of which is reflected in the sharp constriction of spatial operations for both. (2) Inmates cannot spend their entire lives in these systems, since they are born elsewhere (at least in the five systems considered).

*Mobility.* The two types of mobility discussed in this section operate in part as a single process. Practically all movement to the total institution (territorial mobility) is also horizontal mobility since a change of group membership is involved. Certainly this statement applies to the inmates. For the staff, there is little information, though their mobility patterns are probably no different from the residents of the five cities.

Mobility of inmates in and out of the total institutions falls into two discrete classes: (1) those who enter and are eventually discharged, and (2) those who accumulate. In Clemmer's prison, the addition of inmates amounts to approximately 26 per cent of the inmate population per year; slightly less than this leave. Fifty-five per cent of the Trenton inmates leave within two years, 85 per cent within four years, and then there are the "lifers." The turnover in asylums is higher, and perhaps for this reason there also can be a more rapid accumulation of "static" personnel. Southern Hospital had a turnover of 40 per cent or more per year, but the accumulating "untreatable" patients comprised more than half of the inmate population (57 per cent). In Caudill's hospital and in Belmont, because of staff policies, patients did not accumulate. The average stay in both places is approximately four months; most of the patients do not stay the year.

No data are available for the prison staffs, but the rates of mobility for the staff of asylums are quite variable. Almost 70 per cent of the physicians and other professionals in Southern Hospital left and were replaced each year. On the other hand, the older "core" of attendants changed at a rate of about 1 per cent per year. Though important as a limiting case, this core group is nevertheless unusual, since the attendants as a whole had the highest turnover in the hospital. Comparable statistics are not available for Caudill's hospital, but the staff there is described as being *less* mobile than the patients (the nurses were least mobile). Somewhat the same situation prevails at Belmont, where at least some nurses stayed from six months to a year.

Thus, mobility in total institutions has sharply distinct facets. High proportions of both staff and inmates move yearly. But once the inmates are in, their mobility is at a minimum. Most come, stay, and go in three well-defined events, widely separated in time. Some come to stay.

Once the inmate is within the custodial system, horizontal mobility does not stop. Although data are lacking, the change in clique membership would have to proceed at a fairly constant rate in view of the high turnover. In the prisons, there is probably some occupational shifting as well, since they contain industrial enterprises. There is a more regular movement of some patients in Southern and in Caudill's hospital, wherein they shift from ward to ward, depending on the progress (or decline) of their mental condition. Similarly, as the patients in Belmont improve, they are granted passes.

In all cases, horizontal mobility for the inmates is rather sharply confined to the total institution. But there is one exception. Large proportions of all the inmate populations had group memberships on the "outside." Regardless of—or in spite of— the geographic move to the institution, a position was maintained in these other groups as well. That position, furthermore, could be altered with changes such as death, divorce, or birth.

*Continuance.* Total institutions are probably at least as old as cities, of which they are most likely products. Prisons were described in biblical times (see Genesis 39–41), and from the fragmentary evidence available, they resembled later prisons. Rasphuis was in operation for more than two centuries (from the late sixteenth to the nineteenth century) and according to the data is quite representative of the prisons described here (Sellin, 1944). The age of asylums may be considerably younger. Bedlam, England's oldest asylum, was established around 1400. Southern Hospital was almost a century old and in fact developed from the older, more purely custodial asylum. Nevertheless, the type represented by Caudill's hospital and by Belmont are creations of this century. Belmont was two to three years old at the time of its study; Caudill's hospital, twenty-five years old. The two prisons approximated the age of Southern Hospital more than the other asylums (Clemmer's prison was 56 and Trenton was 164 years old).

Thus, custodial institutions in general are as old as vills. However, the more recent forms represented by Caudill's hospital and Belmont are sufficiently different to warrant special notice. They may be indicative of a trend, one which will either show the limits to which total institutions can develop or the avenue toward its eventual modification and even possible dissolution.

SENTIMENT

*Ethnocentrism.* Attitudes of hostility and conflict towards other segments of the system appear in all of the total institutions. Such attitudes in fact become a major concern of staff, such that, in functional terms, *a manifest function of staff dominance is to minimize the manifest dysfunctions of inmate disloyalty.* A closer examination of the implications of this principle is instructive. One of the reasons why society keeps staff in a dominant position is that the inmates intend to be disloyal. Staff has as part of its main job, therefore, the task of (1) keeping the acts of inmate disloyalty to a minimum in order (2) to minimize the repercussions of this disloyalty.

The total institutions vary markedly in the extent of inmate disloyalty. Belmont represents one extreme of solidarity. The staff was enthusiastic concerning their experiment in psychotherapy—the therapeutic "community." Much of this enthusiasm was communicated to the patients. Unfortunately, the reader is not told whether the patients were ethnocentric concerning Belmont, but it is probable that many had positive attitudes toward the staff. And yet, in speaking of the daily discussion group which was held for the entire population, it is noted that: "At almost every such meeting hostility is expressed towards the doctor" (Jones *et al.*, 1953, p. 41). There is also evidence of hostility towards the patients by patients. Typically, this hostility was focused on one particularly objectionable patient who then became a scapegoat, facilitating the expression of goodwill and comradeship among the haters. Perhaps because of this scapegoating, even manifestly hostile patients were able to identify with the whole group (apparently the Unit) to some degree.

In short, the staff-inmate split is in a weakened condition at Belmont. Some loyalty exists, but evidence for its existence is clearest for the staff. The patients quite often and consistently display attitudes that at best should be characterized as ambivalent—at worst as hostility.

Belmont is the extreme case, the case of *highest apparent* ethnocentrism. Caudill records a greater variation in attitude. Among all role groups, a pessimism is manifest which extends to the hospital's physical structure, its emotional climate, and its general social organization. And yet Caudill notes that by and large the hospital is seen in a favorable light. In terms of the ambivalence and conflict mentioned above, this contradiction is understandable. It is perhaps best summarized by the comment one patient made upon leaving: "I feel like I am stepping off into quicksand. I don't know how a person can hate a place so and still feel so squeamish about leaving" (Caudill, 1958,

p. 330). When such information is considered together with the characteristic staff-inmate split, the divided nature of the population's views is apparent.

In Southern, extremes are more often encountered. At the center of the hospital's organization is the core of attendants previously discussed. Their long tenure is but one manifestation of a considerable solidarity and in-group feeling, a feeling which is also directed against both patients and professionals. The ideology and tradition of this core extends over a period of at least seventy years. The attitudes of the patients are not recorded, but the professional people experience frustration, loss of esteem, and a not unexpected hostility toward the attendants. Whatever loyalty there is in Southern is not universal.

The prisoners are generally disloyal toward the prison as a whole (staff reactions are not discussed in either of the studies). Of course, as Sykes indicates, too much solidarity among the prisoners undermines the power of staff. It can even increase the dangers of revolt and thus act as a threat to the most central goal of the staff—custody. But the prisoners' sentiment is one of dissension. On the one hand, there are the members of primary groups who show loyalty to each other. And there is the one value shared by most prisoners directed against "rats," "squealers," "center men," or "stoolies": persons who take the side of the staff against the inmates. The names themselves are suggestive enough; the reaction is institutionalized and extremely negative. But, on the other hand, the names show dramatically that the prisoners expect disloyalty. They recognize that a sizable proportion of the population is frankly looking out for themselves. This sentiment is most vividly put by the "eleventh commandment" recorded as part of the prison argot by Clemmer: "Thou shalt not get caught." More to the point is the habitual cheering of the visitor's team when playing against the prison team (again recorded by Clemmer). Absence of ethnocentrism in such a situation is quite obvious.

But one qualitative observation is simple to make: who would expect prisoners to like their prison? Whatever occasional exceptions there may be, the observations of Clemmer and Sykes make sense. Prisoners are loyal mainly to themselves, and even then, "themselves" often means solely the individual. Such sentiments, if they occurred in vills, would lead to civil war or at

least abandonment. Similarly, if the asylums were suddenly deprived of staff control, none of them could be expected to act
like stable folk villages or cities.

*Awareness.* A consideration of awareness in total institutions
raises problems both of types and degrees. The fact that there is
a concern with custody is in itself evidence of one type: the
awareness of the total institution as a whole. Of course, for those
in stricter confinement, awareness becomes distorted to the
extent of the limitation of mobility. A locked-ward patient will
be most aware of the locked ward. Further, staff and inmates
view the prison from different vantage points, and thus they
will be aware of different aspects of the same thing. They will
also view each other from a different perspective, as Clemmer
notes in his clinically laconic remark: "A good proportion of
the inmates feel critically towards officials, and their emotions
are likely to influence their objectiveness" (Clemmer, 1940,
p. 161). Thus the second type of awareness is an awareness of the
staff-inmate split.

There remains the interesting question, what is the degree of
awareness, especially among the inmates? That it is a peculiar
awareness is obvious. But on an a priori basis, one might believe
that large proportions of inmates, at least in asylums, may be
unconscious of their surroundings. There is no foundation for
such a conclusion. The patients in Belmont are of course completely aware of where they are and why they are there. Caudill
never gives one the impression of such "unconsciousness" in the
asylum he studied, even for patients in seclusion. Belknap comes
closest in describing patients without privileges at Southern:
"patients who are almost completely stuporous, some who are
clearly mentally deficient, some who are passive and listless,
senile and deteriorated largely through physical aging, some
who are frequently disturbed, and some who are nearly always
uncooperative" (1956, p. 167). The "stuporous" are most
likely unaware, but these were not completely stuporous.
Furthermore, all except the highly disturbed were able to
adjust to ward life. Thus, even in Southern, the "unaware"
are apparently rare.

Strangely, the clearest evidence of lack of awareness comes
not from an asylum but from a prison: "About the prison yard
and the shops one sees . . . men who seldom smile, who seldom

talk, who stumble as they walk in lines, whose errors in their tasks cause small concern, and who respond normally to social stimuli only when a stimulus is strong or different. Status or social approbation is as nothing" (Clemmer, 1940, p. 244). This condition Clemmer calls "reverie-plus." It is an escape mechanism, including perhaps 15 or 20 per cent of the inmates, that places one "so socially out of touch with the instant environment that it causes little pain" (p. 247).

Though Sykes does not refer to a condition like reverie-plus in Trenton, the major point is established. Withdrawal to the point of unawareness does not occur in all total institutions, not even in all asylums. When it does occur, it affects only a minority.

*Homogeneity and heterogeneity.* Heterogeneity in custodial systems is not a symptom of either organic or mechanical solidarity, per se, but of antagonism. There is mechanical heterogeneity among both staff and inmates, and organic heterogeneity among staff, and inmates even have some mechanical solidarity against staff.[1] Further, the staff may organize the inmates, as when prisons develop industries, or when asylums employ occupational therapy. But the mechanical solidarity is born of antagonism, and such organic heterogeneity among inmates as exists is imposed by the staff and thus cannot be considered organic *solidarity*.

Apart from the homogeneity arising from sexual segregation, the only common trait among all inmates is that they are considered abnormal by the larger society: all prisoners have been convicted of some crime (they are not merely or even necessarily criminals), whereas mental patients essentially lack the ability to communicate meaningfully. These are the only necessary qualifications for entering prisons and asylums, and total institutions are far from being otherwise homogeneous (for example, Clemmer's prison included burglars, robbers, murders, confidence men, and sex deviates; Belmont contained "psychopaths," schizoid personalities, drug addicts, sex perverts, and chronic psychoneurotics).

Accordingly, the homogeneity of inmates can be traced in one way or another to the fact that they are dominated by staff.

[1] See Fig. 4 and Table 12 in Appendix A for the relationship between heterogeneity and solidarity.

This gives the inmates a common enemy and thus unites them to some degree. The unity is admittedly slight and erratic, but to the extent that it is there, we may speak of mechanical solidarity.

The organic heterogeneity of the staff is plainly evident; for example, psychiatrist, nurse, attendant, etc., or warden, guard, chaplain, etc. And it is well known that prisoners may have a division of labor. Both Trenton and Clemmer's prison were also industrial concerns, as was Southern Hospital. Caudill's hospital and Belmont had occupational therapy, which is essentially no different from the other custodial systems in being an imposed division of labor. Furthermore, Caudill notes that the entire patient population could be treated as a unit when working in occupational therapy, and thus no division of labor was *needed*. Witness the comment of the occupational therapist: "I wanted to invite the entire patient group down to the occupational therapy shop. . . . I wanted to say we are just going to work on pottery this morning" (Caudill, 1958, p. 105). Whatever division of labor exists among inmates, it does not bind them together. It exists because it is wanted, required, or otherwise brought about by the staff.

Thus, though there is solidarity in custodial systems, both organic and mechanical, one cannot speak of solidarity in custodial systems as a whole. More basic is hostility, a quite different sentiment. Hostility pervades the total institution so completely that it is difficult to discuss any aspect of these systems without encountering it. It has received most discussion in reference to the components of interaction, spatial integration, base of operations, and ethnocentrism, and it will be developed further in connection with the institutions of government and cooperation.

INSTITUTIONS

Though institutions are discussed with the same concepts and definitions as used for the vills, the treatment of specific institutions differs at times radically. In some cases, specific institutions are not found in total institutions, for example, the family, and one new institution is introduced because it is a peculiar necessity for custodial systems: the institution of maintenance.

*The absence of family.* None of the inmates lived with their families in the custodial systems. There were homosexual unions, but to broaden the definition of the family to include them would be a gross distortion for at least two reasons. First, such "units" lack children of their own. Furthermore, in practically all cases, the element of sanction is absent. The family is also absent in a third way. Even were prisons, for example, to permit wives free access to the prison, the wife would still not be a member of the prison.

An important variation on this point is provided by Giallombardo in her study of a prison for women (1966). Here, probably most of the women established homosexual "marriages" which were socially recognized as legitimate relationships.[2] Further, the inmates attached themselves to other inmates in kinship roles, that is, they assumed the positions of father, mother, brother, sister, uncle, etc. Although it is still true of course that children are not produced by such unions, socialization of new inmates did occur in the "family" groups. But, as Giallombardo clearly indicates, the marital and familial units are *substitute* relationships for those that would normally occur in the outside world. Thus, inmate "families" are not only pseudo in the biological sense (as in the absence of children and in the act of women assuming male roles), but they are pseudo *in the eyes of the inmates*. Second, the familial units are not cooperating units. They are formed so that the inmates may cooperate within them, not between them. In fact, cooperating between familial units is strongly discouraged by the inmates. Thus, the inmate population cannot be described as "a localized system integrated by cooperation and families," as can the vill. Third, whatever may be said about the presence of "families" in women's prisons, one could not conclude that families are essential to total institutions, since families are not generally (or even usually) found in such systems—and particularly not among inmates.

Finally, it is important to note that the women's prison studied by Giallombardo fits the model of the total institution in every one of the other components. In particular, there is the staff-inmate split noted for the other systems. This means that the staff and inmates are conflicting rather than cooperating units and that they are not united by familial ties.

[2] The relationships were actually more comparable to "going steady" among adolescents, except for perhaps a greater intensity.

As a rule, families are absent among the staff as well, although Southern Hospital provides an exception. One of the few stable points in its organization was a core of families which provided many of the asylum's ward attendants. The members of these families, having grown up on the hospital grounds, found it natural to work there. Seventy per cent lived on the grounds, and six out of ten were married to other attendants employed in the hospital. By no means were all the staff so related. Physicians, nurses, social workers, psychologists, therapists, etc., were excluded. But the presence of this core demonstrates that a custodial system may be operated by families, at least in part. On the other hand, absence of such relationships in the custodial systems also demonstrates that such a type of management is not necessary.

Although it is true that the family is not a part of the inmate population and is unnecessary to the staff, the relation of families to the total institution is nevertheless significant. First, large proportions of the inmate populations described by Clemmer, Sykes, and Belknap had family contacts with the outside world. Doubtless, this relation holds for all total institutions. The significance of such connections is that they give the inmate status in a group other than the custodial system.

This influence is seen further in the malfunctioning of the family. If the inmates do not relish their stay in the total institutions, it is not the total institution, alone, that disturbs them. Clemmer notes that 40 per cent of the prisoners come from broken homes. There is a strong probability, according to Belknap, that the patient in Southern Hospital will have a family that is less well integrated than average. And one of the observers in Belmont concluded from a follow-up study of discharged patients that the cause of much of the desocialization noted in the hospital was "due to the absence of any real family life" (Jones et al., 1953, p. 161). Even with data lacking from the other two systems, it is apparent that the family is related significantly to the present condition of the inmate.

The inmate therefore is not just an inmate. In many total institutions—and probably in all—he is often a family member, though this status is outside the custodial system But, whatever is done to the inmate, it cannot be and is not done to him solely as an inmate. Indeed, it is most probably the rather severe attempts by the staff to rule out the family that helps to set total institutions apart from other systems.

*Institutions of maintenance.* The four institutions of maintenance to be considered are recruitment, custody, treatment, and discharge. All of the total institutions have institutions of maintenance. They do not, however, all have the same institutions.

*Recruitment.* Recruitment pertains to the first contact, both direct and indirect, that the future inmate has with the custodial system. In the present systems, two processes are involved: entrance and screening. Screening is designed to fit the inmate into the system. The entrance process, on the other hand, is seldom a part of the total institution. It generally involves actions by some segment in the larger society or by the prospective inmate. For the prisons, one must be convicted of some crime. The emphasis is on conviction; none can say with certainty that all inmates are criminals. Further, not all are professional criminals. Less than half of Clemmer's prison is composed of technical recidivists (42 per cent). "The great bulk of the penal population is comprised of awkward, amateurish and occasional offenders" (Clemmer, 1940, p. 56).

Patients in Southern Hospital (including the criminally insane) were committed rather than convicted. Commitment could be either voluntary or involuntary and was accompanied by either court or medical action (or both). The process was most involved in Belmont, and here the hospital took much of the initiative. Likely sources of inmates all over England were informed of the existence of the Unit. Prospective patients submitted an application, had an interview with Disablement Resettlement Officers, and applicants with specific occupational disturbances were admitted. A psychiatric report accompanied the "commitment" procedure.

Commitment at Caudill's hospital was generally haphazard, and thus there is little in the entrance process that could be called institutionalized. The screening process was institutionalized, however. Psychiatric observation, diagnosis, and treatment were parts of the ongoing life in the hospital, and the inmate would thus be subjected to a psychiatric screening rather early in the admission process. The psychiatric report has been mentioned for Belmont. Screening in Southern Hospital was a relatively confused process, since patients were classified according to both psychiatric and custodial requirements, and these often conflicted. The core of attendants previously discussed intensified this conflict: they had power over the inmates since they were closer to them; while the psychiatrists had the authority, they had no time to supervise.

Screening for the prisons was done largely by the outside society. Both were maximum security prisons, and thus the presence of maximum security risks was accepted as part of the system. Little more was done than to compile records on the entering prisoners and assign them to various duties.

Thus, recruitment is institutionalized in some sense for all of the organizations, but it is not consistently in the hands of the staff.

*Custody and treatment.* Once within the boundaries of the custodial systems, the one common institution was that of custody. By "custody" is meant all efforts to retain the inmates within a sharply limited territory. This institution was not always dominant, but it was always present—and always in a highly patterned form.

In Clemmer's prison, Trenton, and Southern Hospital, custody was the first and major concern. The psychiatrists in Caudill's hospital regarded the task (particularly on the locked ward) as both a necessity and a nuisance. Belmont had the task of custody, also. Patients were given passes only for certain hours, others were denied passes, and all were expected to be in certain places at certain times. But although the custodial *task* was present, the *problem* was solved simply: patients who violated the custodial requirements were discharged. Admission might be voluntary, but once in, the staff was dominant, and custodial obedience was required by all.

The total institution may either treat custody as an end in itself or as a means to an end. Society in general charges its prisons with the task of maintaining inmates in a certain area, a task in which the prisons are largely successful. Custody thus becomes an end. But custody can also be a means, particularly to the end of treatment. By treatment is meant attempts by the staff to change the inmates' behavior to conform to certain norms and (preferably) to certain sentiments. These attempts can include the more ideal concept of treatment, that is, "the process by which the individual is helped to a greater use of his own capacities or social resources" (Fairchild, 1961, p. 323). In this sense, the total institution becomes a "forcing house," as Goffman maintained (1957). The change sought has variously gone under such names as retribution, reform, rehabilitation, adjustment, and cure. These diverse terms suggest that treatment differs markedly in various total institutions, and such is indeed the case.

Prisons are generally recognized failures as treatment centers, especially when treatment includes a change in both norms and sentiments. But the failure is not from the point of view of the prison staff, for they do not conceive of their role as treatment. All they intend to accomplish—at least most of them—is a change in the behavior of the inmates towards certain norms. They *might* like to see a change in sentiments, but most staff members are probably more realistic. Clemmer found that less than 5 per cent of the staff ever consider the reformative aspect of prison experience. The warden may be concerned, and perhaps a few others, but such thought is utterly foreign to the average guard (Clemmer, 1940, pp. 183–84). Trenton had much the same pattern of sentiment. Whether correctly or not, the prevention of deviant behavior among inmates while in prison was viewed by the warden as the most potent device for preparing prisoners to conform to the dictates of society upon release. At least for the warden, custody was a means for reformation. It was not so viewed by the staff in general.

Southern Hospital, as previously indicated, was also mainly a custodial institution. Medical ends were secondary, and these were more physical than psychiatric. Caudill's hospital, on the other hand, was dedicated chiefly to psychotherapy, and custodial problems were conceived with the end of psychotherapy in view. In Belmont, the transition proceeds further. Therapy was viewed as arising from the normal interactions of "healthy community life." In this effort to produce normality, custody understandably *should* be reduced to a minimum. That it was *not* eliminated is itself significant for including Belmont with the other systems. However, though custodial requirements are present, therapy is the dominant concern, group therapy being employed extensively. Patients spent at least four-fifths of their time with the nurses, occupational therapists, other medical auxiliaries—and other patients.

The continuum for custody is thus the reverse of a similar continuum for treatment. Most emphasis on custody is found in the prisons, the least in Belmont and Caudill's hospital, with Southern Hospital in between.

*Discharge.* The institutions of discharge are more complicated than they may at first seem. Basically, variations depend on differences in custody. A summary of the types of discharge is given in Table 21. Release from the total institution differs quite markedly according to whether the inmate's term of sentence has expired (the prisons) or whether the inmate has conformed to certain expectations of the staff. Even in this last type (which occurs in all the systems), the speed of an inmate's release depends, on the one hand, on conditions that are rather rigorously set forth by statute (in prisons) and, on the other, according to the patient's demonstration of "rationality."

*Table 21.* Types of release from total institutions

|  | Clemmer's prison | Trenton Prison | Southern Hospital | Caudill's hospital | Belmont |
|---|---|---|---|---|---|
| Expiration | X | X | | | |
| Parole | X | X | X | | |
| Escape | X | X | X | X | |
| Death | X | X | X | X | X |
| Transfer | X | X | X | X | X |
| Conformance | X | X | X | X | X |
| Furlough | | | X | X | X |
| Rejection | | | | | X |

Escape is possible in all of the total institutions except Belmont, though it is rare in Caudill's hospital. And release by death is rare in both Belmont and Caudill's hospital primarily because of the rapid turnover of inmates. Belmont is the only total institution that "discharges" inmates when they refuse to conform (that is, it "rejects" them). On the other hand, all of the total institutions can transfer inmates to other total institutions.

The difference between parole and furlough hinges on the degree of supervision. A furlough is essentially a visit, and though it *may* add the quality of supervision, parole *must* contain this quality. Finally, furloughs have the expectation of return. The parolee in contrast, returns only after he has broken the norms of supervision.

The types of discharge are arranged in Table 21 according to whether custody is terminated from the point of view of law or through the efforts of the inmate. Thus, when a sentence expires, custody has completely ceased through the action of the law. Parole is a partial cessation of custody by this means. Escape is illegal cessation of custody—the law still considers the inmate subject to the staff. Death is an extralegal removal of custody, and transfer is a cessation of custody by changing the inmate to another system. Release through conformance (on "good time" or because the patient is "cured") comes about through the actions of the inmate, though it is just as legally binding as release through expiration of sentence. Furlough is a temporary cessation of custody, with the inmate more or less acting on his own initiative. Rejection, finally, is a refusal by the staff to bring a former inmate into the system because he has shown a lack of willingness or an inability to conform to the system's norms.

Thus, at one pole, the inmate is released entirely because of the actions of the legal system. At the other pole, the inmate has refused to conform to regulations, and he is in a sense discharged entirely because of his own actions (recognizing that the total institution made the rule in the first place).

By means of the four institutions of recruitment, custody, treatment, and discharge, the custodial system is able to maintain the type of population for which it was intended. A breakdown in the operation of any one of these institutions would mean either that the population would disappear or that it would quickly grow to unmanageable proportions. Treatment is not effective in prisons, but in the asylums it becomes very much a part of the institutions of maintenance, not only in contributing to the functioning of discharge but in attracting the kind of inmate for which it was organized.

*Captive economics.* Total institutions violate the economic requirements of the larger society more often than they fulfill them. Superficially, all of the systems have some industry. The staff form occupational categories in their own right, but the occupational structure of the inmates varies from "an enforced mimicry of the free community" (Sykes, 1958, p. 26) to an attempt to use this "mimicry" as a therapeutic device.

The prisons are industrial concerns with a division of labor comparable to that found in cities (though not nearly as complete). Neither of the prisons, however, was self-supporting. Whether Southern Hospital returned a profit is unknown, but it had occupational therapy and charged fees to the patients able to pay. The extent to which its occupational therapy was really therapeutic, and not a disguised form of labor (or even a diversionary pastime), is not apparent. But the fees from the "workers" certainly would be an unusual practice for the typical business concern.

The therapeutic nature of work probably received more emphasis in the other two asylums. Occupational therapy in Belmont is the chief form of treatment and one of the major concerns of staff. No attempt is made to train people for a trade. The aim is rather to have conditions of work approximating semi-skilled or unskilled work in factories, although work assignments are compulsory. When one compares the aspects of contracts found in cities (see Appendix B), the non-contractual nature of the work becomes evident: There is no concern with degree of risk; agreements (that is, means of assent) pertain to admission to the Unit, not to work; content of work is irrelevant —the therapeutic nature is the chief concern. Perhaps most important, societal interest in this "work" is therapeutic rather than economic. Similar considerations apply to the other total institutions.

Total institutions do not lack economic consequences. The staff makes its living by means of the system. And the inmates may be better economic producers upon release (though not necessarily, particularly in the case of prisons). But the total institution cannot be described as a means whereby one makes a living. If anything, it is a means for supporting people who cannot make a living. Though the forced labor of inmates may contribute to this end, it is not so employed in all of the systems. More often than not, and in several ways, both the inmates and the staff are economic liabilities.

That inmates are economic failures is obvious. They fail either because they are immoral or amoral; that is, they act contrary to societal norms and sentiments or they cannot live up to them. But, in a special sense, staff are often economic liabilities also, since their productive time must be used in non-productive ways, especially in the supervision of "uneconomic" inmates. If staff were not required to perform this supervision, they could, theoretically, be released for more productive ends.

At times, some staff members help to produce useful citizens and may thus be regarded as economically productive, even if indirectly. But the high rate of recidivism and social failures that come from total institutions stands as a forceful argument against attributing such an "economic productivity" to staff in general. Even if Belmont may be described as economically more "productive" than Trenton Prison, one could still not argue the point for total institutions in general. Further, though it is at times profitable to operate a business with convict or slave labor (cf. Mouledous, 1962, 1963), one must still conclude that economic profit is not necessarily a concern of total institutions (not to mention that such a business is not profitable to the inmates).

*Religion.* Information concerning religion—either as an institution or sentiment—is very meager. Clemmer gives the only systematic and adequate treatment. He states categorically that the majority of prisoners have no religious preference (51 per cent). The inmates take little or no part in church activities, with the exception of Roman Catholics and certain sex offenders. Church was treated more as entertainment than as religious experience.

Clemmer's observations suggest that religion is of only incidental interest to total institutions. Certainly the other investigators maintain this position, in effect, for they either do not give significant attention to religion or they come to the conclusion that it is peripheral to the operation of the system. Caudill, Belknap, Jones and his associates, and Sykes all minimize the importance of religion by giving it little space in their discussion. Belknap provides concrete evidence that the institution of religion was poorly developed at Southern Hospital— that is, chaplains were "too new" to permit adequate analysis. Sykes does no more than mention that religious services were held, both Protestant and Catholic, and that a chaplain was present. Most investigators virtually ignore the subject.

From the reactions both of the investigators as well as the inmates and staff, where there are data, the evidence seems to indicate that the religious institution is of minor importance in total institutions.

*The hierarchy of government.* When government is considered as the institution which enforces norms, then it is seen to be one of the most central institutions in custodial systems. The types of cooperation, the basic staff-inmate antagonism, and the system of stratification all develop as they do primarily because of the nature of power relations. Thus, attention is directed first to the hierarchy of formal power. (For a diagram of this hierarchy, see Fig. 5, p. 343.)

The governmental functions of total institutions are divided into the administrative, judicial, enforcement, and maintenance aspects. In most cases, administrative and judicial functions are combined to some degree. Southern Hospital separated these functions by having a director who specialized in administration. In all of the mental institutions, however, the psychiatrists perform judicial as well as administrative tasks. The warden has a similar combination of roles.

The administrators (or administrative judges) are primarily responsible for the maintenance tasks of custody and treatment. Some maintenance positions, however, such as chaplain or occupational therapist, are outside of the direct line of authority from administrator to enforcer. The role of enforcer is given to the guards in the prisons, the attendants at Southern Hospital, and the nurses at Belmont and Caudill's hospital. This role is comparable in numerous ways to the foreman in industry. He (or she) is the wheelhorse around which the institution functions, the closest contact with the inmates and with administrative and judiciary branches. Perhaps the term "enforcer" seems too harsh for nurses but, in essence, enforcement is precisely their task; that is, they see that the psychiatrist's orders materialize. They are assisted by aides in Caudill's hospital, but at Belmont their contact with the patients is more direct.

Even though at Belmont there is a decided attempt to reduce the distance between staff and inmate, one nurse there made the following comment: "Our uniform and title play a considerable part . . . in helping us to walk our tight rope, making it plain that we are not just friendly women who happen to be around the place; we may not be 'proper' nurses, but we share something of the respect due to the stripy cloth" (Jones *et al.*, 1953, p. 35). Apparently, there is a limit to which the distance between staff and inmate can be eliminated.

This is the staff-inmate split already noted so often. It is more openly acknowledged by the other investigators, and it symbolizes better than anything else the kind of control that the total institutions have over their inmates. This control is a curious mixture of force, authority, and power. The staff in each of the systems are invested with authority by the larger society. But the inmates do not always recognize the authority and, consequently, the staff of the prisons and of Southern and Caudill's hospital must be ever ready to use force. This is one of the major distinctions between Belmont and the other four total institutions. In Belmont, the authority of the staff is clearly recognized by the inmates. Power is manifested only in the act of discharging the recalcitrant, and the force used in such cases was minimal.

Inmates of course are not powerless. Sykes speaks of a strong pressure toward the corruption of guards in the form of friendship, reciprocity, and the transfer of duties to trusted inmates (Sykes, 1958, p. 61). Clemmer notes the prisoners' communication grapevine and the information it puts at the prisoners' disposal. And though little such information is given for Southern Hospital, both in Caudill's hospital and in Belmont there are instances where power shifts to some degree to the patients, even if only slightly or momentarily (see the discussion of interaction earlier in this Appendix).

But staff still retains control—and significantly so. They are immediately responsible for the inmate being in the system at all, and whatever power the inmate may obtain is essentially in reference to the system of power of the staff. Finally, even should an inmate gain extensive personal power, its impact would be effectively blunted by the unorganized nature of the inmate population.

Force, in the sense of a reduction of alternatives, is in use in all of the systems—Belmont included—through the institution of custody. But the appearance of force is much greater in the other total institutions, reaching its height in the maximum security prison of Trenton. There, force is continually applied to the prisoners in the sense of reducing alternatives to those which the staff, and particularly the guards, consider best for the interest of the prison: within the walls at all times (unless accompanied by a guard on the outside), confinement to place of work, to chapel, to recreational areas, and to their cells, and here the force continues through the night as the prisoners' alternatives to movement are reduced to hardly more than a minimal area.

At the other extreme, at Belmont, force is reduced considerably—but it is still there. Some patients are denied passes. All patients must be at their occupations at specified hours; if granted passes, they may leave the grounds only at other specified hours. Such custodial limitations are manifestations of force—milder than those employed with a club, to be sure, but force nevertheless. The force is used with authority, but in this case an authority the patients recognize. The authority also helps to maintain the staff-inmate split in that it produces ambivalent attitudes in the patients. To them, the doctor "is a miracle worker who should be able to solve all their problems; but he is also a figure of authority who may be feared and distrusted" (Jones *et al.*, 1953, p. 40).

*Institutional strata.* The system of stratification in the total institutions is based essentially on authority and power. The *general* layers are depicted in Figure 5. Each total institution has numerous additional positions within each category. To give only one example (chosen because it is one of the simplest), Belmont's professional staff contains four psychiatrists, one psychologist, two psychiatric social workers, two disablement resettlement officers, five occupational instructors, one research technician, and a nursing staff of about twenty. The maintenance personnel are placed to one side in Figure 5 because they are not really a part of the status system; their position has little relevance to authority.

The positions of administrators and judges can be attained both by appointment and by achievement. The status of physicians is a case in point. Initially obtained by achievement, in a mental hospital or prison the position is customarily filled by appointment. Wardens, on the other hand, as well as superintendents, may achieve their position from promotions "within the ranks."

Inmates, themselves, may develop a status structure, although this is not necessarily to be expected and it is seldom permanent. Both Clemmer and Sykes describe a power structure among the inmates, but the structure is unstable. The only institutionalized system of stratification among the patients was at Southern Hospital, where the positions of "privileged," "limited privileged," and "unprivileged" patients had been established. This system, however, was largely maintained by the attendants rather than the high-ranking staff and it had only quasi-legal status. Further, it was not developed by the patients.

The double line separating inmates from staff in Figure 5 represents, first, the qualitatively different nature of the inmate's position in the hierarchy relative to the staff. Second, it

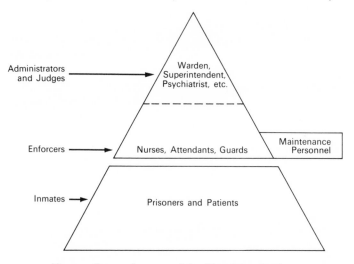

*Fig. 5*—Status System of the Total Institutions

indicates the staff-inmate split, a separation which renders the total institution a thing of two discrete populations in more ways than in just a hierarchical sense. As will be shown in the next section, this split is not the same for all inmates, but nevertheless, all experience it in some sense. And third, the double line represents a caste-like quality relative to social mobility. Inmates as inmates can never move into the category of staff. Even the position of trusty is really one in which certain staff powers (and privileges) are delegated. The trusty is still an inmate. This caste-like structure may even be found on the enforcement level. Nurses, in order to become physicians, must leave the hospital and receive further training. And Clemmer notes that guards have almost no chance for advancement.

*Cooperation and hostility.* Cooperation occurs within both the staff and inmate populations but is markedly reduced between them. Further, the type is qualitatively different in each segment. Cooperation among staff is basically contractual and heavily institutionalized. Cooperation among inmates is just as "heavily" informal, that is, uninstitutionalized, and depends on mutual aid rather than contract. One is never certain of trust in the inmate population, and prior trust is no reason to be certain of future trust. (This condition is not quite as prevalent at Belmont.)

Cooperation between layers is rare. Hostility, as indicated in previous sections, is more usual. But cooperation does occur among the more stable and mentally more reorganized patients and, in prisons, among trusties, "stool pigeons," "rats," "center men," etc. For most inmates, the reaction to the stool pigeon is one of hostility—with the exception of mental patients. According to psychiatric interpretation, the greater the adjustment of patients, the more readily they cooperate. Belmont is a good example of this principle—as well as an example of its limits. Patients were particularly ready to help new nurses adjust to life on the Unit. When engaged in therapeutic sessions of psychodrama, the nurses were sometimes asked to play parts. Yet the nurses maintained their distance; so did the patients in relation to the doctors. There was a limit to the cooperation, whether set by staff or patients.

In each of the five systems, however, it is better to refer to staff-inmate cooperation as accommodation. The distinction is in the nature of accommodation as an adjustment to conflict, whereas neither mutual aid nor contractual cooperation presuppose hostility. The guard or attendant must necessarily look upon the inmate as a potential combatant. True cooperation may develop in individual cases, but such exceptions do not result in a suspension of the rule: *Staff cannot afford to ignore the potential hostility of inmates*—the inmate as a class is to be trusted only at the peril of the system. That the trusty is a special case is apparent, but even this position develops from a condition of conflict, and thus accommodation is the more correct label.

In general, the type and even the existence of cooperation depends on the position the respective members occupy in the system's hierarchy. In other words, whether one encounters mutual aid, contractual relations, accommodation, or hostility depends on his position relative to the configuration of power in the staff-inmate split and whether he is encountering a staff member or an inmate. This distinction is one of the crucial distinctions between total institutions and vills.

*Socialization.* Inmates in each of the total institutions are involved in some type of educational process, proceeding from both staff and inmates. Socialization by staff is institutionalized, but not necessarily that from inmates. The prisons engage in two types of educational ventures: orienting the prisoner to the system and providing formal education in the usual sense. The first type is compulsory; the second may be optional. In the asylums, socialization concerning rehabilitation is in the hands of psychiatrists. This structuring (that is, use of a particular role in socialization) is an aspect of institutionalization, but it varies in the degree to which it is used. Patients probably have maximum contact with therapists in Caudill's hospital and in Belmont. Few patients see the psychiatrist at Southern.

The prisoners institutionalize indoctrination in several ways. In Clemmer's prison, new inmates are called "fish," bringing attention to their special position. And in both prisons, the term "rat" is a common designation for traitor, symbolizing again a standardized reaction which was expected to be learned. Most of the indoctrination, however, is more informal, especially in the asylums.

The general process of indoctrination is an aspect of that which Goffman terms "mortification," a change in status experienced by the inmate in moving from the "outside" to the inmate world. Goffman contends that mortification is a change to a *lower* status. There is some evidence to suggest that this occurs in the prisons. The asylums, however, present a mixed picture. When certain patients in Caudill's hospital initially denied that they were in a mental institution (for example, claiming they were in a country club), the other patients quickly corrected them. Mortification is quite evident here. In Southern Hospital, however, though an adjustment process was described, nothing specifically referring to a change in status was noted. Similarly, in Belmont, the only status change mentioned was the custom of newer patients introducing themselves by giving an outline of their histories.

It should be mentioned that all of the asylums had training programs for the staff. There was undoubtedly some sort of orientation for the prison guards, but nothing is apparent concerning a formal program.

*Recreation.* This institution is heavily subject to staff control. The various types of recreation found in folk villages and cities appear to survive in custodial systems, though the data are incomplete. Games of varying kinds are specifically mentioned, as was music (though nothing is said of music in Southern Hospital). In addition, these organizations are within Western culture, and accordingly feasts and festivals (for example, Christmas and New Year) are no doubt present in all of the systems, though rarely described.

More important, however, is the attempt by staff to regulate recreation. In the prisons, for example, gambling is prohibited, whereas other forms such as games were prescribed (though attendance and participation may be optional). The asylums, on the other hand, employ recreation as a type of therapy.

An interesting variation in the degree of staff dominance may be observed. The staff of both prisons and asylums attempt some regulation. But in the prisons, much attention is given to proscribing recreation as well as to prescribing it. Prohibition decreases progressively from Southern Hospital, to Caudill's hospital, to Belmont (where the minimum of controls is encountered). However, even in the prisons, restrictions are not completely successful. For example, gambling is prohibited in both prisons—and is widely practiced in both. There are, apparently, effective limits to staff dominance.

# References

Alihan, Milla A. 1938. *Social ecology*. New York: Columbia Univ. Press.

Ammar, Hamed. 1954. *Growing up in an Egyptian village: Silwa Province of Aswan*. London: Routledge & Kegan Paul.

Anderson, Nels. 1959. *The Urban Community*. New York: Henry Holt and Co.

Arensberg, Conrad M. 1955. American communities. *American Anthropologist* 57:1143–62.

Arensberg, Conrad M., and Kimball, Solon T. 1940. *Family and community in Ireland*. Cambridge: Harvard Univ. Press.

Arrington, Leonard J. 1958. *Great Basin kingdom*. Cambridge: Harvard Univ. Press.

Aurbach, Herbert A. 1955. A Guttman scale for measuring isolation. *Rural Sociology* 20:142–45.

———. 1960. An empirical study in the application of the folk-urban typology to the classification of social systems. Ph.D. dissertation, University of Kentucky.

Barber, Bernard. 1961. Family status, local-community status, and social stratification: Three types of social ranking. *Pacific Sociological Review* 4:3–10.

Becker, Howard. 1950. *Through values to social interpretation*. Durham, N.C.: Duke Univ. Press.

Belknap, Ivan. 1956. *Human problems of a state mental hospital*. New York: McGraw-Hill.

Bell, Wendell, and Greer, Scott. 1962. Social area analysis and its critics. *Pacific Sociological Review* 5:3–9.

Benyon, Erdmann Doane. 1943. Budapest: An ecological study. *Geographical Review* 33:256–75.

Bierstedt, Robert. 1950. An analysis of social power. *American Sociological Review* 15:730–38.

Blau, Peter M., and Scott, W. Richard. 1962. *Formal organizations: A comparative approach*. San Francisco: Chandler Publishing Co.

Blumer, Herbert. 1939. *Critiques of research in the social sciences. I, An appraisal of Thomas and Znaniecki's " The Polish peasant in Europe and America."* Social Science Research Council, Bulletin 44. New York.

Bogue, Donald J., and Beale, Calvin L. 1961. *Economic areas of the United States*. New York: The Free Press of Glencoe.

Brown, James S. 1950. The social organization of an isolated Kentucky mountain neighborhood. Ph.D. dissertation, Harvard University.

Brown, James S. 1951. Social class, intermarriage, and church membership in a Kentucky community. *American Journal of Sociology* 57:232–42.

———. 1952a. *The family group in a Kentucky mountain farming community.* University of Kentucky Agricultural Experiment Station Bulletin no. 588. Lexington.

———. 1952b. The conjugal family and the extended family group. *American Sociological Review* 17:297–306.

———. 1952c. *The farm family in a Kentucky mountain neighborhood.* University of Kentucky Agricultural Experiment Station Bulletin no. 587. Lexington.

Brown, James S.; Schwarzweller, Harry K.; and Mangalam, Joseph J. 1963. Kentucky mountain migration and the stem-family: An American variation on a theme by Le Play. *Rural Sociology* 28:48–69.

Burgess, Ernest W. 1925. The growth of the city: An introduction to a research project. In *The City*, edited by Robert E. Park, Ernest W. Burgess, and R. D. McKenzie. Chicago: Univ. of Chicago Press.

Caplow, Theodore. 1952. Urban structure in France. *American Sociological Review* 17:544–49.

Caudill, William. 1958. *The psychiatric hospital as a small society.* Cambridge: Harvard Univ. Press.

Clemmer, Donald. 1958. *The prison community.* New York: Rinehart & Co.

Coleman, James S. 1957. *Community conflict.* Glencoe, Ill.: The Free Press.

Davis, Kingsley. 1949. *Human society.* New York: Macmillan.

Dube, S. C. 1955. *Indian village.* Ithaca, N.Y.: Cornell Univ. Press.

Duncan, Otis Dudley. 1959. Human ecology and population studies. In *The study of population*, edited by P. Hauser and O. D. Duncan. Chicago: Univ. of Chicago Press.

———. 1961. From social system to ecosystem. *Sociological Inquiry* 31:140–49.

Duncan, Otis Dudley, and Reiss, Albert J., Jr. 1956. *Social characteristics of urban and rural communities, 1950.* New York: John Wiley & Sons.

Durkheim, Emile. 1933. *The division of labor in society.* Glencoe, Ill.: The Free Press.

Embree, John F. 1939. *Suye Mura: A Japanese village.* Chicago: Univ. of Chicago Press.

Etzioni, Amitai. 1961. *Complex organizations: A sociological reader.* New York: Holt, Rinehart & Winston.

Fairchild, Henry Pratt, ed. 1961. *Dictionary of sociology.* Patterson, N.J.: Littlefield, Adams & Co.

Fei, Hsiao-Tung. 1939. *Peasant life in China: A field study of country life in the Yangtze Valley.* London: Kegan Paul, Trench, Trubner & Co.

Fichter, Joseph H. 1951. *Southern parish: Dynamics of a city church.* Chicago: Univ. of Chicago Press.

Firey, Walter. 1957. *Land use in central Boston.* Cambridge: Harvard Univ. Press.

Fleming, J. B. 1954. An analysis of shops and service trades in Scottish towns. *Scottish Geographical Magazine* 60:97–106.

Ford, Thomas R., ed. 1962. *The southern Appalachian region: A survey.* Lexington: Univ. of Kentucky Press.

Ford, Thomas R., and Sutton, Willis A., Jr. 1964. The impact of change on rural communities and fringe areas: Review of a decade's research. In *Our changing rural society: Perspectives and trends,* edited by James H. Copp. Ames, Iowa: Iowa State Univ. Press.

Fried, Morton H. 1953. *Fabric of Chinese society: A study of the social life of a Chinese county seat.* New York: Friederick A. Praeger.

Giallombardo, Rose. 1966. *Society of women: A study of a women's prison.* New York: John Wiley & Sons.

Gibbs, Jack P., and Martin, Walter T. 1959. Toward a theoretical system of human ecology. *Pacific Sociological Review* 2:29–36.

Gilmore, Harlan W. 1944. The old New Orleans and the new: A case for ecology. *American Sociological Review* 9:385–94.

Gladwin, Thomas, and Sarason, Seymour B. 1953. *Truk: Man in paradise.* Viking Fund Publications in Anthropology, no. 20. New York: Wenner-Gren Foundation for Anthropological Research.

Goffman, Erving. 1957. The characteristics of total institutions. In *Symposium on preventive and social psychiatry,* sponsored jointly by the Walter Reed Army Institute of Research, Walter Reed Army Medical Center, and the National Research Council. Washington, D.C.: U.S. Government Printing Office.

———. 1961. *Asylums: Essays on the social situation of mental patients and other inmates.* Garden City, N.Y.: Doubleday.

Goldenweiser, Alexander. 1937. *Anthropology.* New York: F. S. Crofts & Co.

Gomme, George L. 1912. *The village community: With special reference to the origin and form of its survivals in Britain.* New York: Charles Scribner's Sons.

Goode, William J., and Hatt, Paul K. 1952. *Methods in social research.* New York: McGraw-Hill.

Goodenough, Ward H. 1951. *Property, kin, and community on Truk.* Yale University Publications in Anthropology, no. 46. New Haven, Conn.: Yale Univ. Press.

Gould, Julius, and Kolb, William L., eds. 1964. *A dictionary of the social sciences.* New York: The Free Press of Glencoe.

Greer, Scott. 1955. *Social organization.* New York: Random House.

Halbwachs, Maurice. 1960. *Population and society: Introduction to social morphology*. Translated by Otis Dudley Duncan and Harold W. Pfautz. Glencoe, Ill.: The Free Press.

Hansen, Asael T. 1934. The economy of a Latin American city. In *Race and culture contacts*, edited by E. B. Reuter. New York: McGraw-Hill.

Hanson, Norwood Russell. 1958. *Patterns of discovery*. Cambridge: Cambridge Univ. Press.

Harris, Chauncy D. 1943. A functional classification of cities in the United States. *Geographical Review* 33:86–99.

Harris, Chauncy D., and Ullman, Edward L. 1945. The nature of cities. *Annals of the American Academy of Political and Social Science* 242:7–17.

Hatch, David L. 1948. Changes in the structure and function of a rural New England community since 1900. Ph.D. dissertation, Harvard University.

Hawley, Amos. 1950. *Human ecology: A theory of community structure*. New York: Ronald Press.

———. 1962. *Principles of sociology*. Flushing, N. Y.: Data Guide.

Heberle, Rudolf. 1951. *Social movements*. New York: Appleton-Century-Crofts.

Heberle, Rudolf; Hillery, George A., Jr.; and Lovrich, Frank. 1953. Continuity and change in voting behavior in the 1952 primaries in Louisiana. *Southwestern Social Science Quarterly* 33:328–42.

Hiller, E. T. 1941. The community as a social group. *American Sociological Review* 6:189–202.

Hillery, George A., Jr. 1951. The presence of community among urban Negroes: A case study of a selected area in New Orleans. Master's thesis, Louisiana State University.

———. 1952. The presence of community among New Orleans Negroes: A case study of a selected area. *Proceedings of the Louisiana Academy of Science* 15:72–84.

———. 1954. The Negro in New Orleans: A demographic analysis. Ph.D. dissertation, Louisiana State University.

———. 1955. Definitions of community: Areas of agreement. *Rural Sociology* 20:111–23.

———. 1957. The Negro in New Orleans: A functional analysis of demographic data. *American Sociological Review* 22:183–88.

———. 1959. A critique of selected community concepts. *Social Forces* 37:237–42.

———. 1961. The folk village: A comparative analysis. *Rural Sociology* 26:337–58.

———. 1963. Villages, cities, and total institutions. *American Sociological Review* 28:779–91.

Himmelhoch, Jercome. 1957. Editor's preface, *Social Problems* 5:67.

Homans, George C. 1950. *The human group.* New York: Harcourt, Brace & Co.

Iklé, Fred Charles. 1951. The effect of war destruction upon the ecology of cities. *Social Forces* 29:383–91.

International Urban Research. 1959. *The world's metropolitan areas.* Berkeley: Univ. of California Press.

Jonassen, Christen T. 1961. Functional unities in eighty-eight community systems. *American Sociological Review* 26:399–407.

Jones, Maxwell; Baker, A.; Freeman, Thomas; Merry, Julius; Pomryn, B. A.; Sandler, Joseph; and Tuxford, Joy. 1953. *The therapeutic community: A new treatment method in psychiatry.* New York: Basic Books.

Krader, Lawrence. 1968. *Formation of the state.* Englewood Cliffs, N.J.: Prentice-Hall, Inc.

Kroeber, Alfred L. 1948. *Anthropology.* New York: Harcourt, Brace & Co.

Kroeber, Alfred L., and Parsons, Talcott. 1958. The concepts of culture and of social systems, *American Sociological Review* 23:582–83.

Lewis, Oscar. 1951. *Life in a Mexican village: Tepoztlán restudied.* Urbana, Ill.: Univ. of Illinois Press.

———. 1953. Tepoztlán restudied: A critique of the folk-urban conceptualization of social change. *Rural Sociology* 18:121–34.

Loomis, Charles P., and Beegle, J. Allan. 1950. *Rural social systems.* New York: Prentice-Hall.

Lynd, Robert S., and Lynd, Helen Merrell. 1929. *Middletown: A study in modern American culture.* New York: Harcourt, Brace & Co.

———. 1937. *Middletown in transition: A study in cultural conflicts.* New York: Harcourt, Brace & Co.

McClenahan, Bessie A. 1929. *The changing urban neighborhood.* Social Science Series, no. 1. Los Angeles: Univ. of Southern California Studies.

McElrath, Dennis C. 1962. The social areas of Rome: A comparative analysis. *American Sociological Review* 27:376–91.

MacIver, Robert M. 1917. *Community.* London: Macmillan.

———, 1931. *Society: Its structure and changes.* New York: Ray Long and Richard R. Smith.

———. 1947. *The web of government.* New York: Macmillan.

MacIver, Robert M., and Page, Charles H. 1949. *Society: An introductory analysis.* New York: Rinehart & Co.

McKinney, John C. 1954. Constructive typology and social research. In *An Introduction to Social Research,* edited by John T. Doby. Harrisburg, Pa.: The Stackpole Co.

Maine, Henry Sumner. 1861. *Ancient law.* London: John Murray.

Maine, Henry Sumner. 1889. *Village communities east and west*. New York: Henry Holt & Co. (1st ed. pub. 1871.)

———. 1963. *Ancient law*. 10th ed. Boston: Beacon Press.

Malinowski, Bronislaw. 1955. *Magic, science and religion and other essays*. Garden City, N. Y.: Doubleday.

Mangus, A. R. 1940. *Rural regions of the United States*. Washington, D. C.: Work Projects Administration.

Martindale, Don. 1960. *American Society*. New York: D. Van Nostrand Co.

Mayer, Kurt B. 1955. *Class and society*. Garden City, N. Y.: Doubleday.

Mayhew, Bruce H., Jr. 1963. The folk-urban continuum: Selected quantitative indices. Master's thesis, University of Kentucky.

Mead, Margaret. 1956. *New lives for old: Cultural transformation— Manus, 1928–1953*. New York: William Morrow & Co.

Meehan, Eugene J. 1968. *Explanation in social science: A system paradigm*. Homewood, Ill.: The Dorsey Press.

Merton, Robert K. 1957. *Social theory and social structure*. Rev. ed. Glencoe, Ill.: The Free Press.

Miner, Horace. 1952. The folk-urban continuum. *American Sociological Review* 17:529–37.

———. 1953. *The primitive city of Timbuctoo*. Memoirs of the American Philosophical Society, vol. 32. Princeton: Princeton Univ. Press.

**Mouledous, Joseph C. 1962. Sociological perspectives on a prison** social system. Master's thesis, Louisiana State University.

———. 1963. Organizational goals and structural change: A study of the organization of a prison social system. *Social Forces* 41:283–90.

Murdock, George P. 1949. *Social structure*. New York: Macmillan.

———. 1958. *Outline of world cultures*. New Haven: Human Relations Area Files Press.

Murdock, George P., *et al*. 1950. *Outline of cultural materials*. 3d rev. ed. New Haven: Human Relations Area Files Press.

Murray, James A. H., ed. 1893. *A new English dictionary on historical principles*. 10 vols. Oxford and New York: Macmillan.

Nelson, Lowry; Ramsey, Charles E.; and Verner, Coolie. 1960. *Community structure and change*. New York: Macmillan.

Odum, Howard W., and Moore, Harry E. 1938. *American regionalism*. New York: Henry Holt & Co.

Ogburn, William Fielding. 1922. *Social change*. New York: Viking Press.

Ogles, Richard H.; Levy, Marion J., Jr.; and Parsons, Talcott. 1959. Culture and social system: An exchange. *American Sociological Review* 24:246–50.

Park, Robert E. 1925. The City. In *The City*, edited by Robert E. Park, Ernest W. Burgess, and R. D. McKenzie. Chicago: Univ. of Chicago Press.

———. 1926. The urban community as a spacial pattern and a moral order. In *The urban community*, edited by Ernest W. Burgess. Chicago: Univ. of Chicago Press.

———. 1936. Human ecology. *American Journal of Sociology* 42:1–15.

Parsons, Talcott. 1951. *The social system*. Glencoe, Ill.: The Free Press.

———. 1953. A revised analytical approach to the theory of social stratification. In *Class, status and power*, edited by Reinhard Bendix and Seymour Martin Lipset. Glencoe, Ill.: The Free Press.

———. 1960. *Structure and process in modern societies*. Glencoe, Ill.: The Free Press.

———. 1966. *Societies: Evolutionary and comparative perspectives*. Englewood Cliffs, N.J.: Prentice-Hall, Inc.

Price, Paul H., and Hillery, George A., Jr. 1959. *The rural-urban fringe and Louisiana's agriculture: A case study of the Baton Rouge area*. Louisiana State University Agricultural Experiment Station Bulletin no. 526. Baton Rouge.

Quinn, James A. 1950. *Human ecology*. New York: Prentice-Hall.

Redfield, Robert. 1930. *Tepoztlán: A Mexican village*. Chicago: Univ. of Chicago Press.

———. 1941. *The folk culture of Yucatan*. Chicago: Univ. of Chicago Press.

———. 1947. The folk society. *American Journal of Sociology* 52:293–308.

———. 1950. *A village that chose progress: Chan Kom revisited*. Chicago: Univ. of Chicago Press.

———. 1955. *The little community*. Chicago: Univ. of Chicago Press.

Redfield, Robert, and Villa Rojas, Alfonso. 1934. *Chan Kom: A Maya village*. Carnegie Institution Publication no. 448. Washington, D.C.

Reiss, Albert J., Jr. 1954. A review and evaluation of research on community. Working memorandum prepared for the Committee on Social Behavior. Mimeographed. Nashville, Tenn.: Social Science Research Council.

———. 1959. The sociological study of communities. *Rural Sociology* 24:118–30.

Rosenfeld, Eva. 1957. Institutional change in the kibbutz. *Social Problems* 5:110–36.

Sanders, Irwin T. 1949. *Balkan village*. Lexington: Univ. of Kentucky Press.

———. 1958. *The community*. New York: Ronald Press.

Sanderson, Dwight. 1919. Democracy and community organization. *Publications of the American Sociological Society* 24:83–93.

Schmid, Calvin F.; MacCannell, Earle H.; and Van Arsdol, Maurice D., Jr. 1958. The ecology of the American city: Further comparison and validation of generalizations. *American Sociological Review* 23:392–401.

Schnore, Leo F. 1958. Social morphology and human ecology. *American Journal of Sociology* 63:620–34.

Sellin, Thorsten. 1944. *Pioneering in penology: The Amsterdam houses of correction in the sixteenth and seventeenth centuries*. Philadelphia: Univ. of Pennsylvania Press.

Seymour, S. Frederick. 1963. Convergence of rural sociology and anthropology in definition of the community. Paper read before the Rural Sociological Society, Los Angeles, August 25, 1963.

Shevky, Eshref, and Bell, Wendell. 1955. *Social area analysis*. Stanford: Stanford Univ. Press.

Sjoberg, Gideon. 1952. Folk and "feudal" societies. *American Journal of Sociology* 58:231–39.

———. 1955. The preindustrial city. *American Journal of Sociology* 60:438–45.

———. 1960a. *The preindustrial city*. Glencoe, Ill.: The Free Press.

———. 1960b. Contradictory functional requirements and social systems. *Conflict Resolution* 4:198–208.

Smith, T. Lynn. 1953. *The sociology of rural life*. 3d ed. New York: Harper & Bros.

———. 1960. *Fundamentals of population study*. New York: Lippincott.

Sorokin, Pitirim A. 1937–41. *Social and cultural dynamics*. 4 vols. New York: American Book Co.

———. 1947. *Society, culture, and personality: Their structure and dynamics*. New York: Harper & Bros.

Sorokin, Pitirim A.; Zimmerman, Carle C.; and Galpin, Charles J., eds. 1930. *A systematic source book in rural sociology*, vol. 1. Minneapolis: Univ. of Minnesota Press.

Spiro, Melford E. 1956. *Kibbutz: Venture in utopia*. Cambridge: Harvard Univ. Press.

———. 1958. *Children of the kibbutz*. Cambridge: Harvard Univ. Press.

Steffens, Lincoln. 1931. *The autobiography of Lincoln Steffens*. New York: Harcourt, Brace & Co.

Stein, Maurice R. 1960. *The eclipse of community: An interpretation of American studies*. Princeton: Princeton Univ. Press.

Steward, Julian H. 1950. *Area research: Theory and practice*. Social Science Research Council, Bulletin no. 63. New York.

Sutton, Willis A., Jr., and Kolaja, Jiri. 1960. The concept of community. *Rural Sociology* 25:197–203.

Sykes, Gresham M. 1958. *The society of captives: A study of a maximum security prison.* Princeton: Princeton Univ. Press.

Tawney, R. H. 1947. *Religion and the rise of capitalism.* Mentor Book ed. New York: New American Library.

Theodorson, George A., ed. 1961. *Studies in human ecology.* Evanston, Ill.: Row, Peterson and Co.

Toennies, Ferdinand. 1957. *Community and society* [Gemeinschaft und Gesellschaft]. Translated by Charles P. Loomis. East Lansing: Michigan State Univ. Press.

Tryon, Robert C. 1955. *Identification of social areas by cluster analysis.* Berkeley: Univ. of California Press.

Udry, J. Richard. 1964. Increasing scale and spatial differentiation: New tests of two theories from Shevky and Bell. *Social Forces* 42:403–13.

United States Bureau of the Census. 1941. *Religious bodies: 1936.* Washington, D. C.: U.S. Government Printing Office.

———. 1952. *U.S. census of population: 1950.* Vol. 2, *Characteristics of the population;* pts. 14, *Indiana,* and 18, *Louisiana.* Washington, D.C.: U.S. Government Printing Office.

Van Arsdol, Maurice D., Jr.; Camilleri, Santo F.; and Schmid, Calvin F. 1958. The generality of urban social area indexes. *American Sociological Review* 23:277–84.

Vogt, Evon Z. 1955. *Modern homesteaders: The life of a twentieth-century frontier community.* Cambridge: The Belknap Press of Harvard Univ. Press.

Vogt, Evon Z., and O'Dea, Thomas F. 1953. A comparative study of the role of values in social action in two southwestern communities. *American Sociological Review* 18:645–54.

Warren, Roland L. 1963. *The community in America.* Chicago: Rand McNally & Co.

Weber, Max. 1930. *The Protestant ethic and the spirit of capitalism.* Translated by Talcott Parsons. London: Allen & Unwin.

———. 1946. *From Max Weber: Essays in sociology.* Translated and edited by H. H. Gerth and C. Wright Mills. New York: Oxford Univ. Press.

———. 1950. *General economic history.* Translated by Frank H. Knight. Glencoe, Ill.: The Free Press.

———. 1958. *The city.* Translated and edited by Don Martindale and Gertrud Neuwirth. Glencoe, Ill.: The Free Press.

West, James, 1945. *Plainville, U.S.A.* New York: Columbia Univ. Press.

Whitman, William. 1947. *The Pueblo Indians of San Ildefonso: A changing culture.* New York: Columbia Univ. Press.

Williams, Robin M., Jr. 1960. *American society: A sociological interpretation.* 2d ed. New York: Alfred A. Knopf.

Wirth, Louis. 1938. Urbanism as a way of life. *American Journal of Sociology* 44:1–24.

Wissler, Clark. 1923. *Man and culture.* New York: Crowell.

Zimmerman, Carle C. 1938. *The changing community.* New York: Harper & Bros.

# Index

357